BILL & TED ARE DOOMED

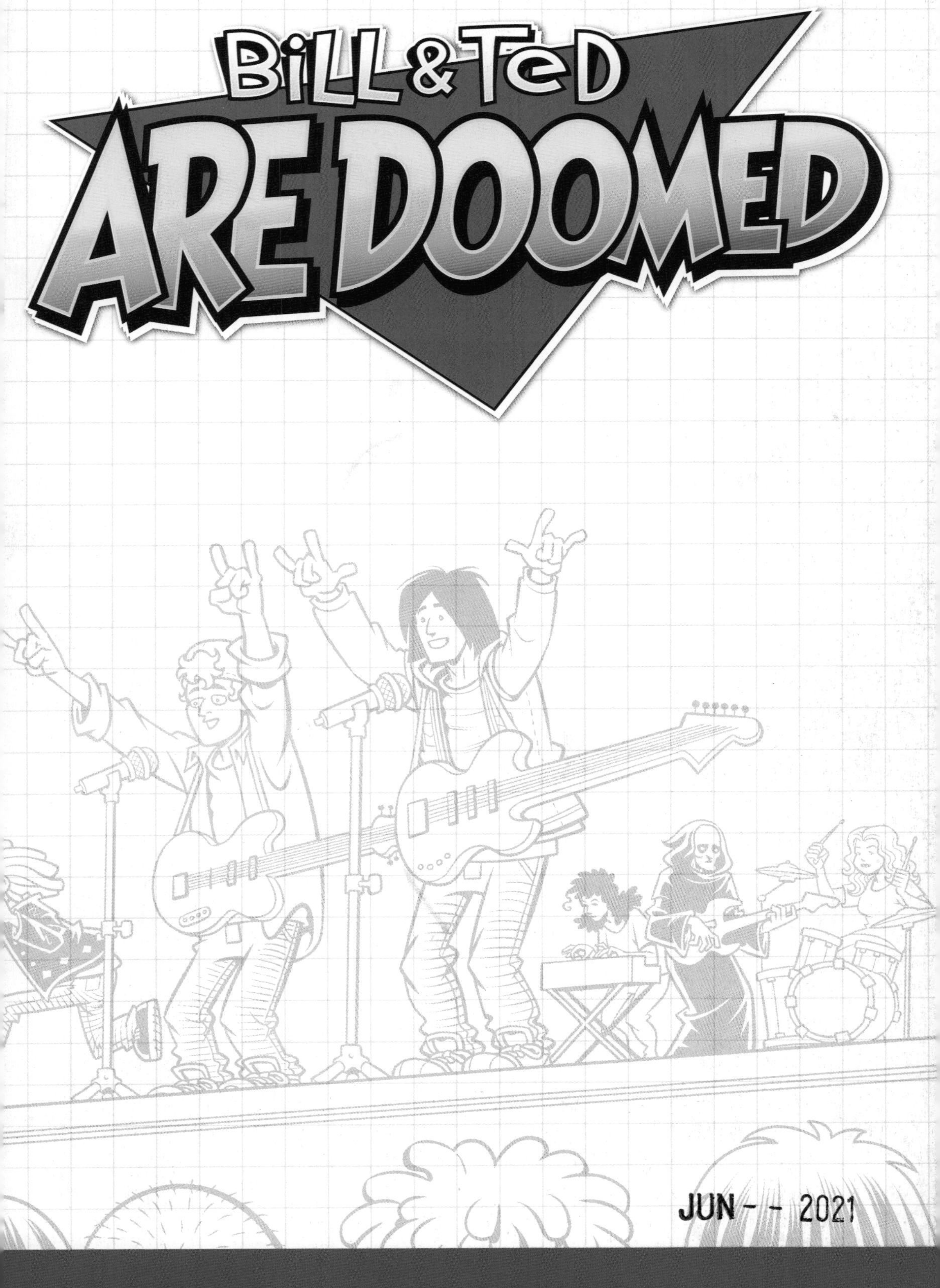

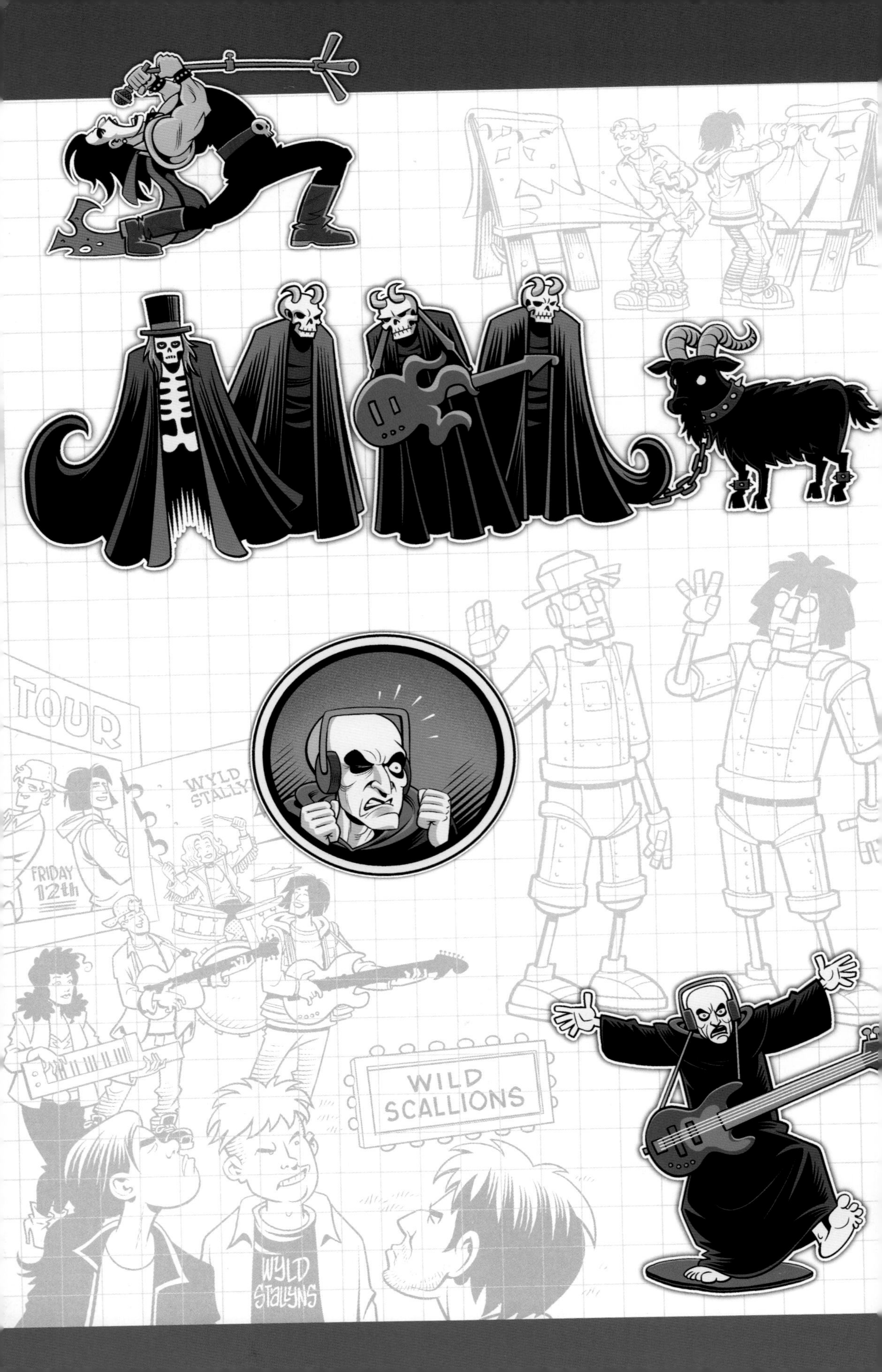

TOUR
WYLD STALLYNS
FRIDAY 12th
WILD SCALLIONS
WYLD STALLYNS

BILL & TED ARE DOOMED

TONITE: MYLD STALLYNS
WIDE HORSES

SCRIPT
EVAN DORKIN

ART AND LETTERS
ROGER LANGRIDGE

CONSULTATION
ED SOLOMON

COVER AND CHAPTER BREAKS BY
EVAN DORKIN WITH SARAH DYER

WYLD STALLYNS

DARK HORSE BOOKS

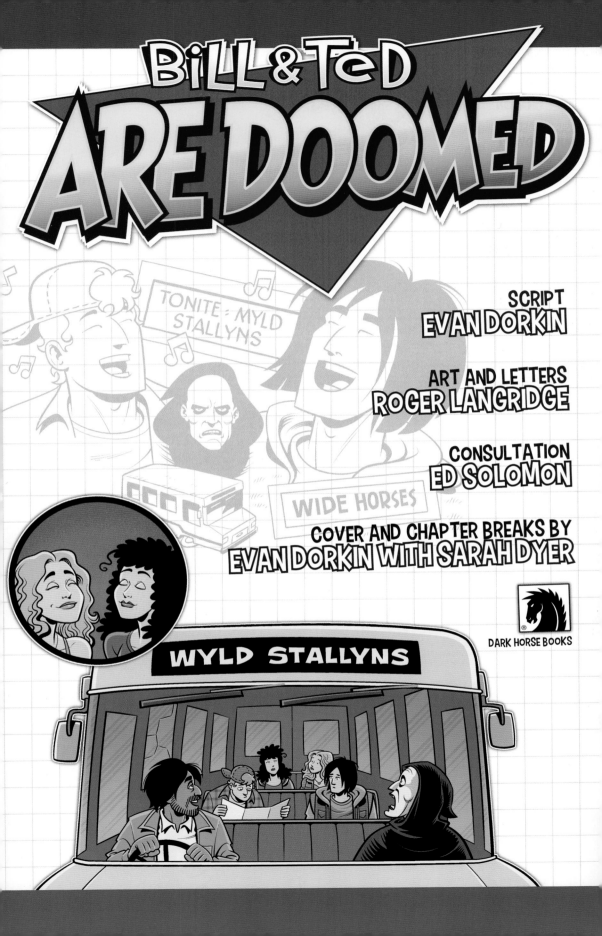

PRESIDENT & PUBLISHER
MIKE RICHARDSON

EDITOR
DANIEL CHABON

ASSISTANT EDITOR
CHUCK HOWITT

DESIGNER
BRENNAN THOME

DIGITAL ART TECHNICIAN
ALLYSON HALLER

SPECIAL THANKS TO APRIL CANLAS EDDY AND RAND MARLIS

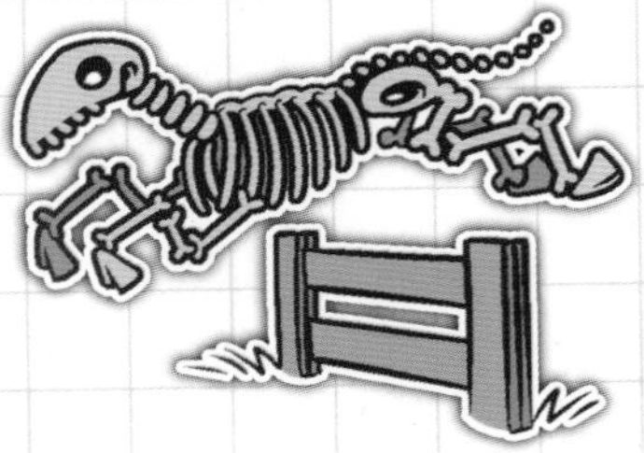

Collects issues #1–#4 of the Dark Horse Comics series *Bill & Ted Are Doomed*.

Published by Dark Horse Books / A division of Dark Horse Comics LLC / 10956 SE Main Street / Milwaukie, OR 97222

DarkHorse.com

To find a comics shop in your area, visit comicshoplocator.com

First edition: March 2021

Ebook ISBN 978-1-50672-253-5 / Trade Paperback ISBN 978-1-50672-252-8

10 9 8 7 6 5 4 3 2 1

Printed in China

Neil Hankerson Executive Vice President • Tom Weddle Chief Financial Officer • Randy Stradley Vice President of Publishing • Nick McWhorter Chief Business Development Officer • Dale LaFountain Chief Information Officer • Matt Parkinson Vice President of Marketing • Vanessa Todd-Holmes Vice President of Production and Scheduling • Mark Bernardi Vice President of Book Trade and Digital Sales • Ken Lizzi General Counsel • Dave Marshall Editor in Chief • Davey Estrada Editorial Director • Chris Warner Senior Books Editor • Cary Grazzini Director of Specialty Projects • Lia Ribacchi Art Director • Matt Dryer Director of Digital Art and Prepress • Michael Gombos Senior Director of Licensed Publications • Kari Yadro Director of Custom Programs • Kari Torson Director of International Licensing • Sean Brice Director of Trade Sales

Library of Congress Cataloging-in-Publication Data
Names: Dorkin, Evan, author. | Langridge, Roger, artist.
Title: Bill & Ted are doomed / script, Evan Dorkin ; art and letters, Roger Langridge.
Other titles: Bill and Ted are doomed
Description: First edition. | Milwaukie, OR : Dark Horse Books, 2021. | "Collects issues #1-#4 of the Dark Horse Comics series Bill & Ted Are Doomed" | Summary: "This new series is a direct sequel to Bogus Journey and prequel to Face the Music and part of the Bill and Ted canon bringing in screenwriter and creator Ed Solomon to the table along with bringing back legendary Bill and Ted comics writer Evan Dorkin and acclaimed artist Roger Langridge!"-- Provided by publisher.
Identifiers: LCCN 2020044053 (print) | LCCN 2020044054 (ebook) | ISBN 9781506722528 (trade paperback) | ISBN 9781506722535 (ebook other)
Subjects: LCSH: Comic books, strips, etc.
Classification: LCC PN6728.B4966 D67 2021 (print) | LCC PN6728.B4966 (ebook) | DDC 741.5/973--dc23
LC record available at https://lccn.loc.gov/2020044053
LC ebook record available at https://lccn.loc.gov/2020044054

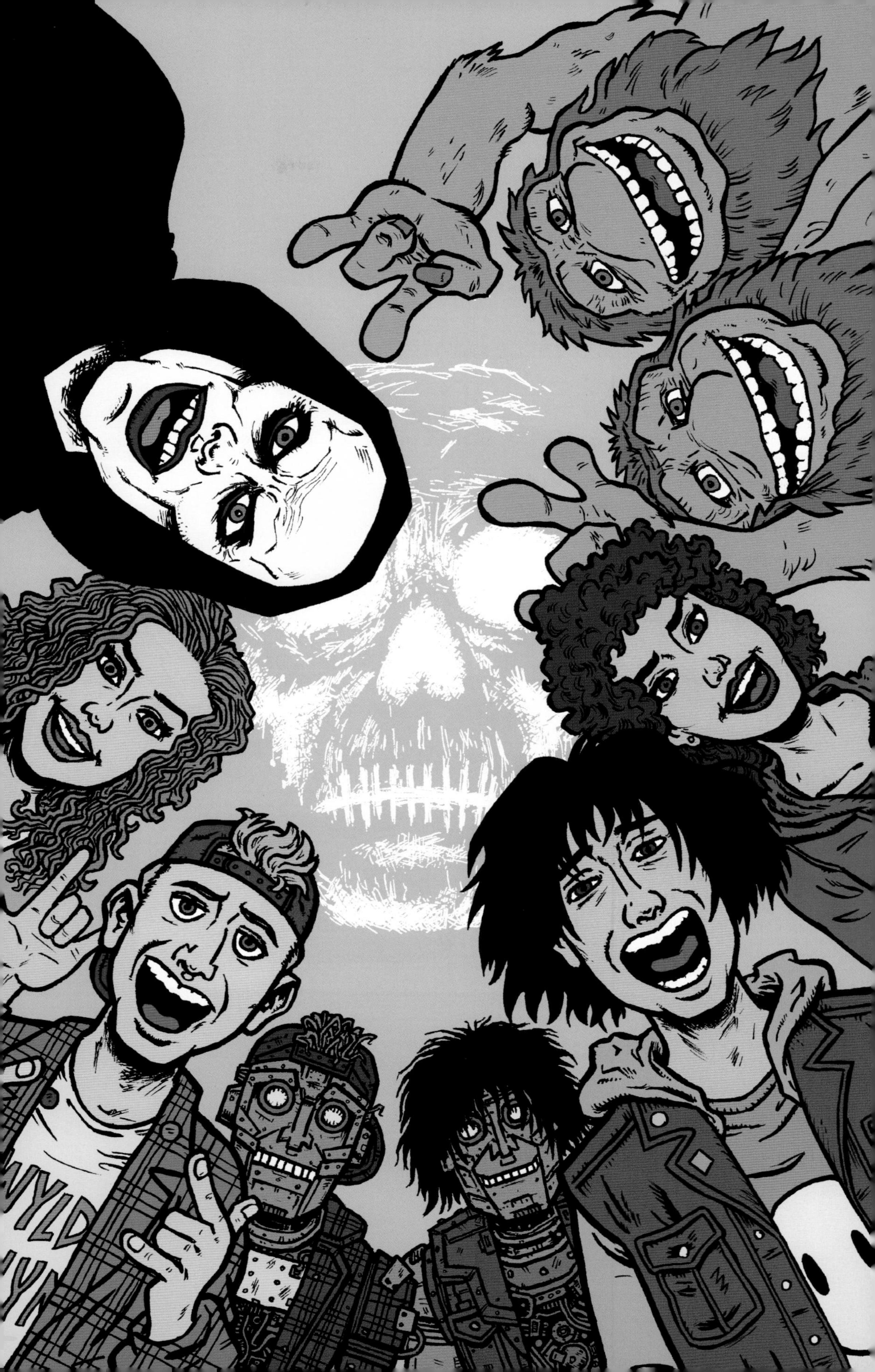

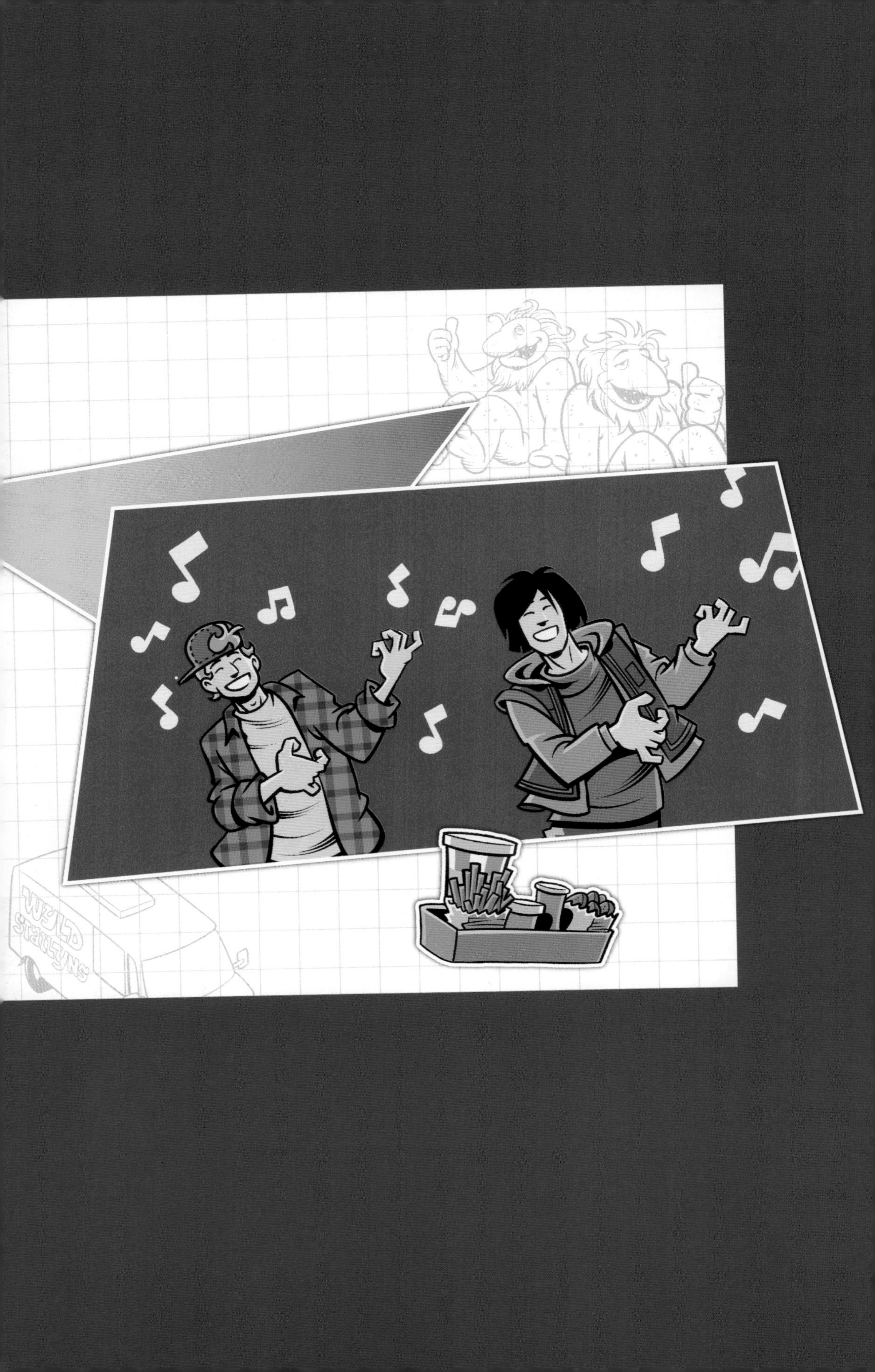
WYLD STALLYNS

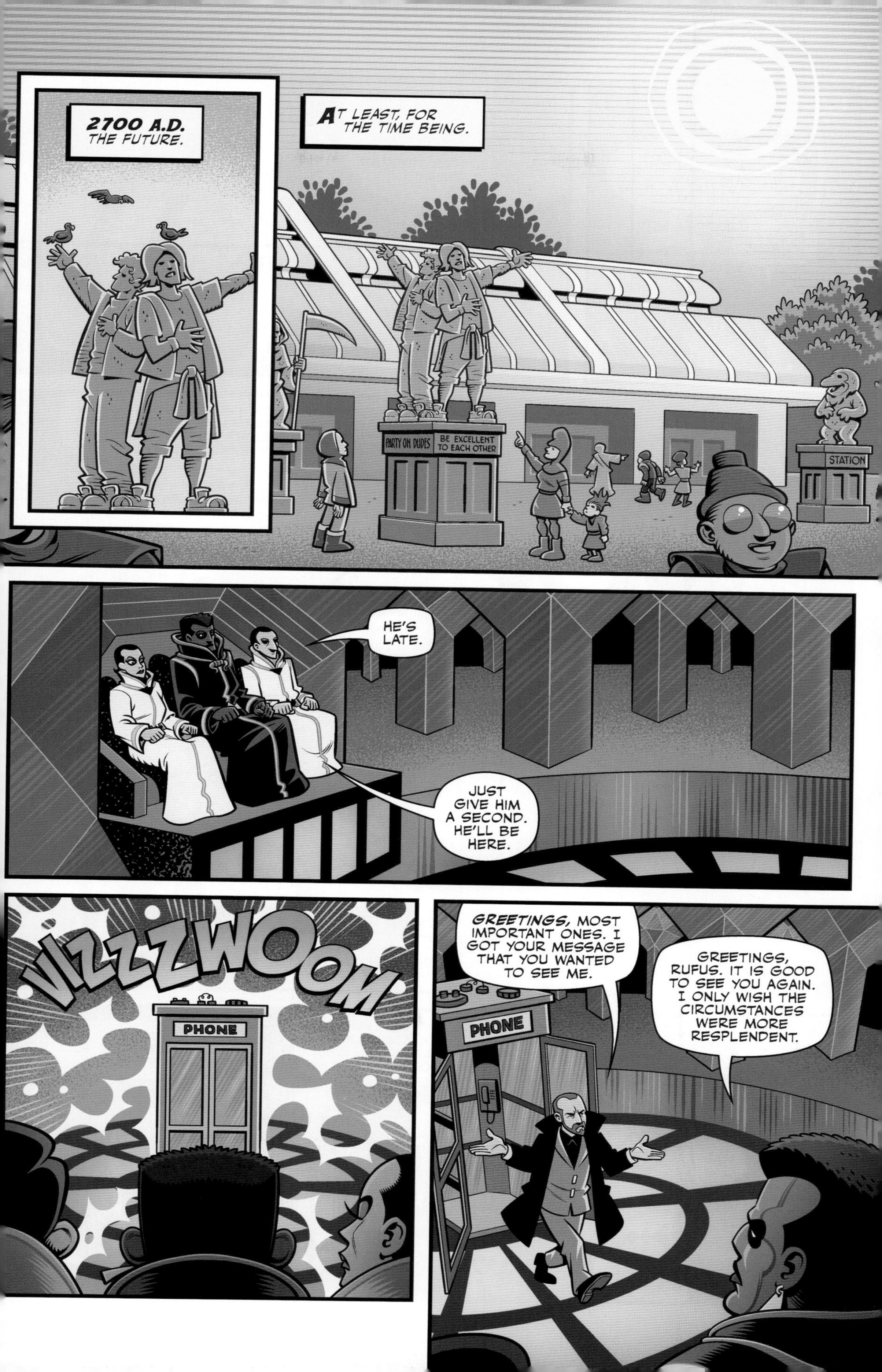
2700 A.D.
THE FUTURE.
AT LEAST, FOR THE TIME BEING.
PARTY ON DUDES
BE EXCELLENT TO EACH OTHER
STATION
HE'S LATE.
JUST GIVE HIM A SECOND. HE'LL BE HERE.
VIZZZWOOM
PHONE
GREETINGS, MOST IMPORTANT ONES. I GOT YOUR MESSAGE THAT YOU WANTED TO SEE ME.
GREETINGS, RUFUS. IT IS GOOD TO SEE YOU AGAIN. I ONLY WISH THE CIRCUMSTANCES WERE MORE RESPLENDENT.
PHONE

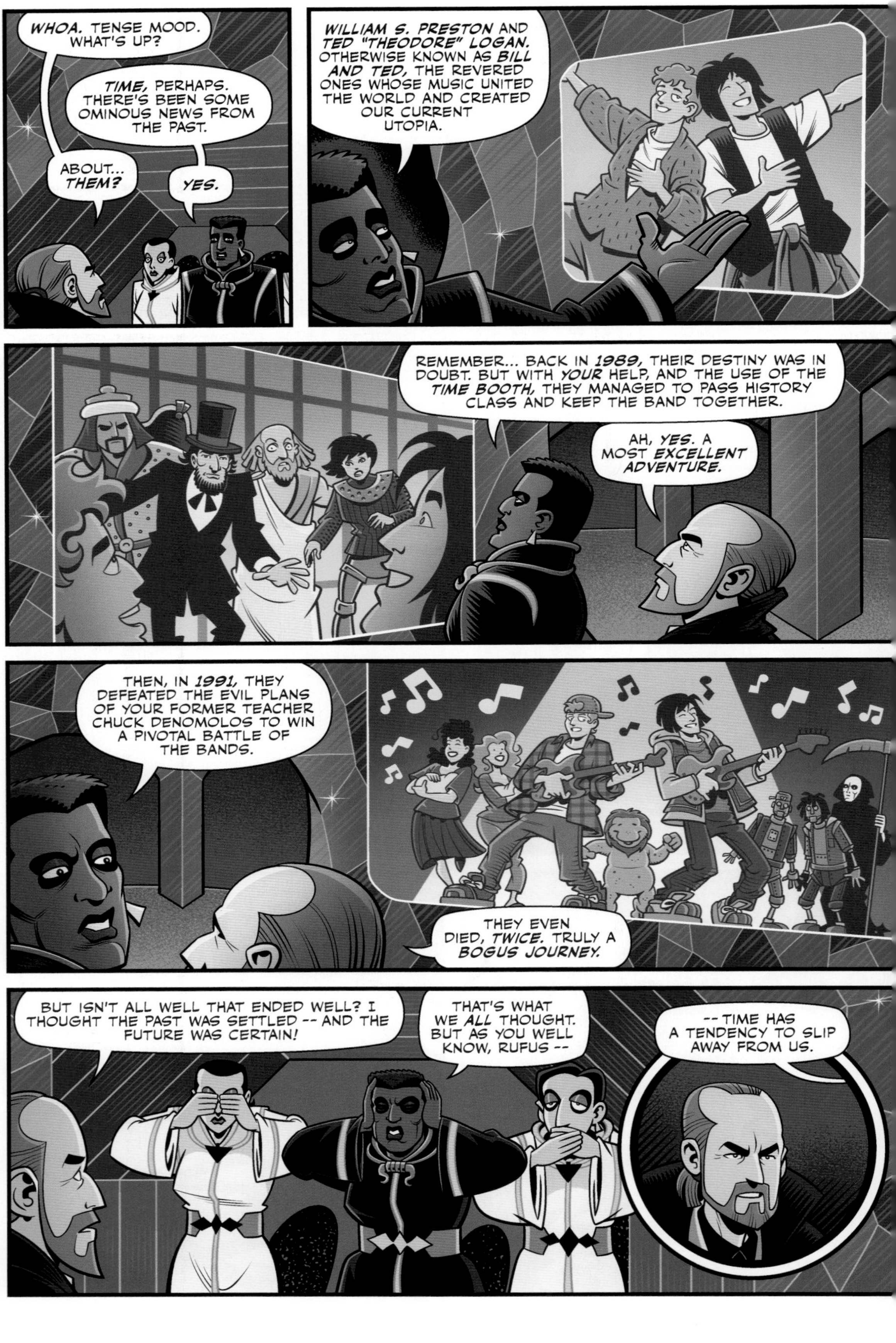
WHOA. TENSE MOOD. WHAT'S UP?
TIME, PERHAPS. THERE'S BEEN SOME OMINOUS NEWS FROM THE PAST.
ABOUT... THEM?
YES.
WILLIAM S. PRESTON AND TED "THEODORE" LOGAN. OTHERWISE KNOWN AS BILL AND TED, THE REVERED ONES WHOSE MUSIC UNITED THE WORLD AND CREATED OUR CURRENT UTOPIA.
REMEMBER... BACK IN 1989, THEIR DESTINY WAS IN DOUBT. BUT WITH YOUR HELP, AND THE USE OF THE TIME BOOTH, THEY MANAGED TO PASS HISTORY CLASS AND KEEP THE BAND TOGETHER.
AH, YES. A MOST EXCELLENT ADVENTURE.
THEN, IN 1991, THEY DEFEATED THE EVIL PLANS OF YOUR FORMER TEACHER CHUCK DENOMOLOS TO WIN A PIVOTAL BATTLE OF THE BANDS.
THEY EVEN DIED, TWICE. TRULY A BOGUS JOURNEY.
BUT ISN'T ALL WELL THAT ENDED WELL? I THOUGHT THE PAST WAS SETTLED -- AND THE FUTURE WAS CERTAIN!
THAT'S WHAT WE ALL THOUGHT. BUT AS YOU WELL KNOW, RUFUS --
-- TIME HAS A TENDENCY TO SLIP AWAY FROM US.

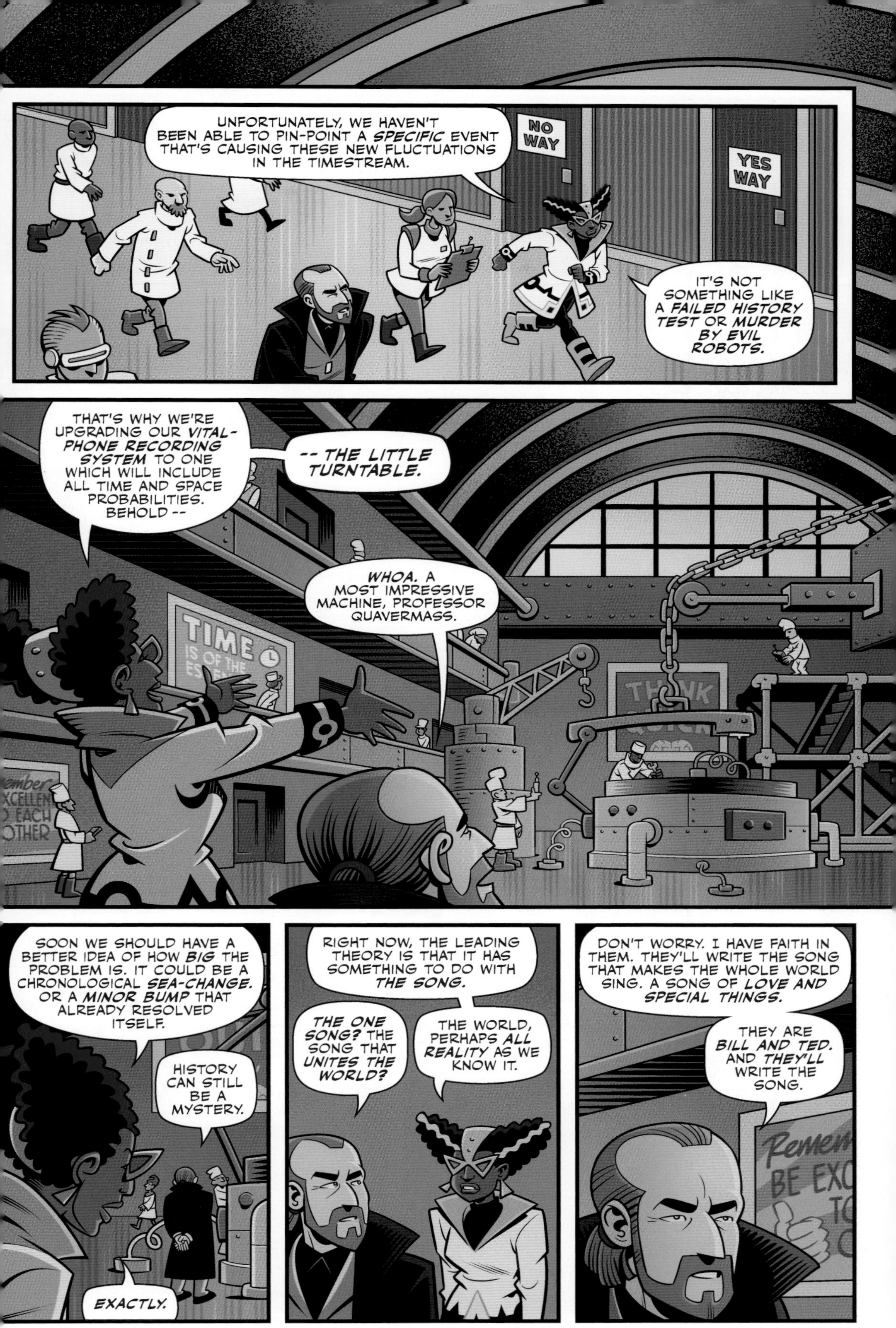
UNFORTUNATELY, WE HAVEN'T BEEN ABLE TO PIN-POINT A *SPECIFIC* EVENT THAT'S CAUSING THESE NEW FLUCTUATIONS IN THE TIMESTREAM.
NO WAY
YES WAY
IT'S NOT SOMETHING LIKE A *FAILED HISTORY TEST* OR *MURDER BY EVIL ROBOTS.*
THAT'S WHY WE'RE UPGRADING OUR *VITAL-PHONE RECORDING SYSTEM* TO ONE WHICH WILL INCLUDE ALL TIME AND SPACE PROBABILITIES. BEHOLD --
-- THE LITTLE TURNTABLE.
WHOA. A MOST IMPRESSIVE MACHINE, PROFESSOR QUAVERMASS.
TIME IS OF THE
SOON WE SHOULD HAVE A BETTER IDEA OF HOW *BIG* THE PROBLEM IS. IT COULD BE A CHRONOLOGICAL *SEA-CHANGE.* OR A *MINOR BUMP* THAT ALREADY RESOLVED ITSELF.
HISTORY CAN STILL BE A MYSTERY.
EXACTLY.
RIGHT NOW, THE LEADING THEORY IS THAT IT HAS SOMETHING TO DO WITH *THE SONG.*
THE ONE SONG? THE SONG THAT *UNITES THE WORLD?*
THE WORLD, PERHAPS *ALL REALITY* AS WE KNOW IT.
DON'T WORRY. I HAVE FAITH IN THEM. THEY'LL WRITE THE SONG THAT MAKES THE WHOLE WORLD SING. A SONG OF *LOVE AND SPECIAL THINGS.*
THEY ARE *BILL AND TED.* AND *THEY'LL* WRITE THE SONG.

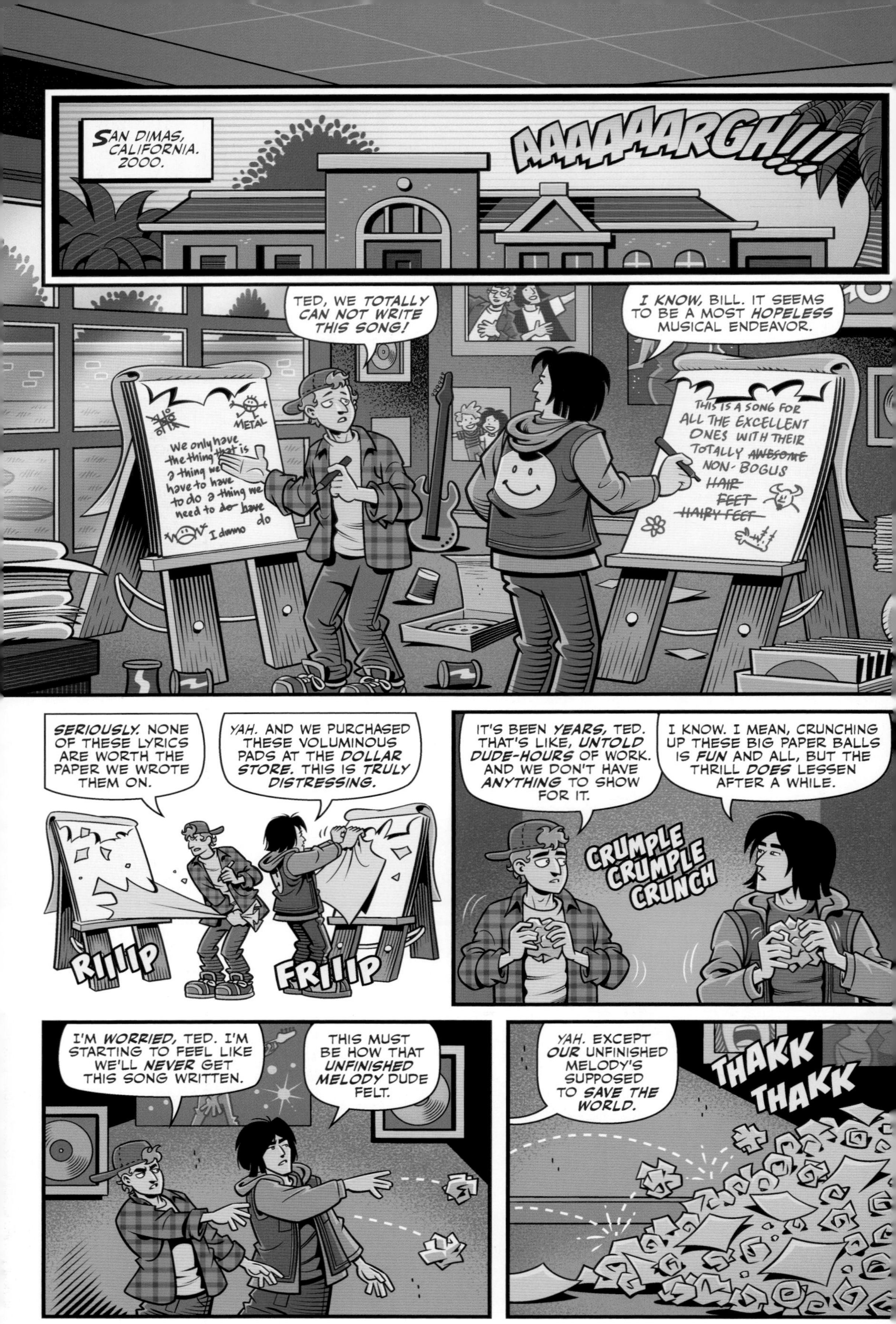
SAN DIMAS, CALIFORNIA. 2000.
AAAAAARGH!!!
TED, WE TOTALLY CAN NOT WRITE THIS SONG!
I KNOW, BILL. IT SEEMS TO BE A MOST HOPELESS MUSICAL ENDEAVOR.
METAL
We only have the thing that is a thing we have to have to do a thing we need to do have do
I dunno
THIS IS A SONG FOR ALL THE EXCELLENT ONES WITH THEIR TOTALLY AWESOME NON-BOGUS HAIR FEET HAIRY FEET
SERIOUSLY. NONE OF THESE LYRICS ARE WORTH THE PAPER WE WROTE THEM ON.
YAH. AND WE PURCHASED THESE VOLUMINOUS PADS AT THE DOLLAR STORE. THIS IS TRULY DISTRESSING.
RIIIP
FRIIIP
IT'S BEEN YEARS, TED. THAT'S LIKE, UNTOLD DUDE-HOURS OF WORK. AND WE DON'T HAVE ANYTHING TO SHOW FOR IT.
I KNOW. I MEAN, CRUNCHING UP THESE BIG PAPER BALLS IS FUN AND ALL, BUT THE THRILL DOES LESSEN AFTER A WHILE.
CRUMPLE CRUMPLE CRUNCH
I'M WORRIED, TED. I'M STARTING TO FEEL LIKE WE'LL NEVER GET THIS SONG WRITTEN.
THIS MUST BE HOW THAT UNFINISHED MELODY DUDE FELT.
YAH. EXCEPT OUR UNFINISHED MELODY'S SUPPOSED TO SAVE THE WORLD.
THAKK THAKK

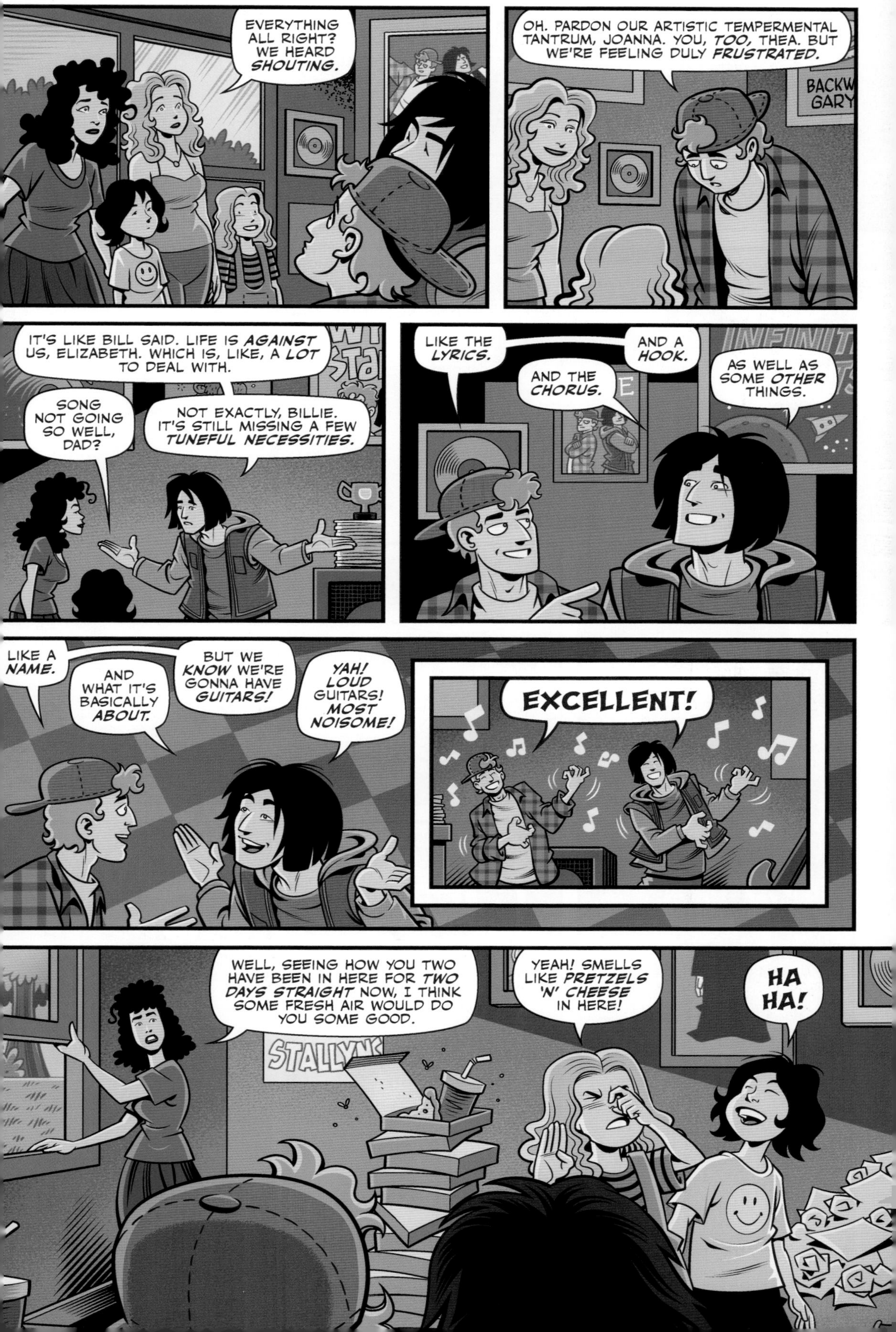
EVERYTHING ALL RIGHT? WE HEARD SHOUTING.
OH. PARDON OUR ARTISTIC TEMPERMENTAL TANTRUM, JOANNA. YOU, TOO, THEA. BUT WE'RE FEELING DULY FRUSTRATED.
IT'S LIKE BILL SAID. LIFE IS AGAINST US, ELIZABETH. WHICH IS, LIKE, A LOT TO DEAL WITH.
SONG NOT GOING SO WELL, DAD?
NOT EXACTLY, BILLIE. IT'S STILL MISSING A FEW TUNEFUL NECESSITIES.
LIKE THE LYRICS.
AND A HOOK.
AND THE CHORUS.
AS WELL AS SOME OTHER THINGS.
LIKE A NAME.
AND WHAT IT'S BASICALLY ABOUT.
BUT WE KNOW WE'RE GONNA HAVE GUITARS!
YAH! LOUD GUITARS! MOST NOISOME!
EXCELLENT!
WELL, SEEING HOW YOU TWO HAVE BEEN IN HERE FOR TWO DAYS STRAIGHT NOW, I THINK SOME FRESH AIR WOULD DO YOU SOME GOOD.
YEAH! SMELLS LIKE PRETZELS 'N' CHEESE IN HERE!
HA HA!

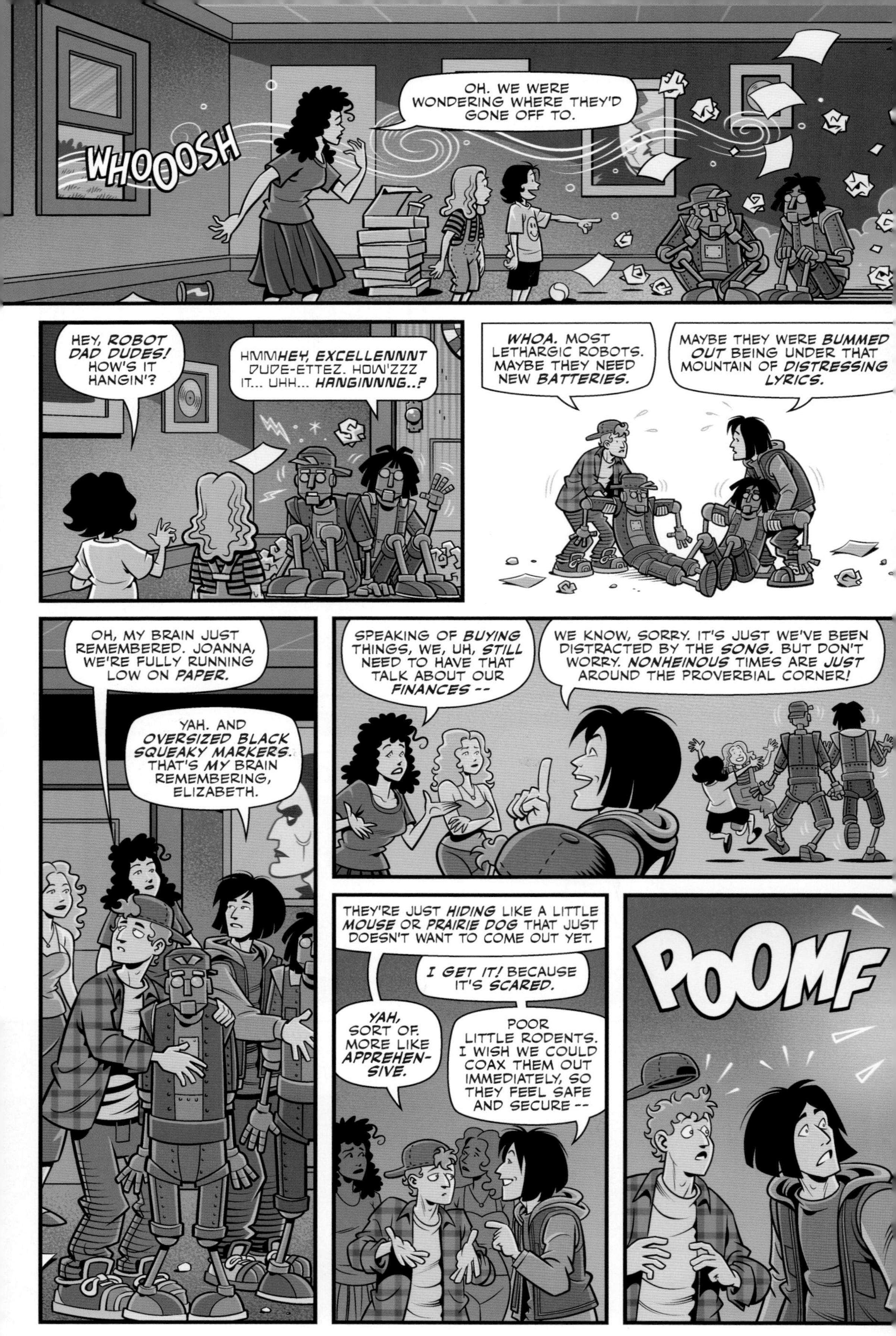
WHOOOSH
OH. WE WERE WONDERING WHERE THEY'D GONE OFF TO.
HEY, ROBOT DAD DUDES! HOW'S IT HANGIN'?
HMMHEY, EXCELLENNNT DUDE-ETTEZ. HOW'ZZZ IT... UHH... HANGINNNG..?
WHOA. MOST LETHARGIC ROBOTS. MAYBE THEY NEED NEW BATTERIES.
MAYBE THEY WERE BUMMED OUT BEING UNDER THAT MOUNTAIN OF DISTRESSING LYRICS.
OH, MY BRAIN JUST REMEMBERED. JOANNA, WE'RE FULLY RUNNING LOW ON PAPER.
YAH. AND OVERSIZED BLACK SQUEAKY MARKERS. THAT'S MY BRAIN REMEMBERING, ELIZABETH.
SPEAKING OF BUYING THINGS, WE, UH, STILL NEED TO HAVE THAT TALK ABOUT OUR FINANCES --
WE KNOW, SORRY. IT'S JUST WE'VE BEEN DISTRACTED BY THE SONG. BUT DON'T WORRY. NONHEINOUS TIMES ARE JUST AROUND THE PROVERBIAL CORNER!
THEY'RE JUST HIDING LIKE A LITTLE MOUSE OR PRAIRIE DOG THAT JUST DOESN'T WANT TO COME OUT YET.
I GET IT! BECAUSE IT'S SCARED.
YAH, SORT OF. MORE LIKE APPREHENSIVE.
POOR LITTLE RODENTS. I WISH WE COULD COAX THEM OUT IMMEDIATELY, SO THEY FEEL SAFE AND SECURE --
POOMF

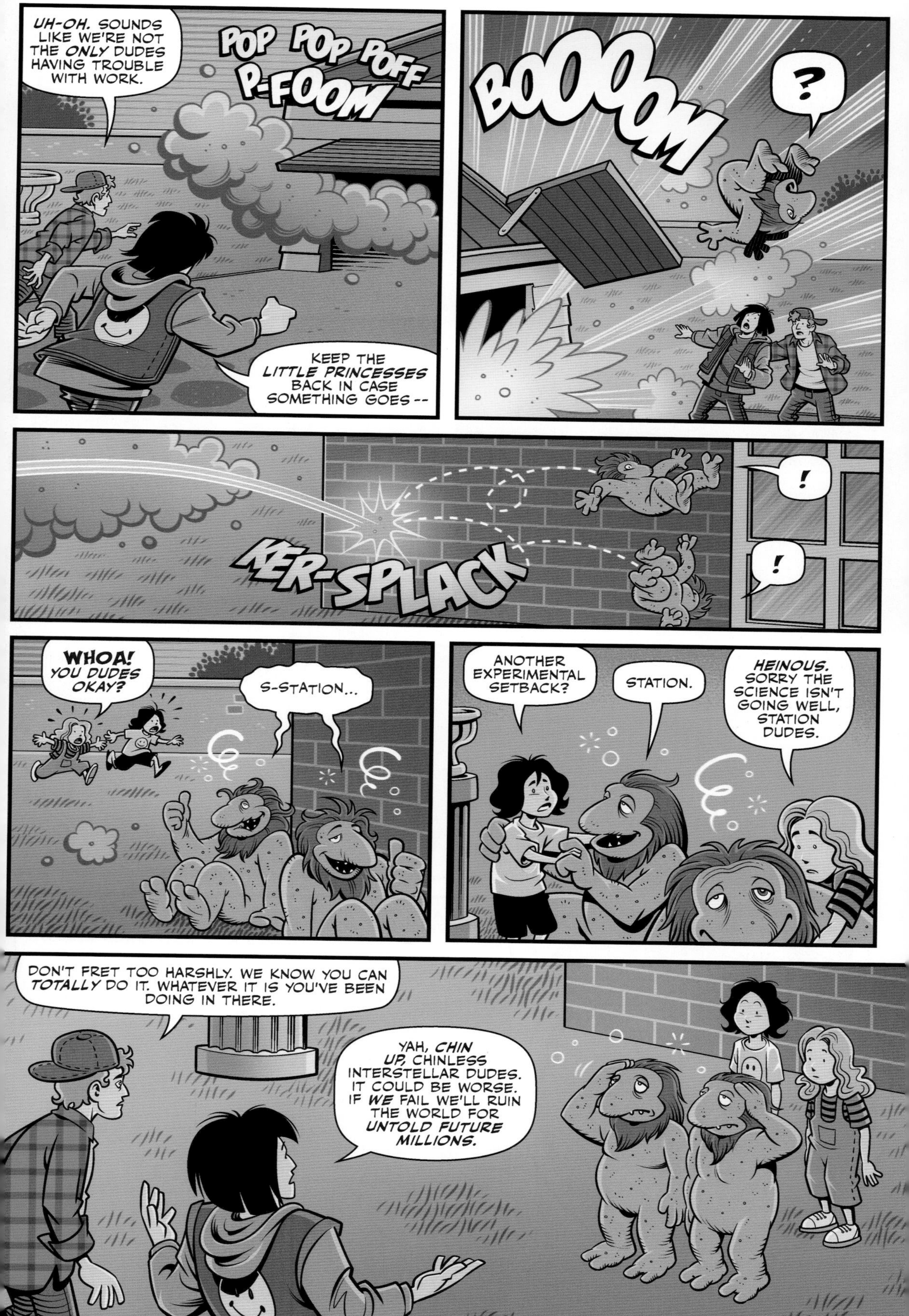
UH-OH. SOUNDS LIKE WE'RE NOT THE ONLY DUDES HAVING TROUBLE WITH WORK.
POP POP POFF P-FOOM
KEEP THE LITTLE PRINCESSES BACK IN CASE SOMETHING GOES --
BOOOOOM
?
KER-SPLACK
!
!
WHOA! YOU DUDES OKAY?
S-STATION...
ANOTHER EXPERIMENTAL SETBACK?
STATION.
HEINOUS. SORRY THE SCIENCE ISN'T GOING WELL, STATION DUDES.
DON'T FRET TOO HARSHLY. WE KNOW YOU CAN TOTALLY DO IT. WHATEVER IT IS YOU'VE BEEN DOING IN THERE.
YAH, CHIN UP, CHINLESS INTERSTELLAR DUDES. IT COULD BE WORSE. IF WE FAIL WE'LL RUIN THE WORLD FOR UNTOLD FUTURE MILLIONS.

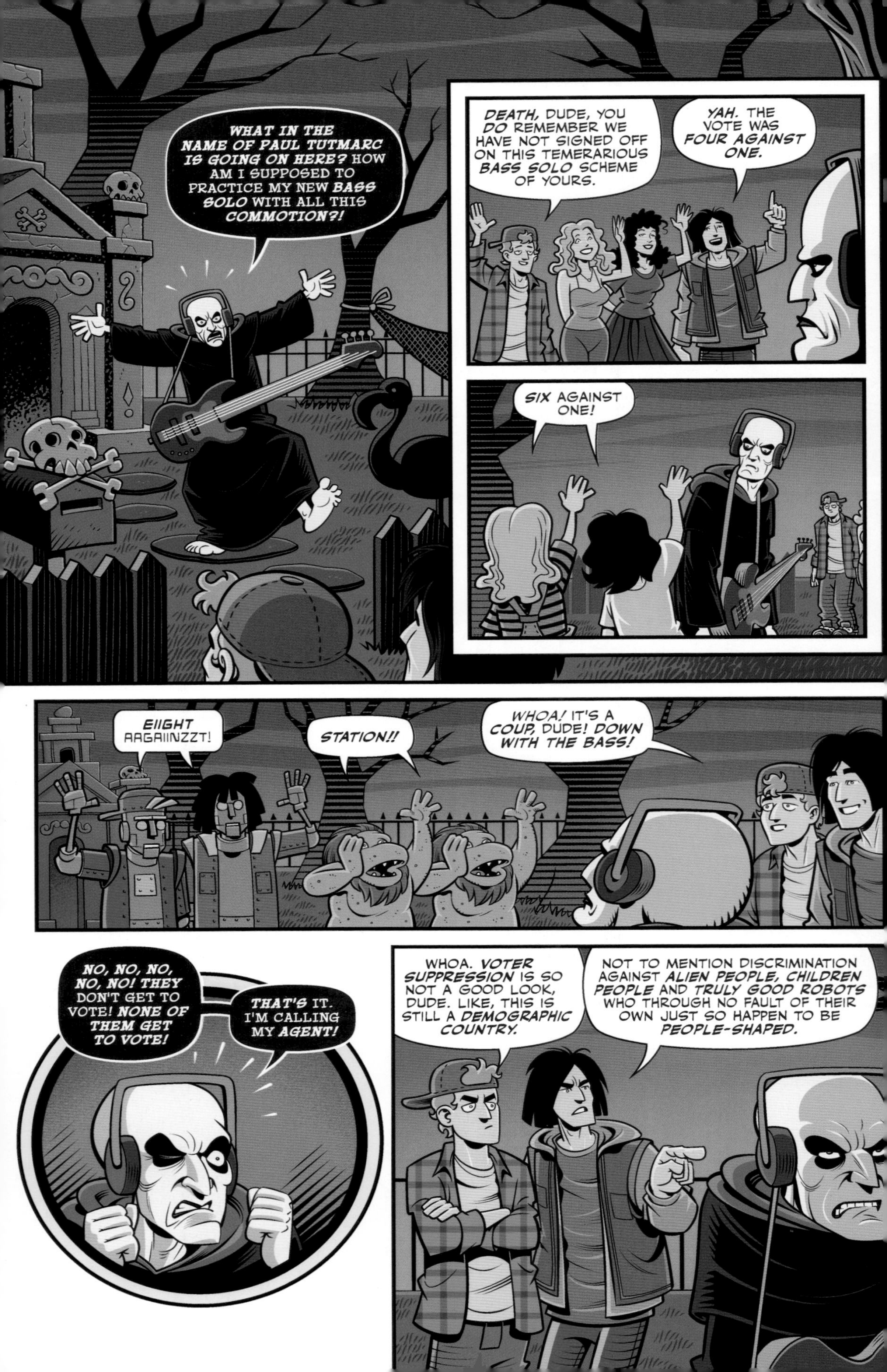
WHAT IN THE NAME OF PAUL TUTMARC IS GOING ON HERE? HOW AM I SUPPOSED TO PRACTICE MY NEW BASS SOLO WITH ALL THIS COMMOTION?!
DEATH, DUDE, YOU DO REMEMBER WE HAVE NOT SIGNED OFF ON THIS TEMERARIOUS BASS SOLO SCHEME OF YOURS.
YAH. THE VOTE WAS FOUR AGAINST ONE.
SIX AGAINST ONE!
EIIGHT AAGAIINZZT!
STATION!!
WHOA! IT'S A COUP, DUDE! DOWN WITH THE BASS!
NO, NO, NO, NO, NO! THEY DON'T GET TO VOTE! NONE OF THEM GET TO VOTE!
THAT'S IT. I'M CALLING MY AGENT!
WHOA. VOTER SUPPRESSION IS SO NOT A GOOD LOOK, DUDE. LIKE, THIS IS STILL A DEMOGRAPHIC COUNTRY.
NOT TO MENTION DISCRIMINATION AGAINST ALIEN PEOPLE, CHILDREN PEOPLE AND TRULY GOOD ROBOTS WHO THROUGH NO FAULT OF THEIR OWN JUST SO HAPPEN TO BE PEOPLE-SHAPED.

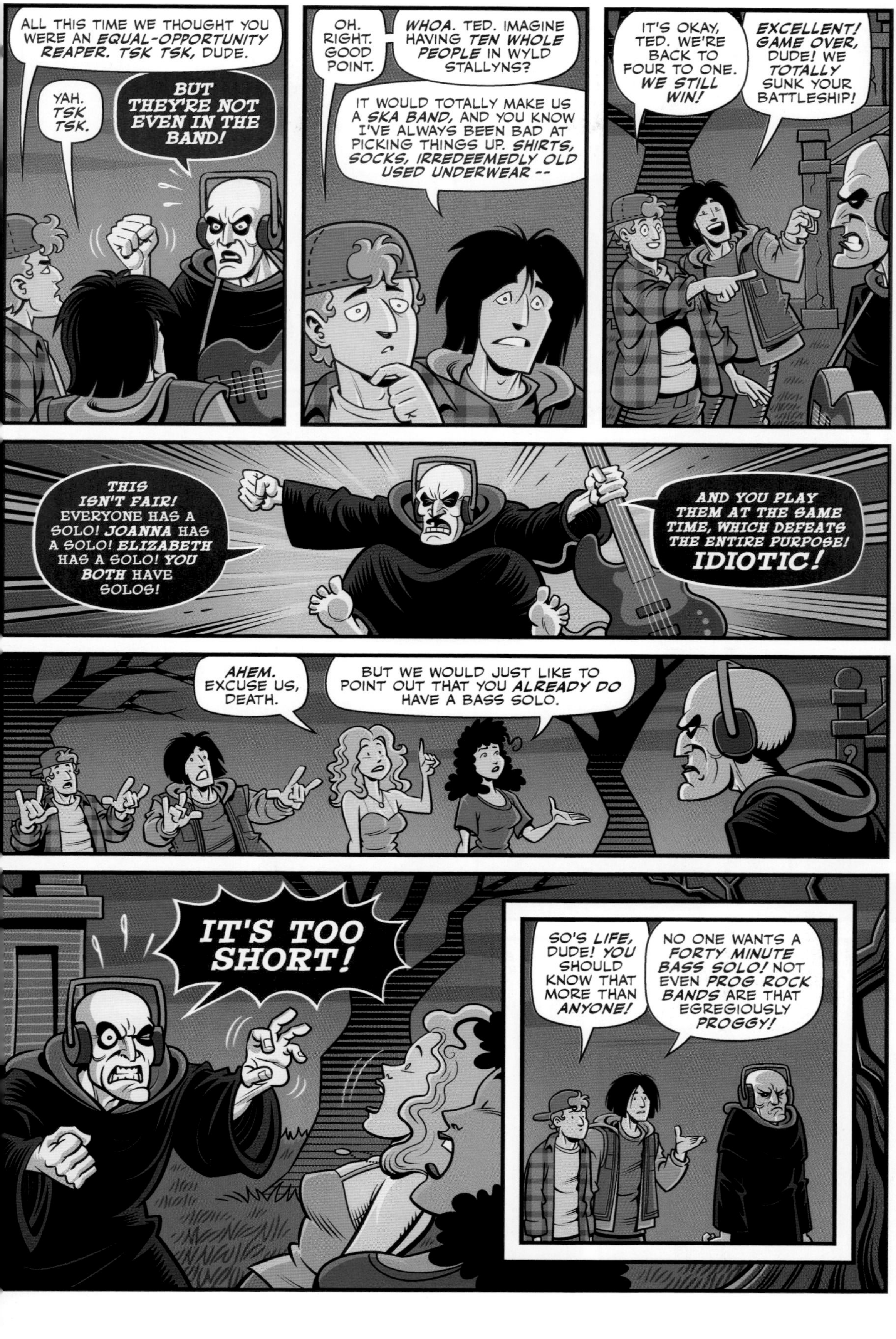
ALL THIS TIME WE THOUGHT YOU WERE AN *EQUAL-OPPORTUNITY REAPER. TSK TSK,* DUDE.
YAH. *TSK TSK.*
BUT THEY'RE NOT EVEN IN THE BAND!
OH. RIGHT. GOOD POINT.
WHOA. TED. IMAGINE HAVING *TEN WHOLE PEOPLE* IN WYLD STALLYNS?
IT WOULD TOTALLY MAKE US A *SKA BAND,* AND YOU KNOW I'VE ALWAYS BEEN BAD AT PICKING THINGS UP. *SHIRTS, SOCKS, IRREDEEMEDLY OLD USED UNDERWEAR --*
IT'S OKAY, TED. WE'RE BACK TO FOUR TO ONE. *WE STILL WIN!*
EXCELLENT! GAME OVER, DUDE! WE *TOTALLY* SUNK YOUR BATTLESHIP!
THIS ISN'T FAIR! EVERYONE HAS A SOLO! *JOANNA* HAS A SOLO! *ELIZABETH* HAS A SOLO! *YOU BOTH* HAVE SOLOS!
AND YOU PLAY THEM AT THE SAME TIME, WHICH DEFEATS THE ENTIRE PURPOSE! IDIOTIC!
AHEM. EXCUSE US, DEATH.
BUT WE WOULD JUST LIKE TO POINT OUT THAT YOU *ALREADY DO* HAVE A BASS SOLO.
IT'S TOO SHORT!
SO'S *LIFE,* DUDE! *YOU* SHOULD KNOW THAT MORE THAN *ANYONE!*
NO ONE WANTS A *FORTY MINUTE BASS SOLO!* NOT EVEN *PROG ROCK BANDS* ARE THAT EGREGIOUSLY *PROGGY!*

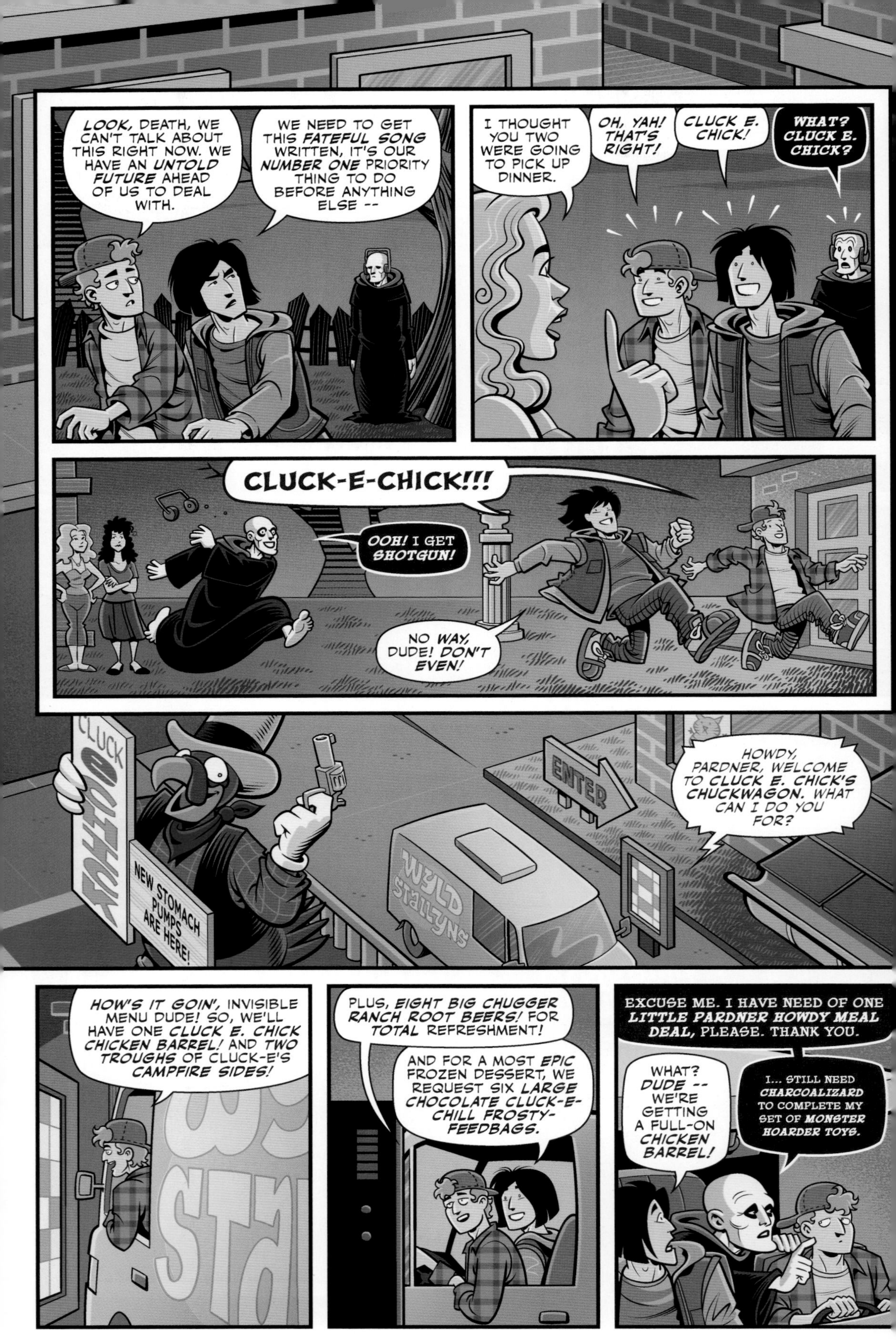
LOOK, DEATH, WE CAN'T TALK ABOUT THIS RIGHT NOW. WE HAVE AN UNTOLD FUTURE AHEAD OF US TO DEAL WITH.
WE NEED TO GET THIS FATEFUL SONG WRITTEN, IT'S OUR NUMBER ONE PRIORITY THING TO DO BEFORE ANYTHING ELSE --
I THOUGHT YOU TWO WERE GOING TO PICK UP DINNER.
OH, YAH! THAT'S RIGHT!
CLUCK E. CHICK!
WHAT? CLUCK E. CHICK?
CLUCK-E-CHICK!!!
OOH! I GET SHOTGUN!
NO WAY, DUDE! DON'T EVEN!
CLUCK
NEW STOMACH PUMPS ARE HERE!
ENTER
WYLD STALLYNS
HOWDY, PARDNER, WELCOME TO CLUCK E. CHICK'S CHUCKWAGON. WHAT CAN I DO YOU FOR?
HOW'S IT GOIN', INVISIBLE MENU DUDE! SO, WE'LL HAVE ONE CLUCK E. CHICK CHICKEN BARREL! AND TWO TROUGHS OF CLUCK-E'S CAMPFIRE SIDES!
PLUS, EIGHT BIG CHUGGER RANCH ROOT BEERS! FOR TOTAL REFRESHMENT!
AND FOR A MOST EPIC FROZEN DESSERT, WE REQUEST SIX LARGE CHOCOLATE CLUCK-E-CHILL FROSTY-FEEDBAGS.
EXCUSE ME. I HAVE NEED OF ONE LITTLE PARDNER HOWDY MEAL DEAL, PLEASE. THANK YOU.
WHAT? DUDE -- WE'RE GETTING A FULL-ON CHICKEN BARREL!
I... STILL NEED CHARCOALIZARD TO COMPLETE MY SET OF MONSTER HOARDER TOYS.

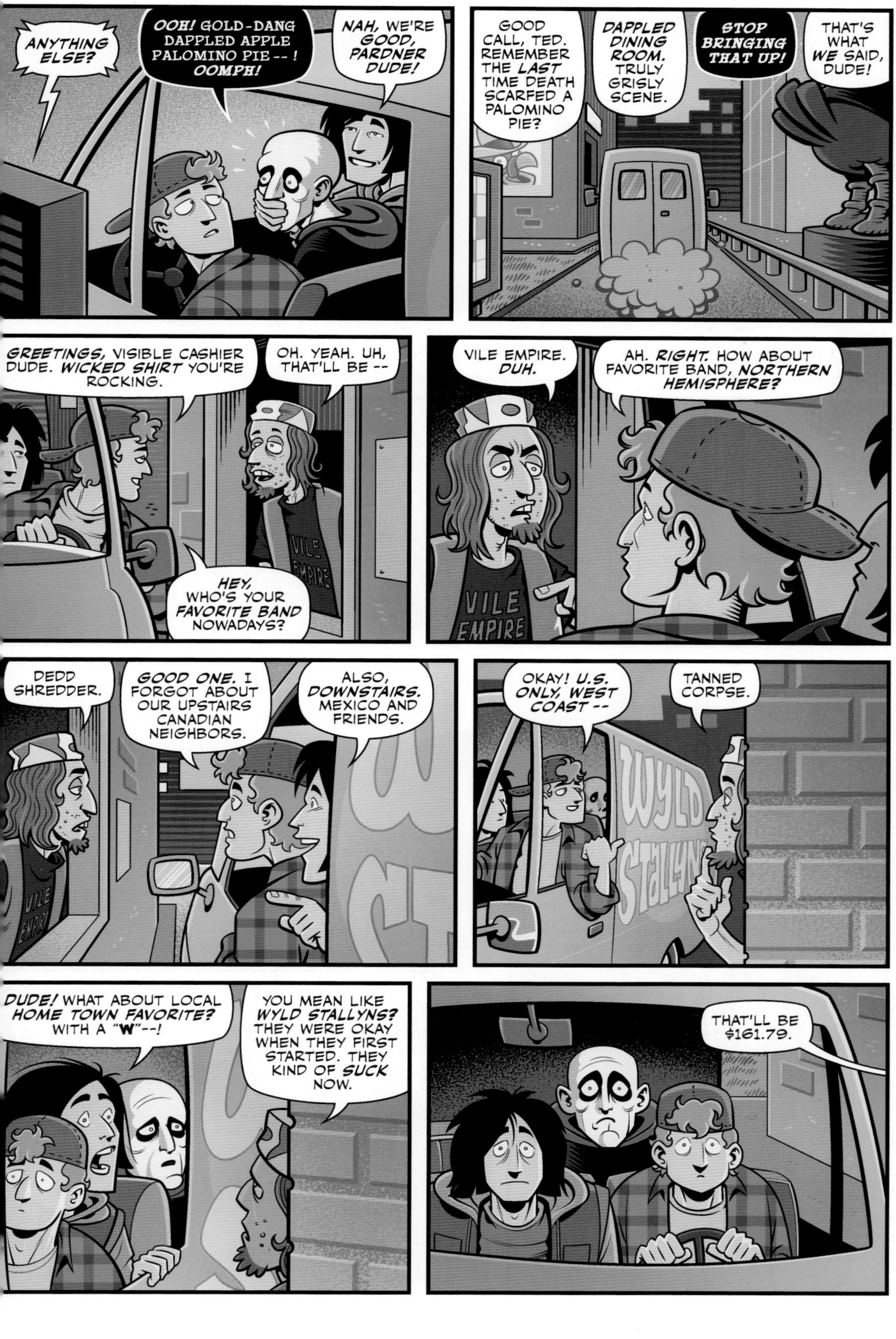

ANYTHING ELSE?
OOH! GOLD-DANG DAPPLED APPLE PALOMINO PIE -- ! OOMPH!
NAH, WE'RE GOOD, PARDNER DUDE!
GOOD CALL, TED. REMEMBER THE LAST TIME DEATH SCARFED A PALOMINO PIE?
DAPPLED DINING ROOM. TRULY GRISLY SCENE.
STOP BRINGING THAT UP!
THAT'S WHAT WE SAID, DUDE!
GREETINGS, VISIBLE CASHIER DUDE. WICKED SHIRT YOU'RE ROCKING.
OH. YEAH. UH, THAT'LL BE --
HEY, WHO'S YOUR FAVORITE BAND NOWADAYS?
VILE EMPIRE
VILE EMPIRE. DUH.
AH. RIGHT. HOW ABOUT FAVORITE BAND, NORTHERN HEMISPHERE?
VILE EMPIRE
DEDD SHREDDER.
GOOD ONE. I FORGOT ABOUT OUR UPSTAIRS CANADIAN NEIGHBORS.
ALSO, DOWNSTAIRS. MEXICO AND FRIENDS.
OKAY! U.S. ONLY, WEST COAST --
TANNED CORPSE.
WYLD STALLYNS
DUDE! WHAT ABOUT LOCAL HOME TOWN FAVORITE? WITH A "W"--!
YOU MEAN LIKE WYLD STALLYNS? THEY WERE OKAY WHEN THEY FIRST STARTED. THEY KIND OF SUCK NOW.
THAT'LL BE $161.79.

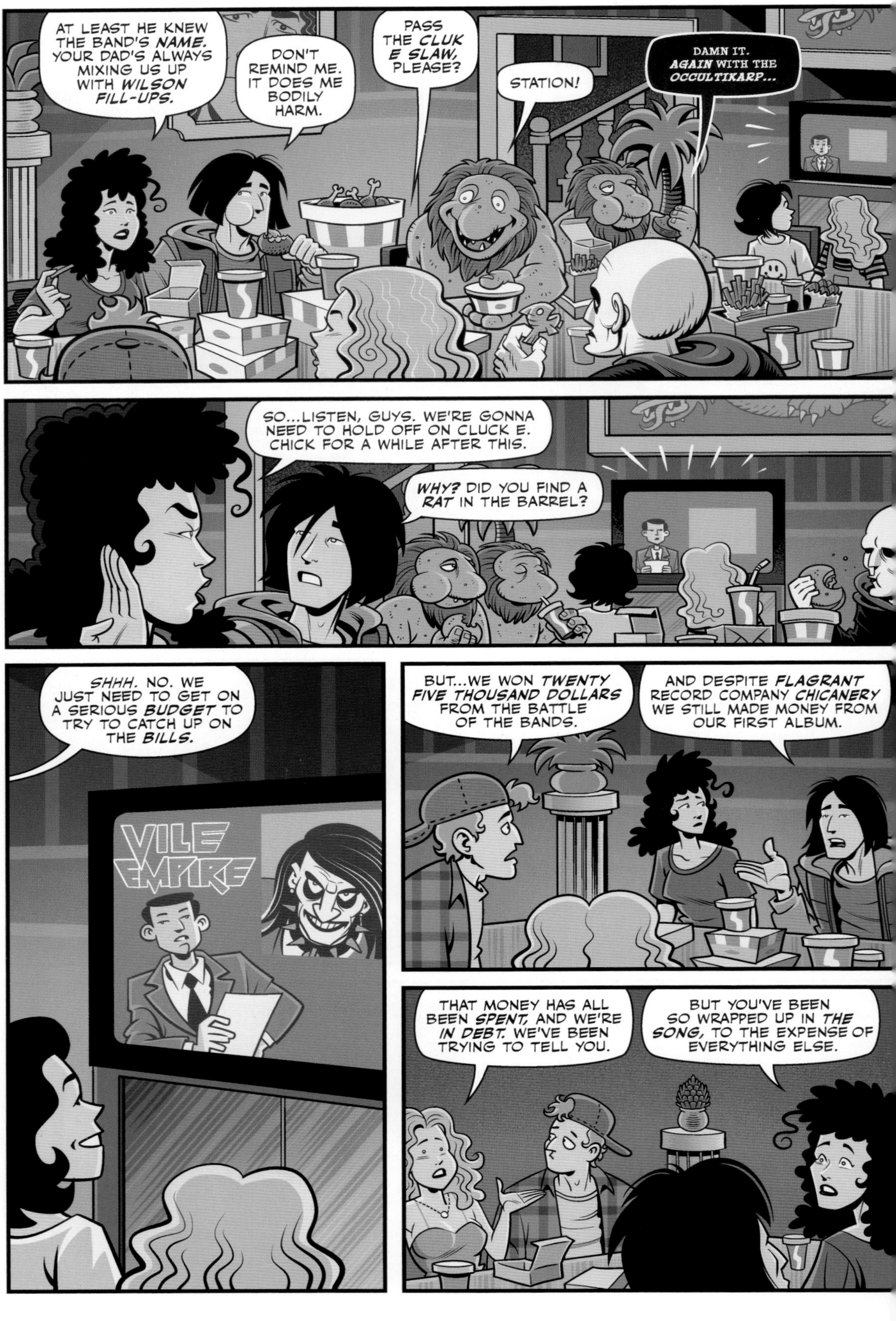
AT LEAST HE KNEW THE BAND'S *NAME.* YOUR DAD'S ALWAYS MIXING US UP WITH *WILSON FILL-UPS.*
DON'T REMIND ME. IT DOES ME BODILY HARM.
PASS THE *CLUK E SLAW,* PLEASE?
STATION!
DAMN IT. *AGAIN* WITH THE *OCCULTIKARP...*
SO...LISTEN, GUYS. WE'RE GONNA NEED TO HOLD OFF ON CLUCK E. CHICK FOR A WHILE AFTER THIS.
WHY? DID YOU FIND A *RAT* IN THE BARREL?
SHHH. NO. WE JUST NEED TO GET ON A SERIOUS *BUDGET* TO TRY TO CATCH UP ON THE *BILLS.*
VILE EMPIRE
BUT...WE WON *TWENTY FIVE THOUSAND DOLLARS* FROM THE BATTLE OF THE BANDS.
AND DESPITE *FLAGRANT* RECORD COMPANY *CHICANERY* WE STILL MADE MONEY FROM OUR FIRST ALBUM.
THAT MONEY HAS ALL BEEN *SPENT,* AND WE'RE *IN DEBT.* WE'VE BEEN TRYING TO TELL YOU.
BUT YOU'VE BEEN SO WRAPPED UP IN *THE SONG,* TO THE EXPENSE OF EVERYTHING ELSE.

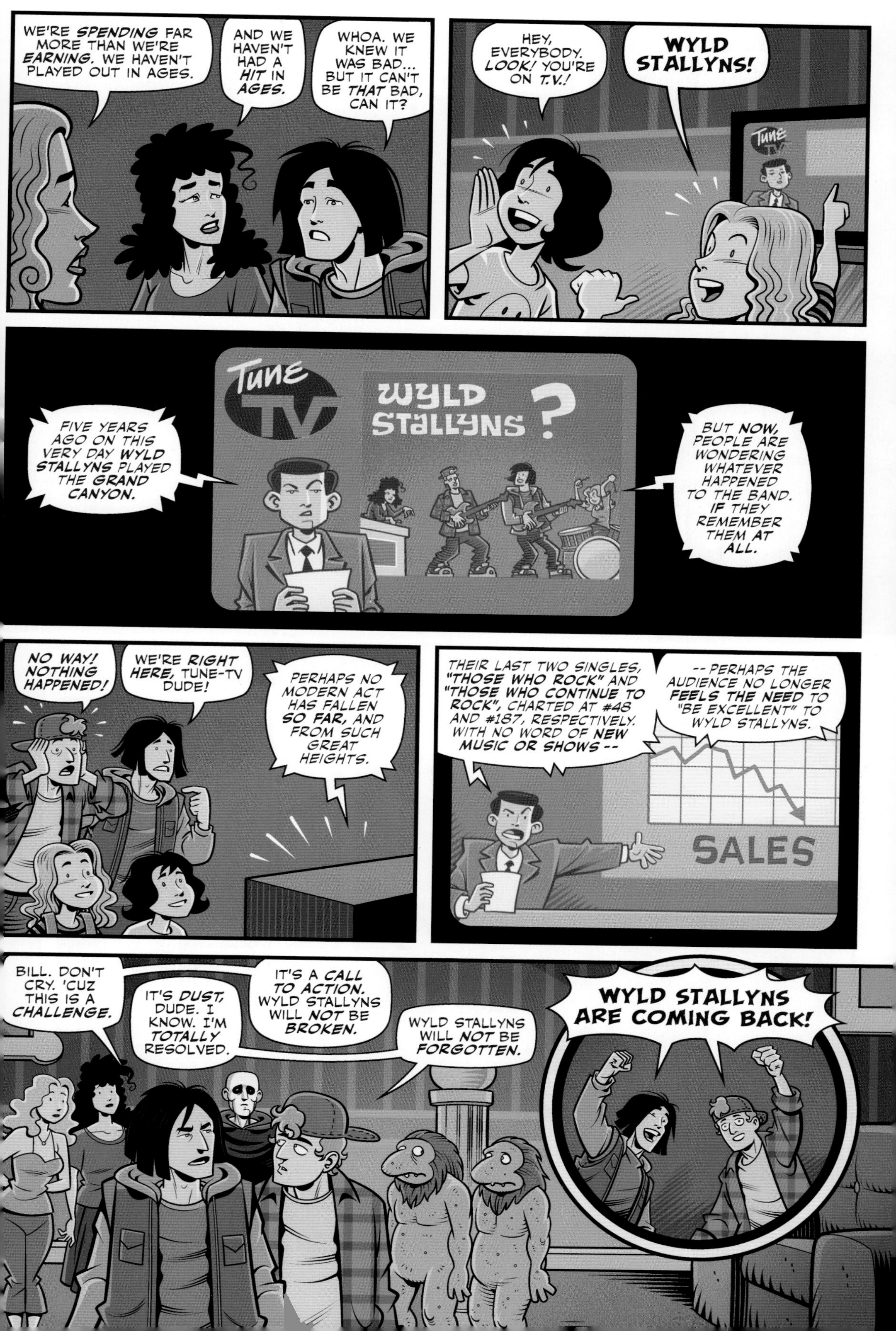
WE'RE SPENDING FAR MORE THAN WE'RE EARNING. WE HAVEN'T PLAYED OUT IN AGES.
AND WE HAVEN'T HAD A HIT IN AGES.
WHOA. WE KNEW IT WAS BAD... BUT IT CAN'T BE THAT BAD, CAN IT?
HEY, EVERYBODY. LOOK! YOU'RE ON T.V.!
WYLD STALLYNS!
TUNE TV
TUNE TV
WYLD STALLYNS ?
FIVE YEARS AGO ON THIS VERY DAY WYLD STALLYNS PLAYED THE GRAND CANYON.
BUT NOW, PEOPLE ARE WONDERING WHATEVER HAPPENED TO THE BAND. IF THEY REMEMBER THEM AT ALL.
NO WAY! NOTHING HAPPENED!
WE'RE RIGHT HERE, TUNE-TV DUDE!
PERHAPS NO MODERN ACT HAS FALLEN SO FAR, AND FROM SUCH GREAT HEIGHTS.
THEIR LAST TWO SINGLES, "THOSE WHO ROCK" AND "THOSE WHO CONTINUE TO ROCK", CHARTED AT #48 AND #187, RESPECTIVELY. WITH NO WORD OF NEW MUSIC OR SHOWS --
-- PERHAPS THE AUDIENCE NO LONGER FEELS THE NEED TO "BE EXCELLENT" TO WYLD STALLYNS.
SALES
BILL. DON'T CRY. 'CUZ THIS IS A CHALLENGE.
IT'S DUST, DUDE. I KNOW. I'M TOTALLY RESOLVED.
IT'S A CALL TO ACTION. WYLD STALLYNS WILL NOT BE BROKEN.
WYLD STALLYNS WILL NOT BE FORGOTTEN.
WYLD STALLYNS ARE COMING BACK!

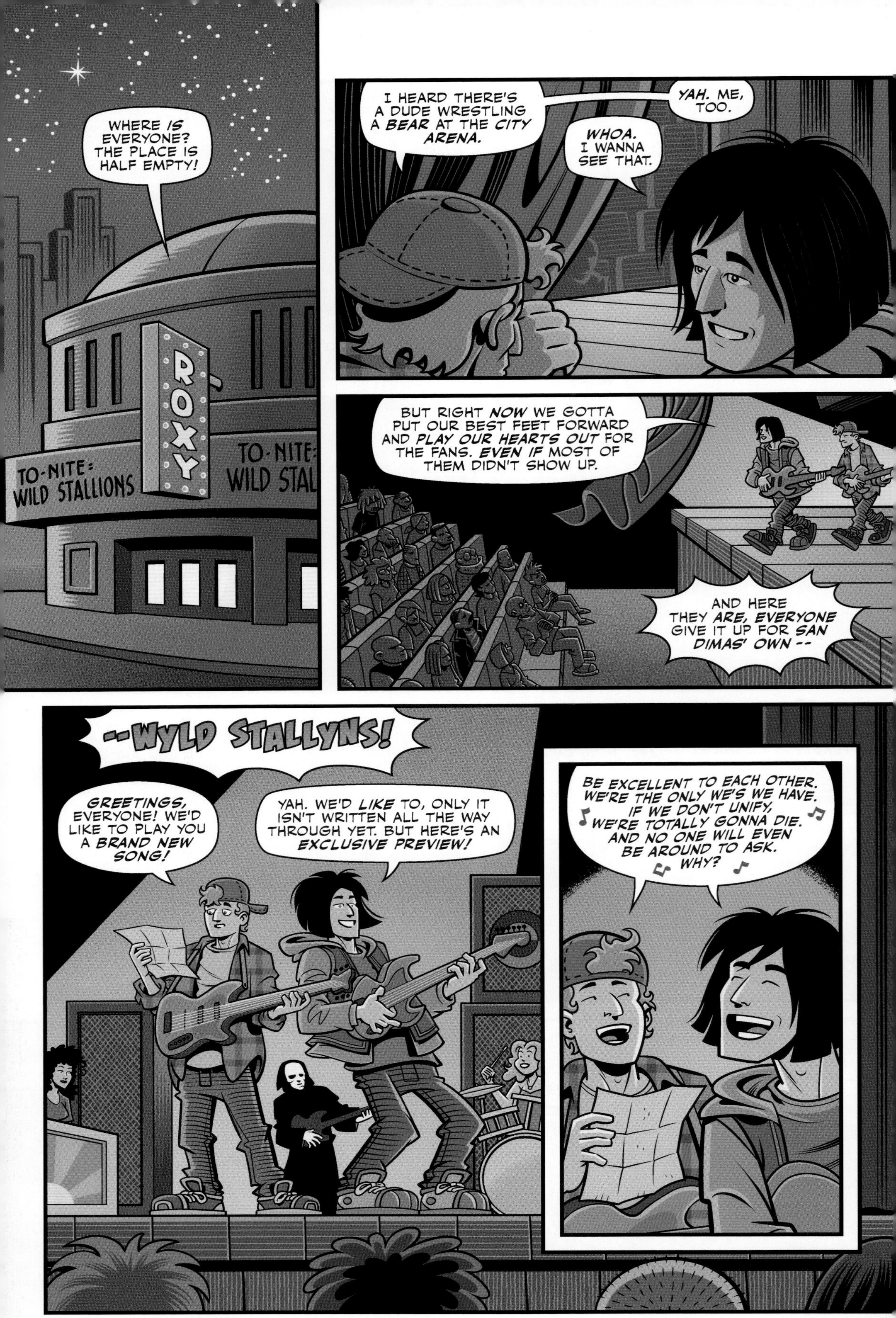
WHERE *IS* EVERYONE? THE PLACE IS HALF EMPTY!
TO-NITE: WILD STALLIONS
ROXY
TO-NITE: WILD STAL
I HEARD THERE'S A DUDE WRESTLING A *BEAR* AT THE *CITY ARENA.*
YAH. ME, TOO.
WHOA. I WANNA SEE THAT.
BUT RIGHT *NOW* WE GOTTA PUT OUR BEST FEET FORWARD AND *PLAY OUR HEARTS OUT* FOR THE FANS. *EVEN IF* MOST OF THEM DIDN'T SHOW UP.
AND HERE THEY *ARE, EVERYONE* GIVE IT UP FOR *SAN DIMAS' OWN* --
--WYLD STALLYNS!
GREETINGS, EVERYONE! WE'D LIKE TO PLAY YOU A *BRAND NEW SONG!*
YAH. WE'D *LIKE* TO, ONLY IT ISN'T WRITTEN ALL THE WAY THROUGH YET. BUT HERE'S AN *EXCLUSIVE PREVIEW!*
BE EXCELLENT TO EACH OTHER. WE'RE THE ONLY WE'S WE HAVE. IF WE DON'T UNIFY, WE'RE TOTALLY GONNA DIE. AND NO ONE WILL EVEN BE AROUND TO ASK. WHY?

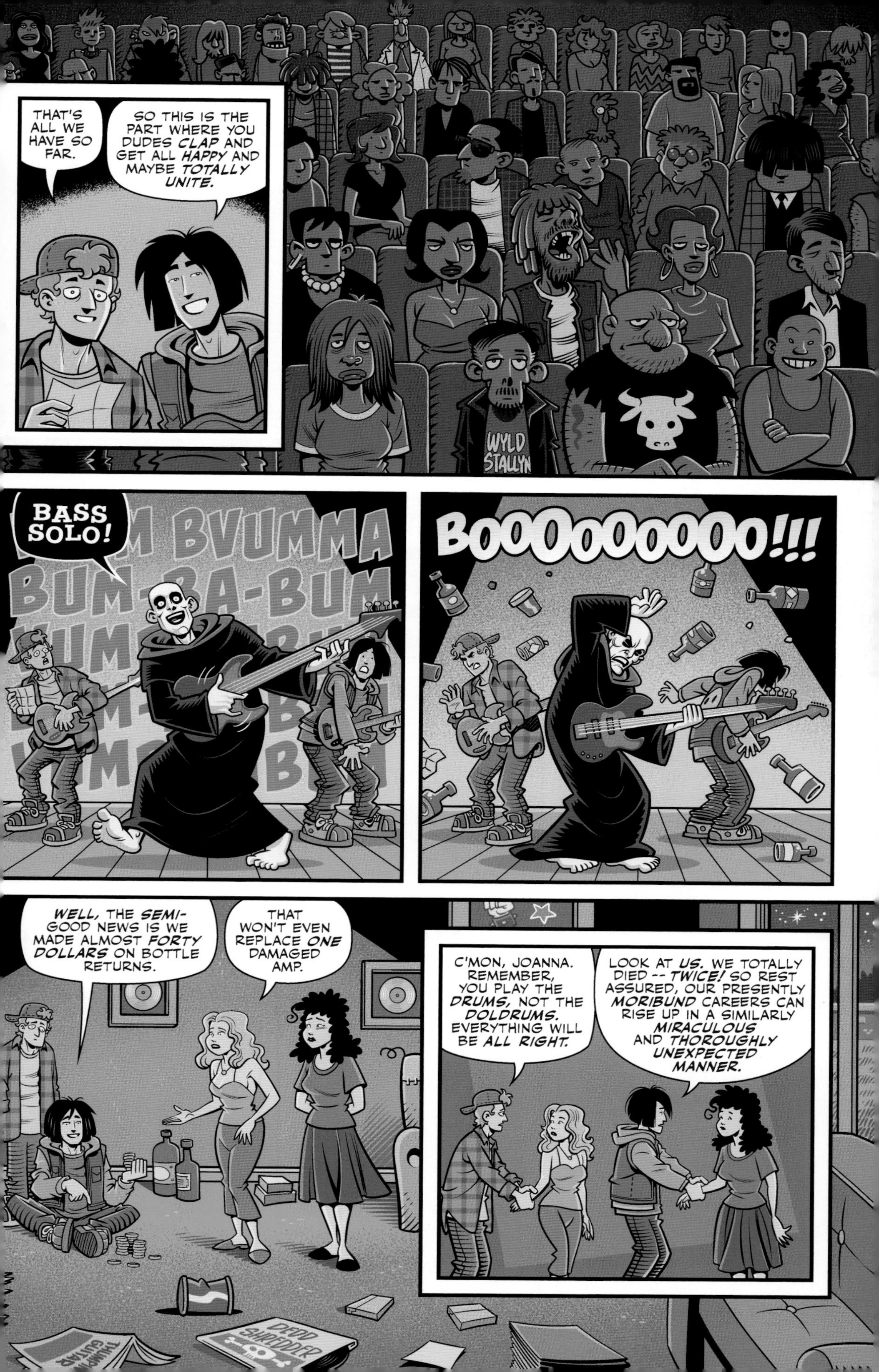
THAT'S ALL WE HAVE SO FAR.
SO THIS IS THE PART WHERE YOU DUDES *CLAP* AND GET ALL *HAPPY* AND MAYBE *TOTALLY UNITE.*
WYLD STALLYN
BASS SOLO!
BVUMMA BUM-BA-BUM
BOOOOOOOOO!!!
WELL, THE *SEMI*-GOOD NEWS IS WE MADE ALMOST *FORTY DOLLARS* ON BOTTLE RETURNS.
THAT WON'T EVEN REPLACE *ONE* DAMAGED AMP.
C'MON, JOANNA. REMEMBER, YOU PLAY THE *DRUMS,* NOT THE *DOLDRUMS.* EVERYTHING WILL BE *ALL RIGHT.*
LOOK AT *US.* WE TOTALLY DIED -- *TWICE!* SO REST ASSURED, OUR PRESENTLY *MORIBUND* CAREERS CAN RISE UP IN A SIMILARLY *MIRACULOUS* AND *THOROUGHLY UNEXPECTED MANNER.*
THUMPIN' GUITAR
DEDD SHREDDER

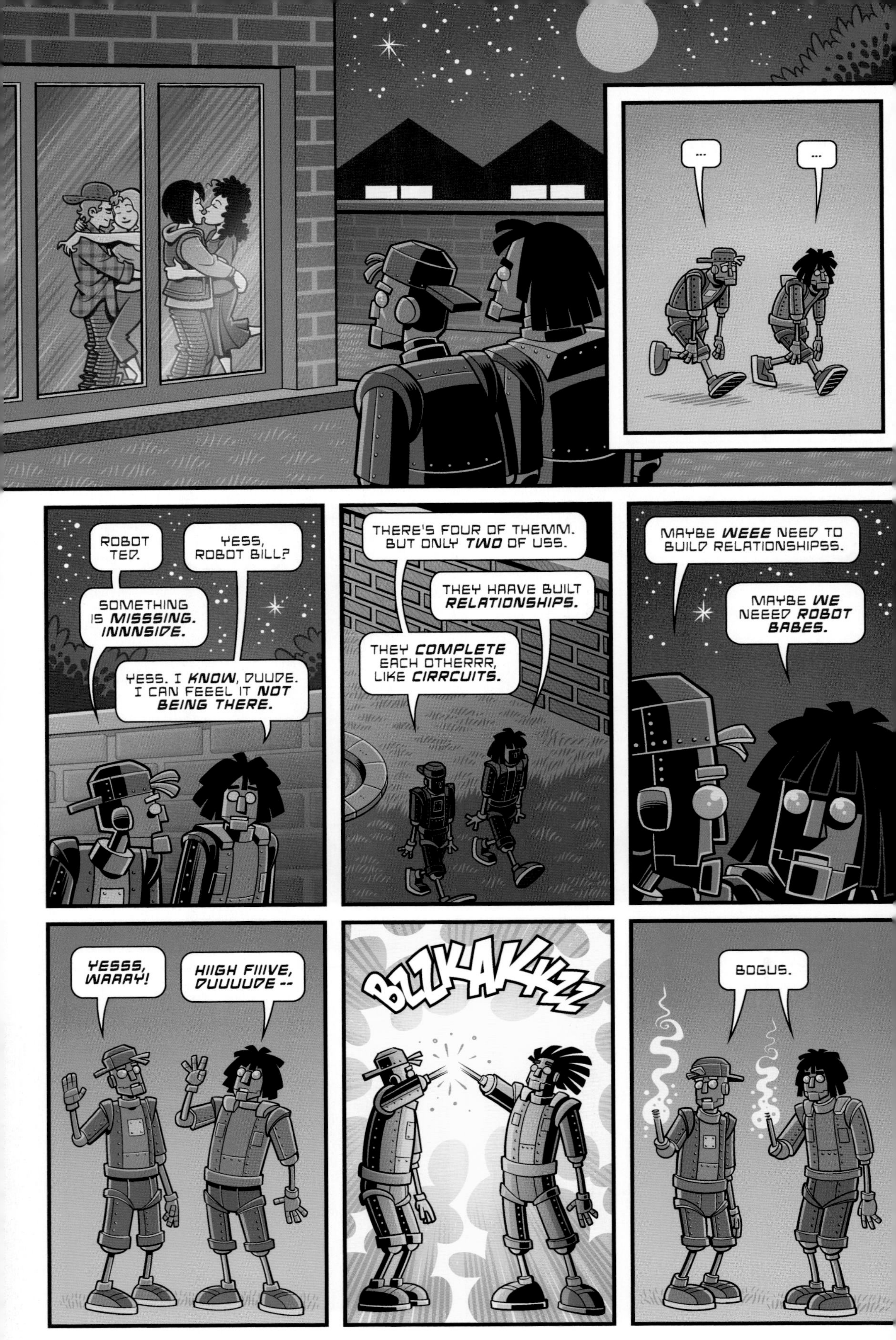
...
...
ROBOT TED.
YESS, ROBOT BILL?
SOMETHING IS MISSSING. INNNSIDE.
YESS. I KNOW, DUUDE. I CAN FEEEL IT NOT BEING THERE.
THERE'S FOUR OF THEMM. BUT ONLY TWO OF USS.
THEY HAAVE BUILT RELATIONSHIPS.
THEY COMPLETE EACH OTHERRR, LIKE CIRRCUITS.
MAYBE WEEE NEED TO BUILD RELATIONSHIPSS.
MAYBE WE NEEED ROBOT BABES.
YESSS, WAAAY!
HIIGH FIIIVE, DUUUUDE --
BZZKAKKZZ
BOGUS.

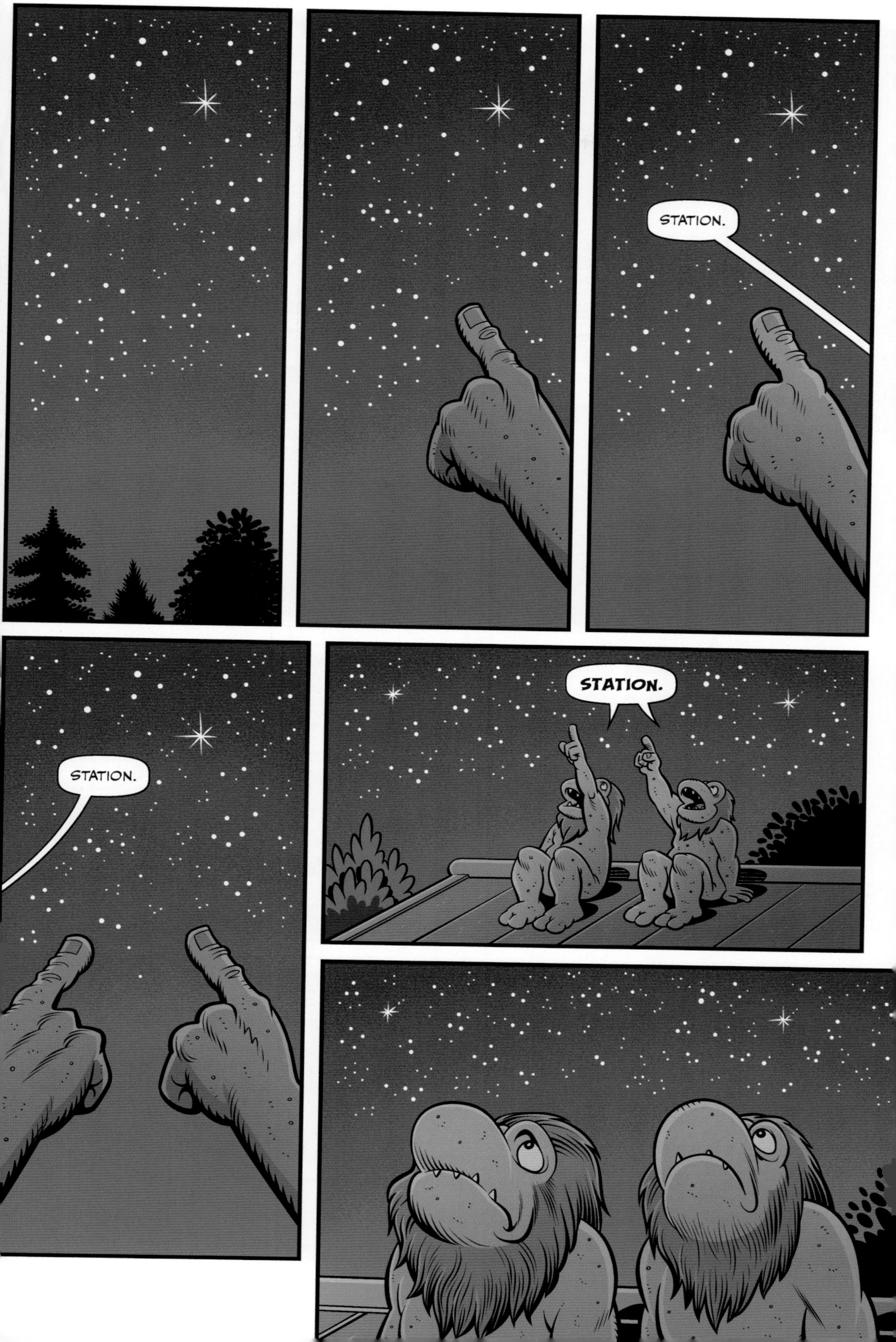
STATION.
STATION.
STATION.

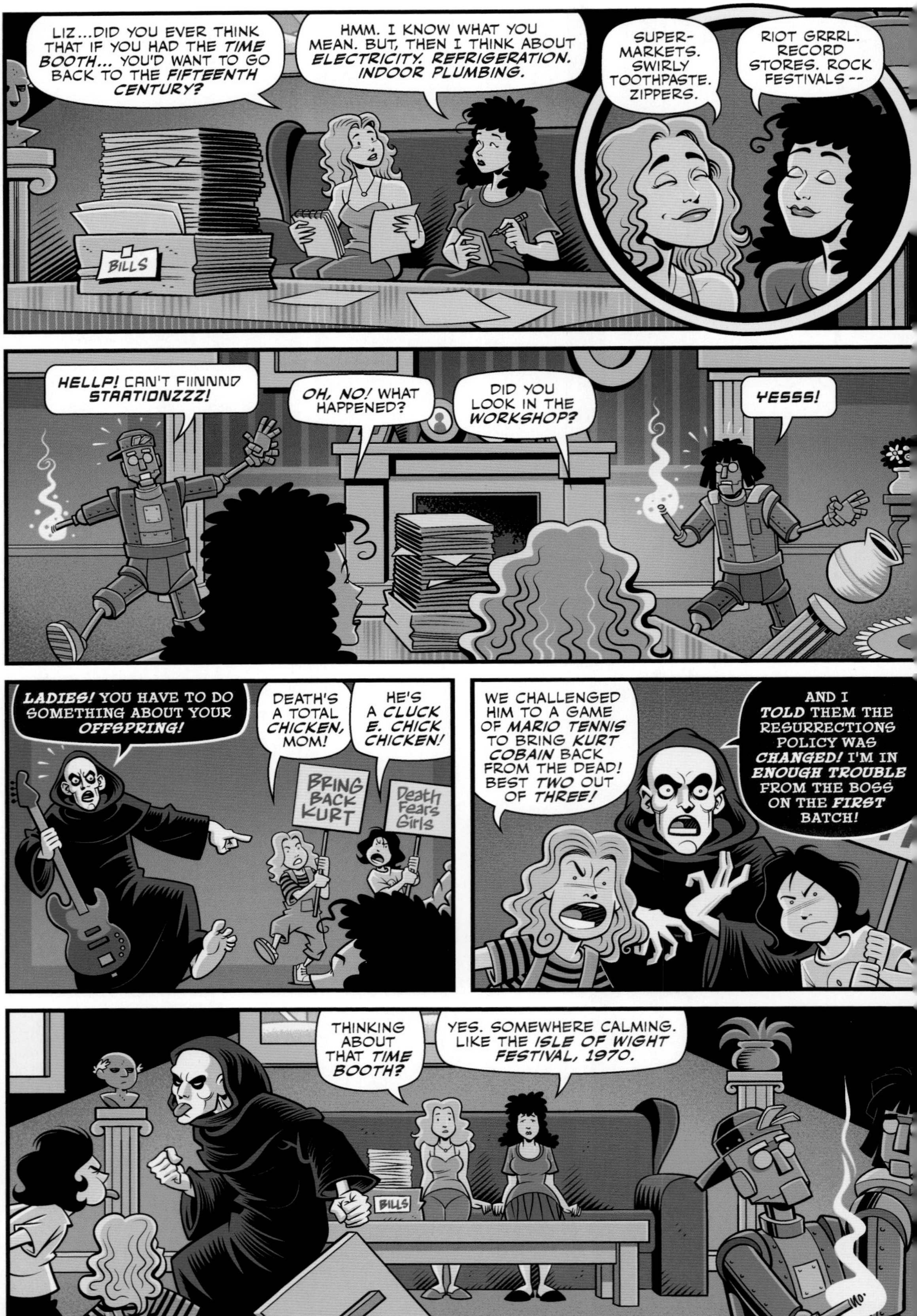

LIZ...DID YOU EVER THINK THAT IF YOU HAD THE TIME BOOTH... YOU'D WANT TO GO BACK TO THE FIFTEENTH CENTURY?
HMM. I KNOW WHAT YOU MEAN. BUT, THEN I THINK ABOUT ELECTRICITY. REFRIGERATION. INDOOR PLUMBING.
SUPER-MARKETS. SWIRLY TOOTHPASTE. ZIPPERS.
RIOT GRRRL. RECORD STORES. ROCK FESTIVALS --
BILLS
HELLP! CAN'T FIINNND STAATIONZZZ!
OH, NO! WHAT HAPPENED?
DID YOU LOOK IN THE WORKSHOP?
YESSS!
LADIES! YOU HAVE TO DO SOMETHING ABOUT YOUR OFFSPRING!
DEATH'S A TOTAL CHICKEN, MOM!
HE'S A CLUCK E. CHICK CHICKEN!
BRING BACK KURT
Death Fears Girls
WE CHALLENGED HIM TO A GAME OF MARIO TENNIS TO BRING KURT COBAIN BACK FROM THE DEAD! BEST TWO OUT OF THREE!
AND I TOLD THEM THE RESURRECTIONS POLICY WAS CHANGED! I'M IN ENOUGH TROUBLE FROM THE BOSS ON THE FIRST BATCH!
THINKING ABOUT THAT TIME BOOTH?
YES. SOMEWHERE CALMING. LIKE THE ISLE OF WIGHT FESTIVAL, 1970.
BILLS

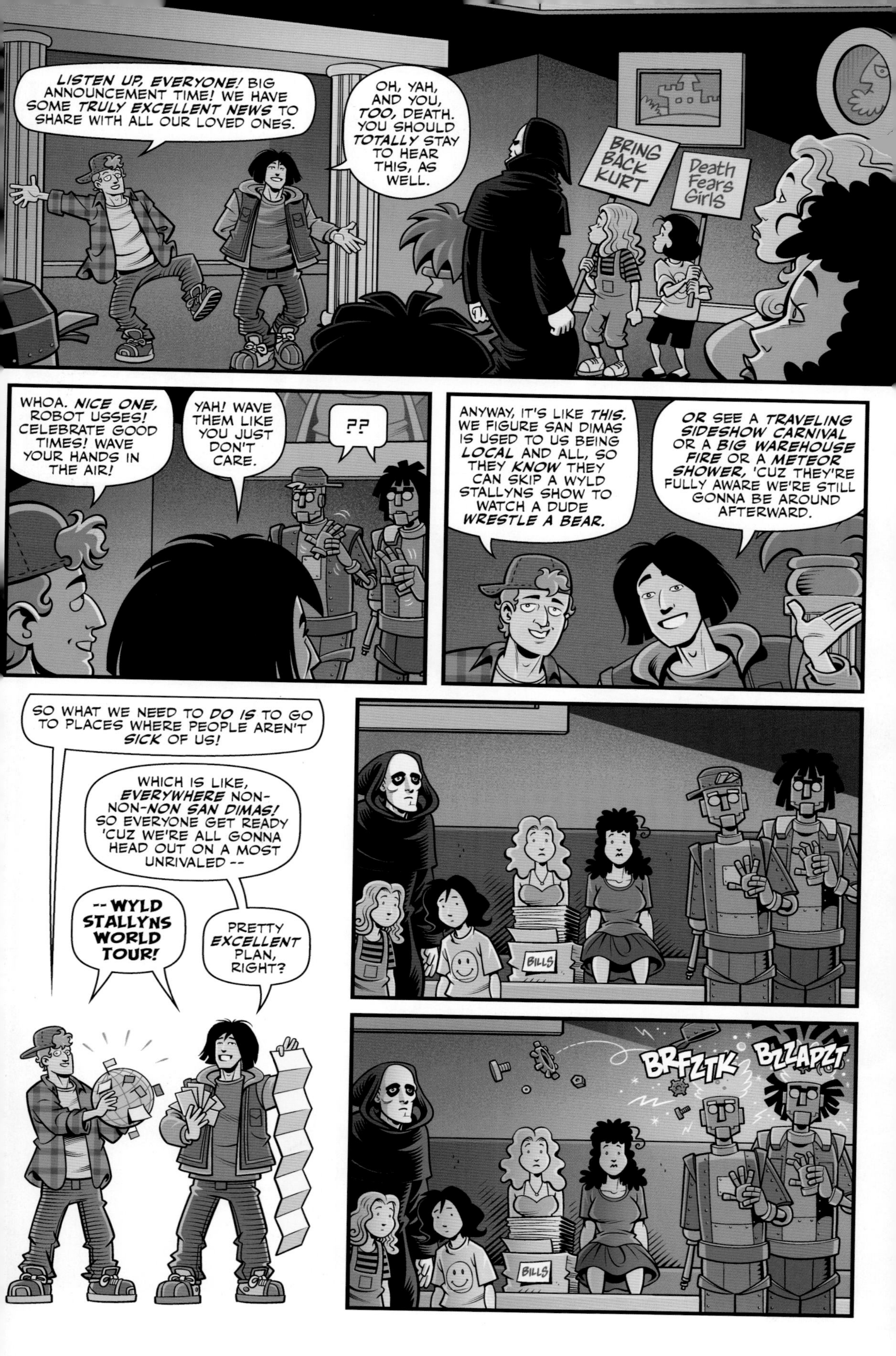
LISTEN UP, EVERYONE! BIG ANNOUNCEMENT TIME! WE HAVE SOME TRULY EXCELLENT NEWS TO SHARE WITH ALL OUR LOVED ONES.
OH, YAH, AND YOU, TOO, DEATH. YOU SHOULD TOTALLY STAY TO HEAR THIS, AS WELL.
BRING BACK KURT
Death Fears Girls
WHOA. NICE ONE, ROBOT USSES! CELEBRATE GOOD TIMES! WAVE YOUR HANDS IN THE AIR!
YAH! WAVE THEM LIKE YOU JUST DON'T CARE.
??
ANYWAY, IT'S LIKE THIS. WE FIGURE SAN DIMAS IS USED TO US BEING LOCAL AND ALL, SO THEY KNOW THEY CAN SKIP A WYLD STALLYNS SHOW TO WATCH A DUDE WRESTLE A BEAR.
OR SEE A TRAVELING SIDESHOW CARNIVAL OR A BIG WAREHOUSE FIRE OR A METEOR SHOWER, 'CUZ THEY'RE FULLY AWARE WE'RE STILL GONNA BE AROUND AFTERWARD.
SO WHAT WE NEED TO DO IS TO GO TO PLACES WHERE PEOPLE AREN'T SICK OF US!
WHICH IS LIKE, EVERYWHERE NON-NON-NON SAN DIMAS! SO EVERYONE GET READY 'CUZ WE'RE ALL GONNA HEAD OUT ON A MOST UNRIVALED --
-- WYLD STALLYNS WORLD TOUR!
PRETTY EXCELLENT PLAN, RIGHT?
BILLS
BRFZTK
BZZAPZT
BILLS

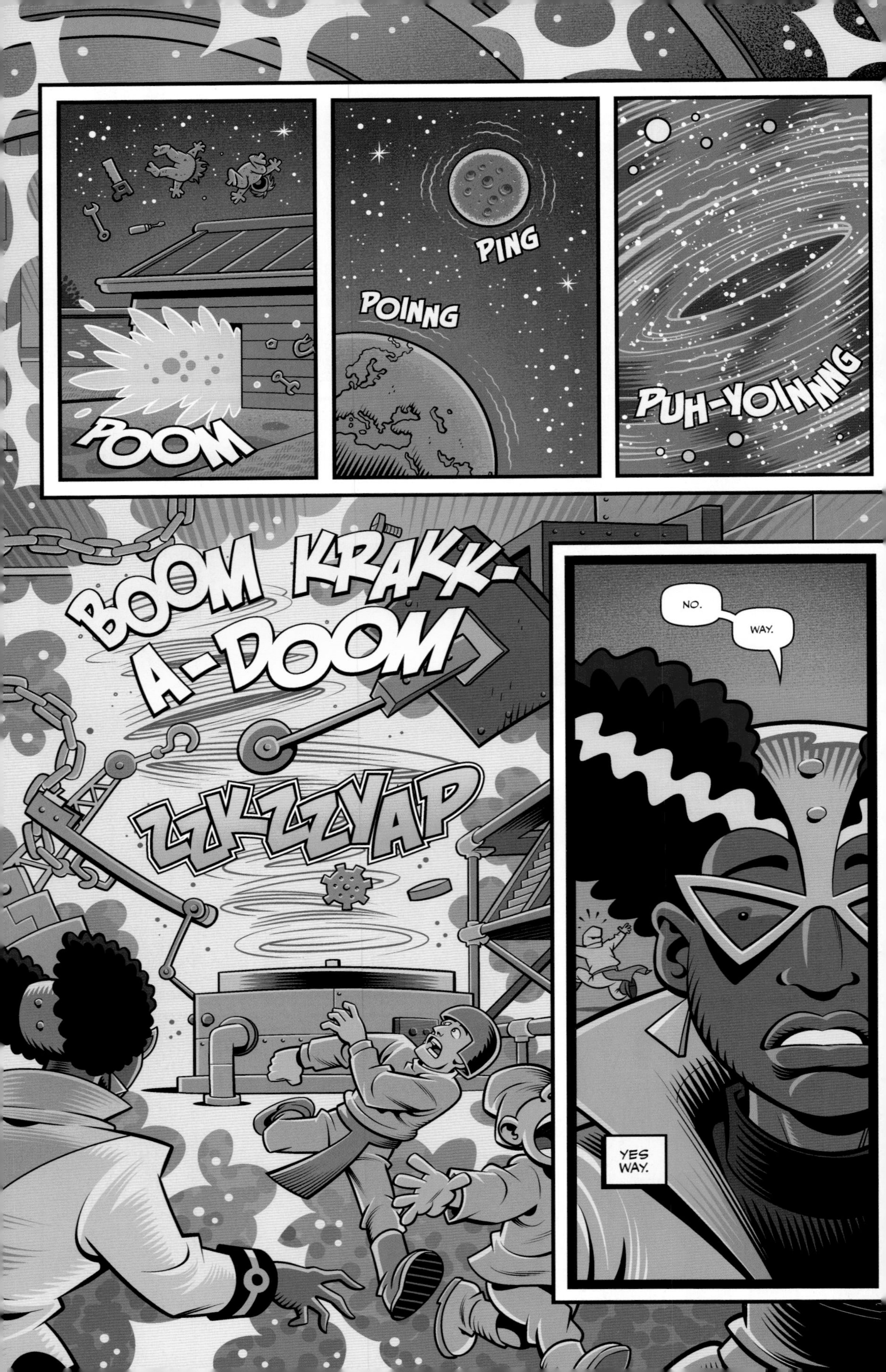
POOM
PING
POINNG
PUH-YOINNNG
BOOM KRAKK-A-DOOM
ZZKZZYAP
NO.
WAY.
YES WAY.

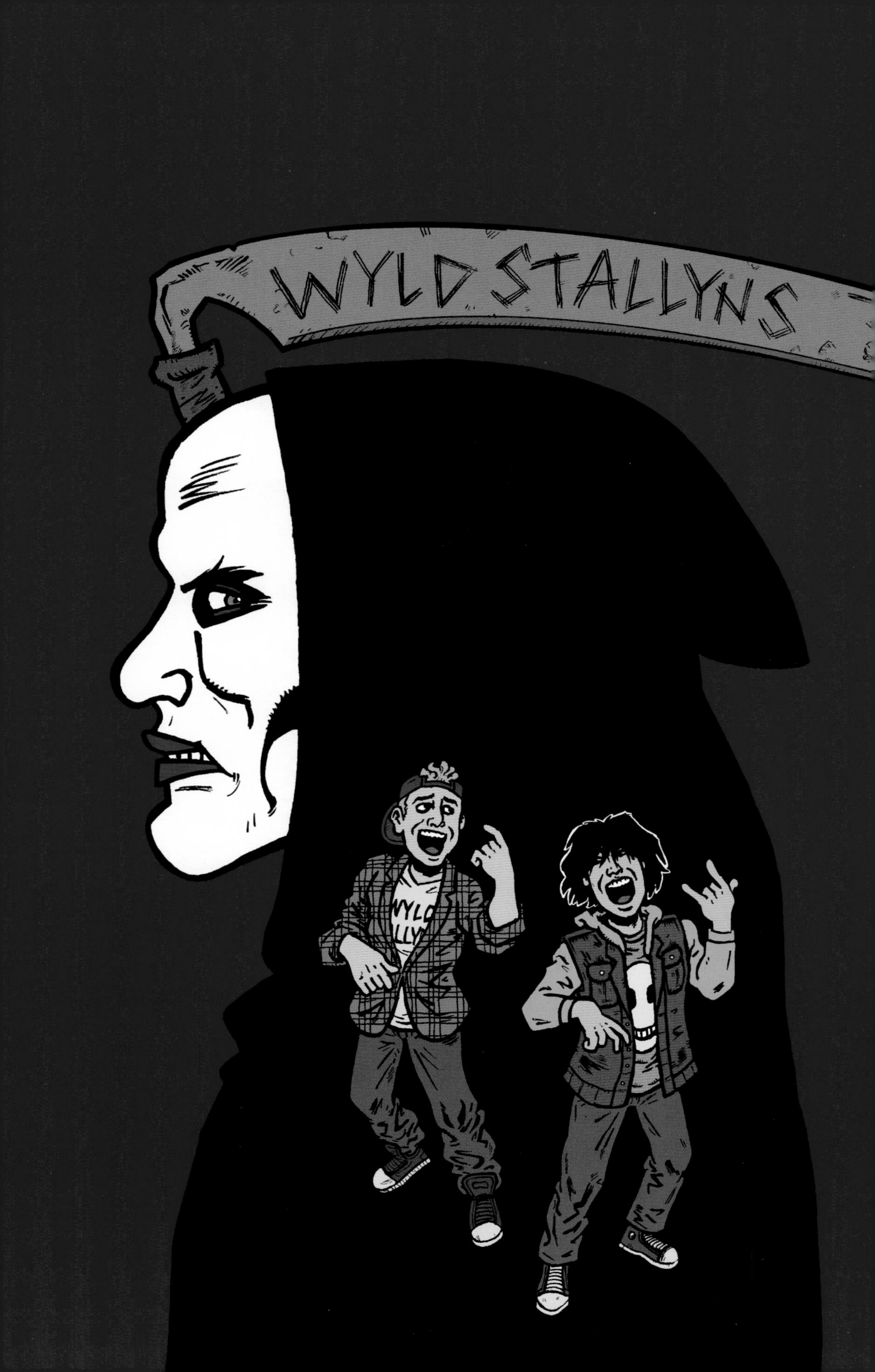
WYLD STALLYNS

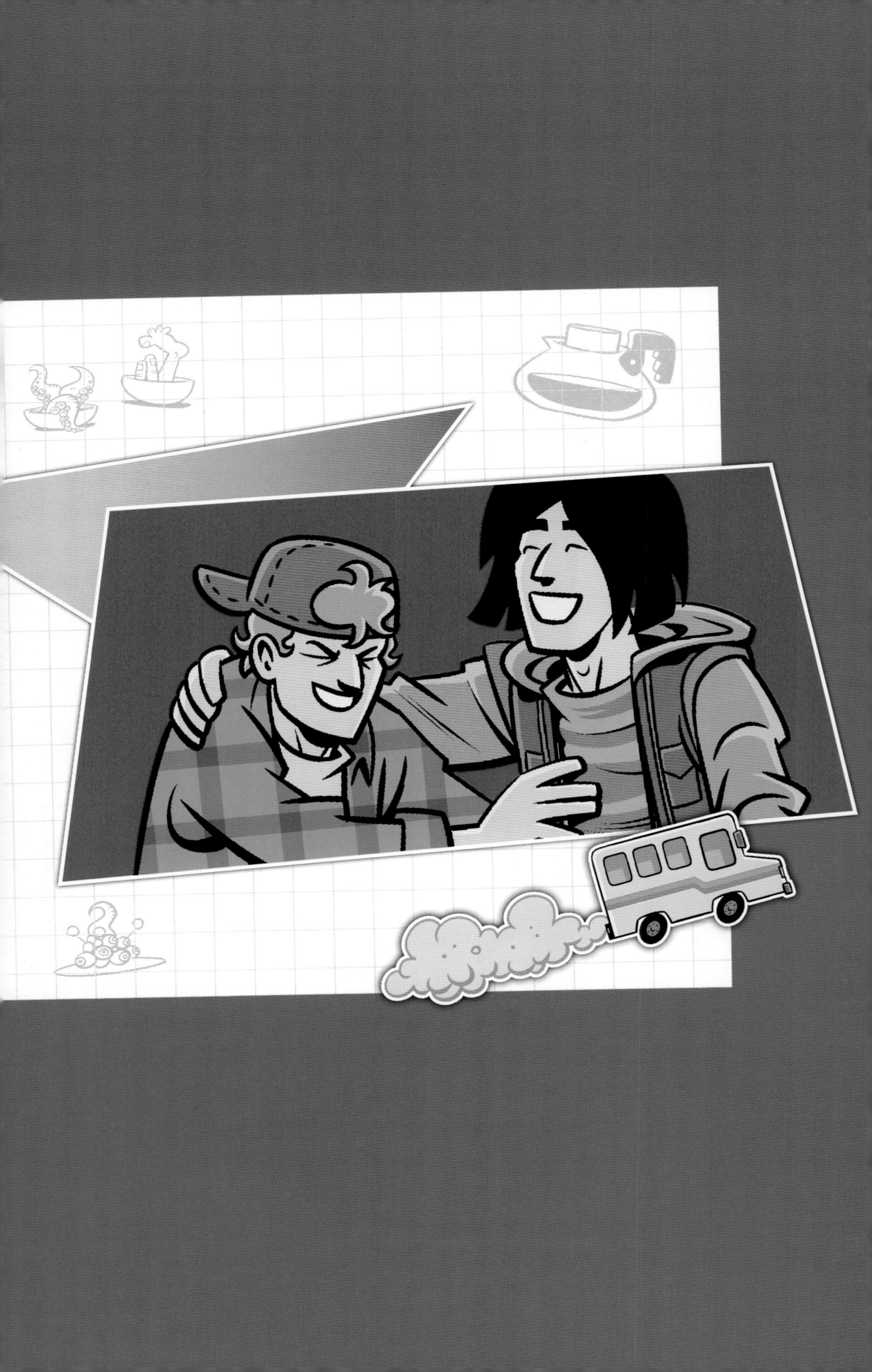

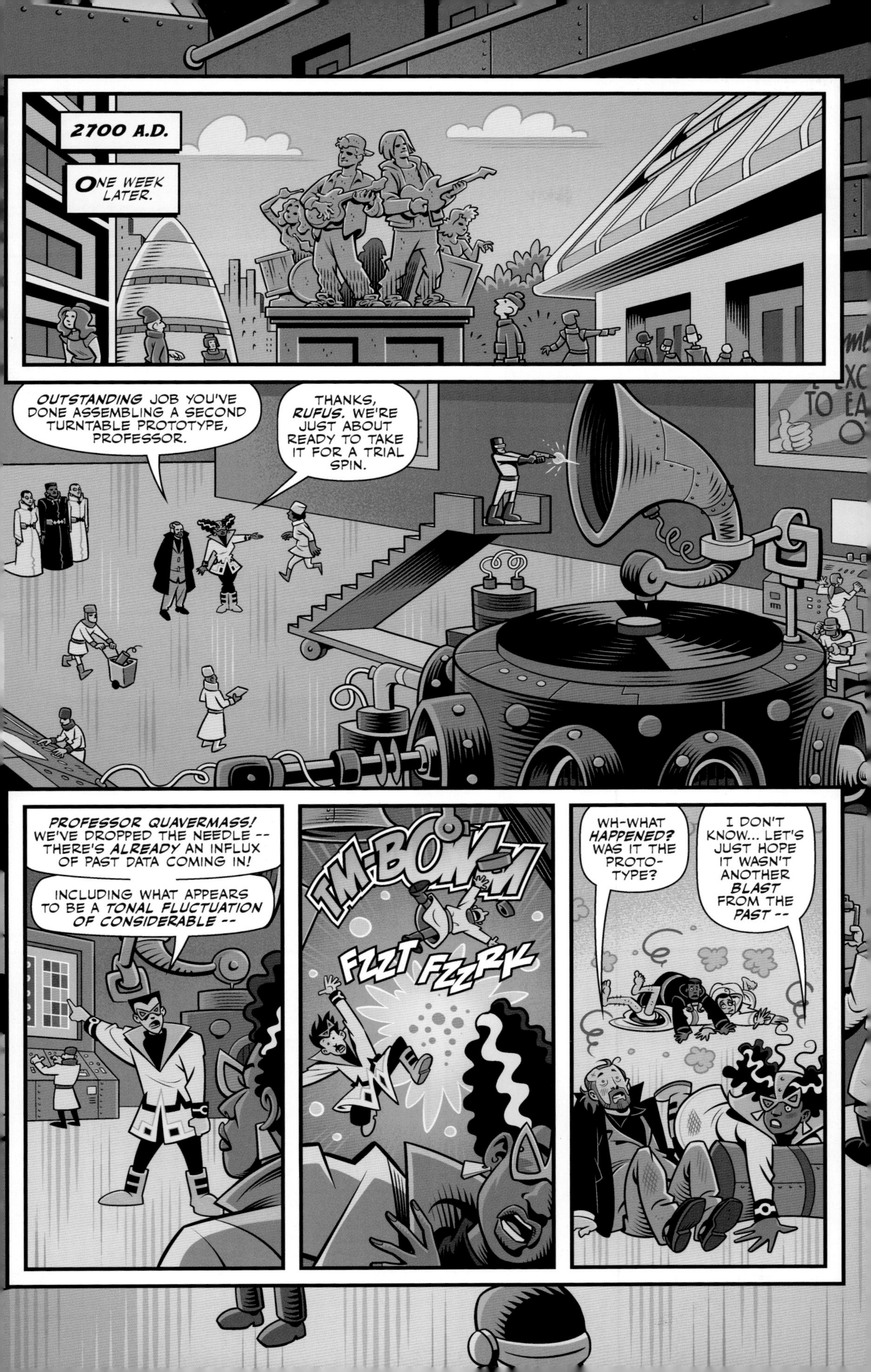

2700 A.D.
ONE WEEK LATER.
OUTSTANDING JOB YOU'VE DONE ASSEMBLING A SECOND TURNTABLE PROTOTYPE, PROFESSOR.
THANKS, RUFUS. WE'RE JUST ABOUT READY TO TAKE IT FOR A TRIAL SPIN.
PROFESSOR QUAVERMASS! WE'VE DROPPED THE NEEDLE -- THERE'S ALREADY AN INFLUX OF PAST DATA COMING IN!
INCLUDING WHAT APPEARS TO BE A TONAL FLUCTUATION OF CONSIDERABLE --
TM-BOWM
FZZT FZZRK
WH-WHAT HAPPENED? WAS IT THE PROTO-TYPE?
I DON'T KNOW... LET'S JUST HOPE IT WASN'T ANOTHER BLAST FROM THE PAST --

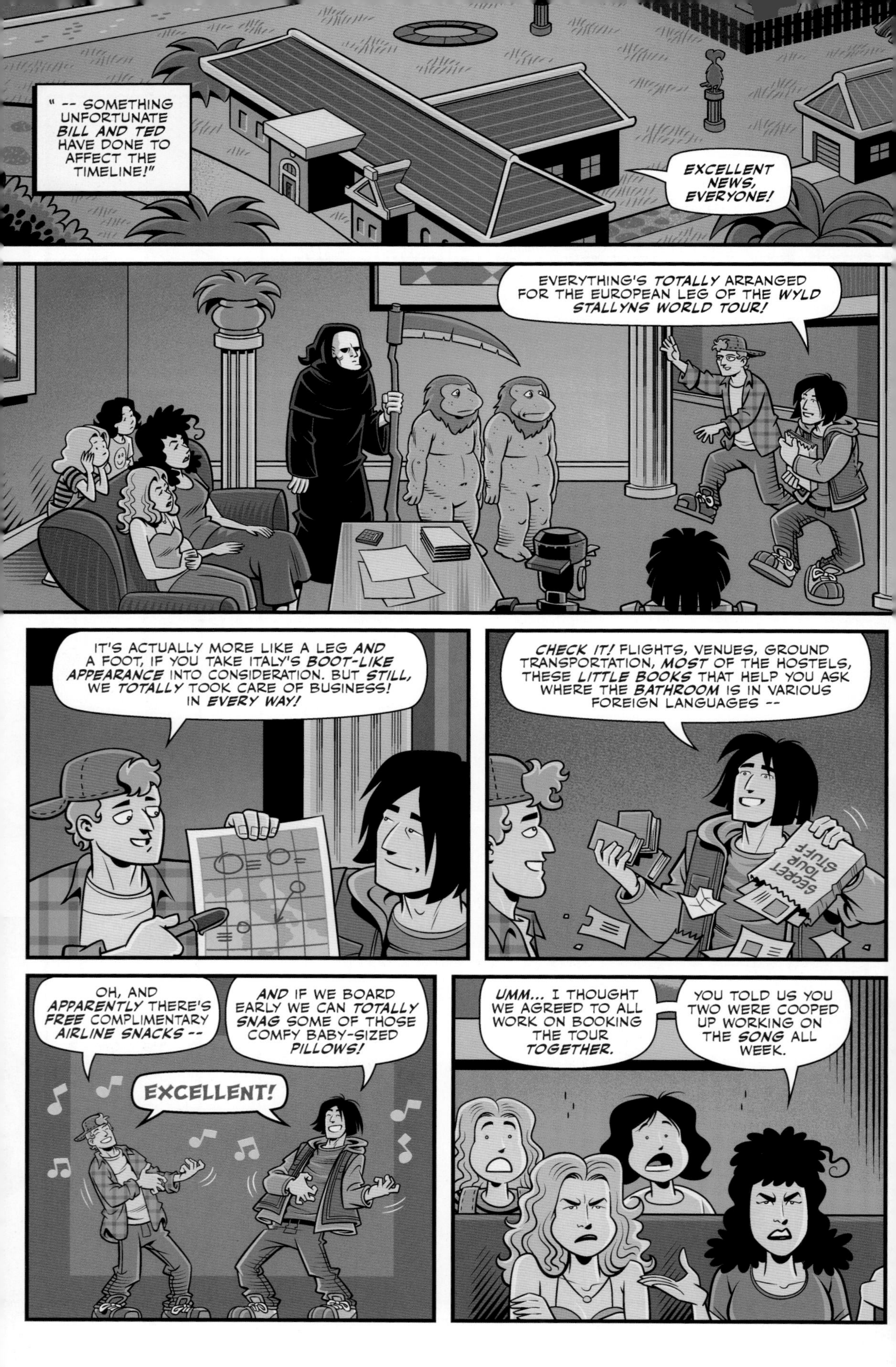
"-- SOMETHING UNFORTUNATE BILL AND TED HAVE DONE TO AFFECT THE TIMELINE!"
EXCELLENT NEWS, EVERYONE!
EVERYTHING'S TOTALLY ARRANGED FOR THE EUROPEAN LEG OF THE WYLD STALLYNS WORLD TOUR!
IT'S ACTUALLY MORE LIKE A LEG AND A FOOT, IF YOU TAKE ITALY'S BOOT-LIKE APPEARANCE INTO CONSIDERATION. BUT STILL, WE TOTALLY TOOK CARE OF BUSINESS! IN EVERY WAY!
CHECK IT! FLIGHTS, VENUES, GROUND TRANSPORTATION, MOST OF THE HOSTELS, THESE LITTLE BOOKS THAT HELP YOU ASK WHERE THE BATHROOM IS IN VARIOUS FOREIGN LANGUAGES --
SECRET TOUR STUFF
OH, AND APPARENTLY THERE'S FREE COMPLIMENTARY AIRLINE SNACKS --
AND IF WE BOARD EARLY WE CAN TOTALLY SNAG SOME OF THOSE COMFY BABY-SIZED PILLOWS!
EXCELLENT!
UMM... I THOUGHT WE AGREED TO ALL WORK ON BOOKING THE TOUR TOGETHER.
YOU TOLD US YOU TWO WERE COOPED UP WORKING ON THE SONG ALL WEEK.

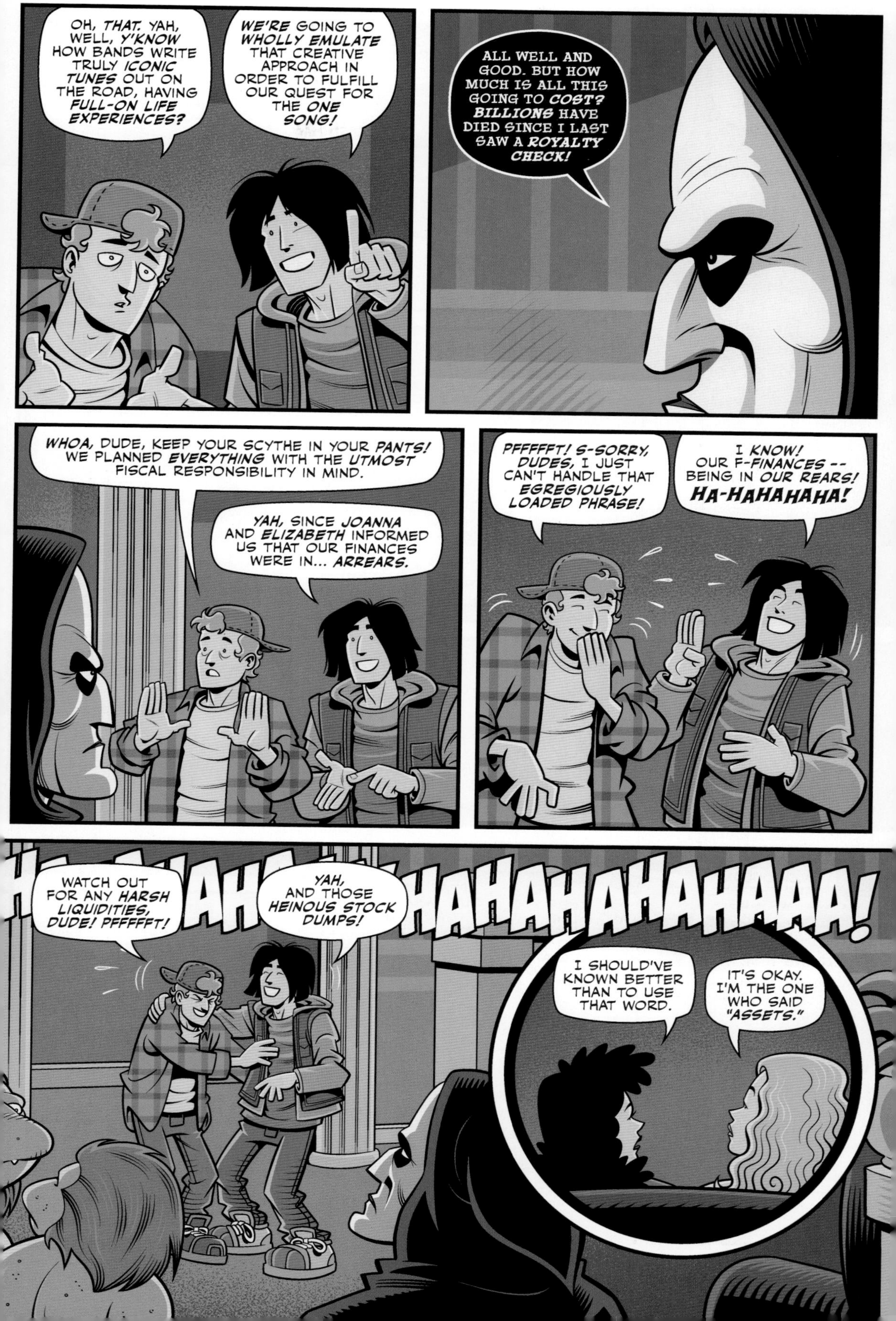
OH, THAT. YAH, WELL, Y'KNOW HOW BANDS WRITE TRULY ICONIC TUNES OUT ON THE ROAD, HAVING FULL-ON LIFE EXPERIENCES?
WE'RE GOING TO WHOLLY EMULATE THAT CREATIVE APPROACH IN ORDER TO FULFILL OUR QUEST FOR THE ONE SONG!
ALL WELL AND GOOD. BUT HOW MUCH IS ALL THIS GOING TO COST? BILLIONS HAVE DIED SINCE I LAST SAW A ROYALTY CHECK!
WHOA, DUDE, KEEP YOUR SCYTHE IN YOUR PANTS! WE PLANNED EVERYTHING WITH THE UTMOST FISCAL RESPONSIBILITY IN MIND.
YAH, SINCE JOANNA AND ELIZABETH INFORMED US THAT OUR FINANCES WERE IN... ARREARS.
PFFFFFT! S-SORRY, DUDES, I JUST CAN'T HANDLE THAT EGREGIOUSLY LOADED PHRASE!
I KNOW! OUR F-FINANCES -- BEING IN OUR REARS! HA-HAHAHAHA!
WATCH OUT FOR ANY HARSH LIQUIDITIES, DUDE! PFFFFFT!
YAH, AND THOSE HEINOUS STOCK DUMPS!
HAHAHAHAHAHAHAHAAAA!
I SHOULD'VE KNOWN BETTER THAN TO USE THAT WORD.
IT'S OKAY. I'M THE ONE WHO SAID "ASSETS."

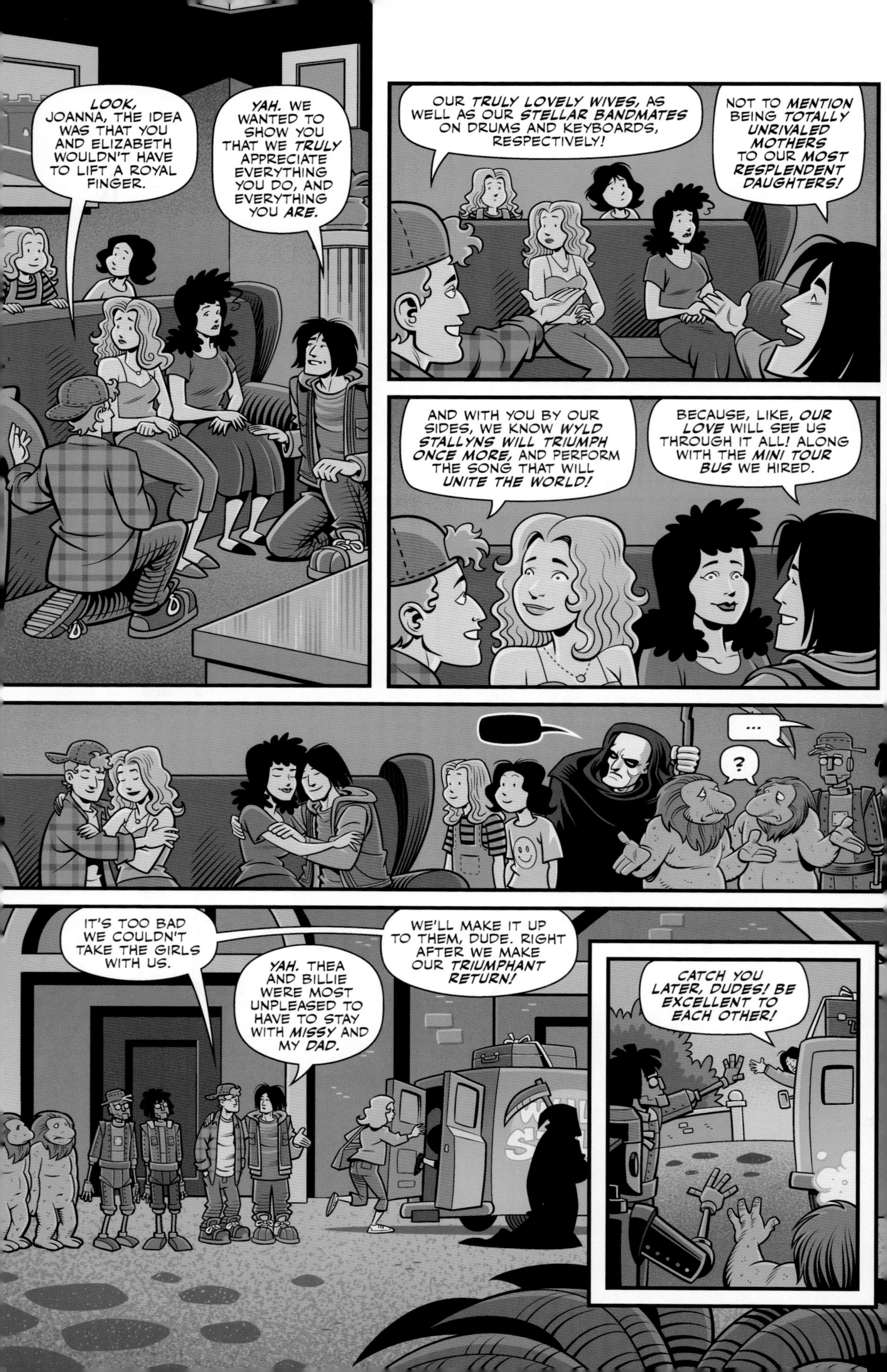
LOOK, JOANNA, THE IDEA WAS THAT YOU AND ELIZABETH WOULDN'T HAVE TO LIFT A ROYAL FINGER.
YAH. WE WANTED TO SHOW YOU THAT WE TRULY APPRECIATE EVERYTHING YOU DO, AND EVERYTHING YOU ARE.
OUR TRULY LOVELY WIVES, AS WELL AS OUR STELLAR BANDMATES ON DRUMS AND KEYBOARDS, RESPECTIVELY!
NOT TO MENTION BEING TOTALLY UNRIVALED MOTHERS TO OUR MOST RESPLENDENT DAUGHTERS!
AND WITH YOU BY OUR SIDES, WE KNOW WYLD STALLYNS WILL TRIUMPH ONCE MORE, AND PERFORM THE SONG THAT WILL UNITE THE WORLD!
BECAUSE, LIKE, OUR LOVE WILL SEE US THROUGH IT ALL! ALONG WITH THE MINI TOUR BUS WE HIRED.
...
?
IT'S TOO BAD WE COULDN'T TAKE THE GIRLS WITH US.
YAH. THEA AND BILLIE WERE MOST UNPLEASED TO HAVE TO STAY WITH MISSY AND MY DAD.
WE'LL MAKE IT UP TO THEM, DUDE. RIGHT AFTER WE MAKE OUR TRIUMPHANT RETURN!
CATCH YOU LATER, DUDES! BE EXCELLENT TO EACH OTHER!

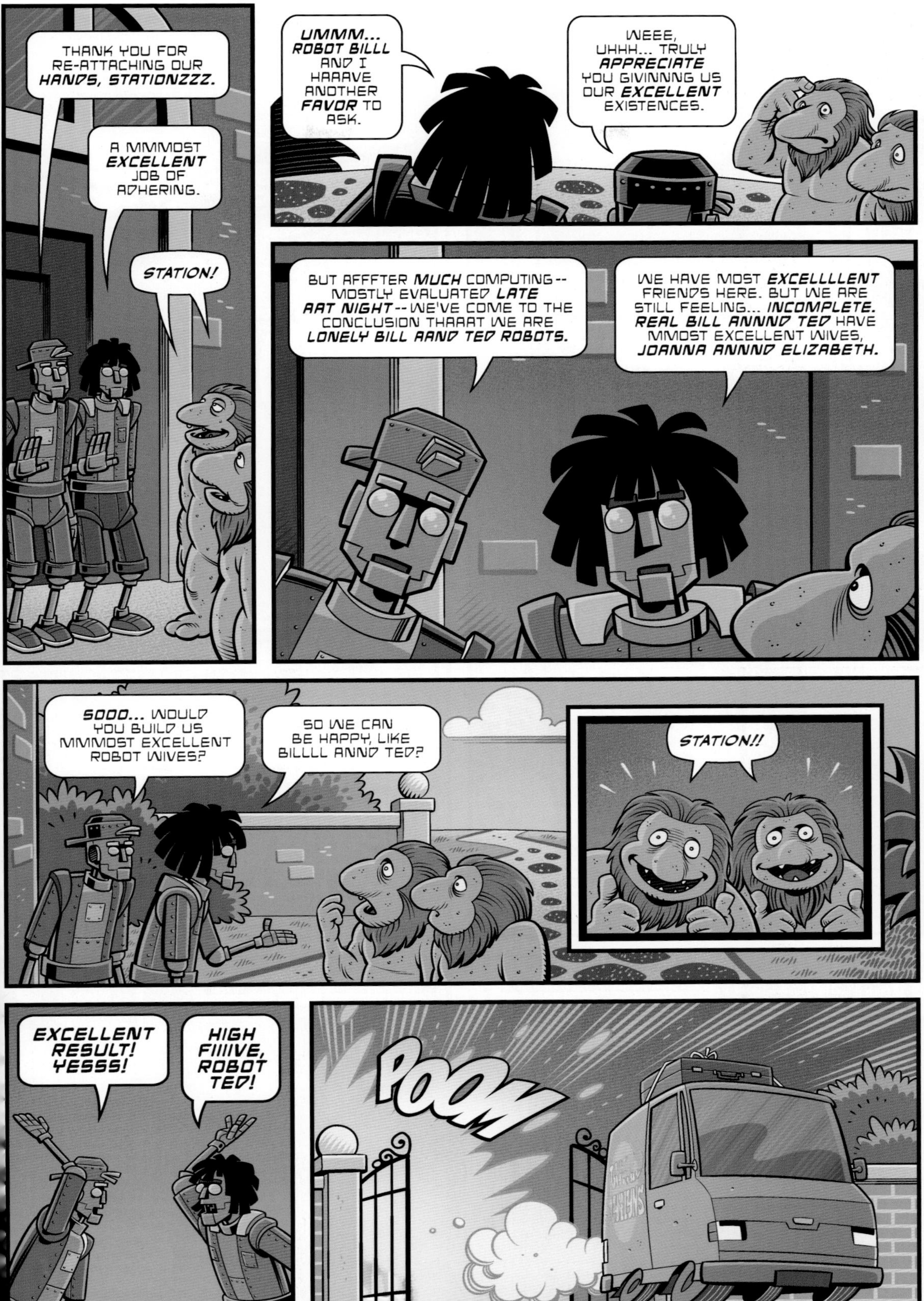
THANK YOU FOR RE-ATTACHING OUR HANDS, STATIONZZZ.
A MMMOST EXCELLENT JOB OF ADHERING.
STATION!
UMMM... ROBOT BILLL AND I HAARAVE ANOTHER FAVOR TO ASK.
WEEE, UHHH... TRULY APPRECIATE YOU GIVINNNG US OUR EXCELLENT EXISTENCES.
BUT AFFFTER MUCH COMPUTING -- MOSTLY EVALUATED LATE AAT NIGHT -- WE'VE COME TO THE CONCLUSION THARAT WE ARE LONELY BILL AAND TED ROBOTS.
WE HAVE MOST EXCELLLLENT FRIENDS HERE. BUT WE ARE STILL FEELING... INCOMPLETE. REAL BILL ANNND TED HAVE MMOST EXCELLENT WIVES, JOANNA ANNND ELIZABETH.
SOOO... WOULD YOU BUILD US MMMOST EXCELLENT ROBOT WIVES?
SO WE CAN BE HAPPY, LIKE BILLLL ANND TED?
STATION!!
EXCELLENT RESULT! YESSS!
HIGH FIIIIVE, ROBOT TED!
POOM

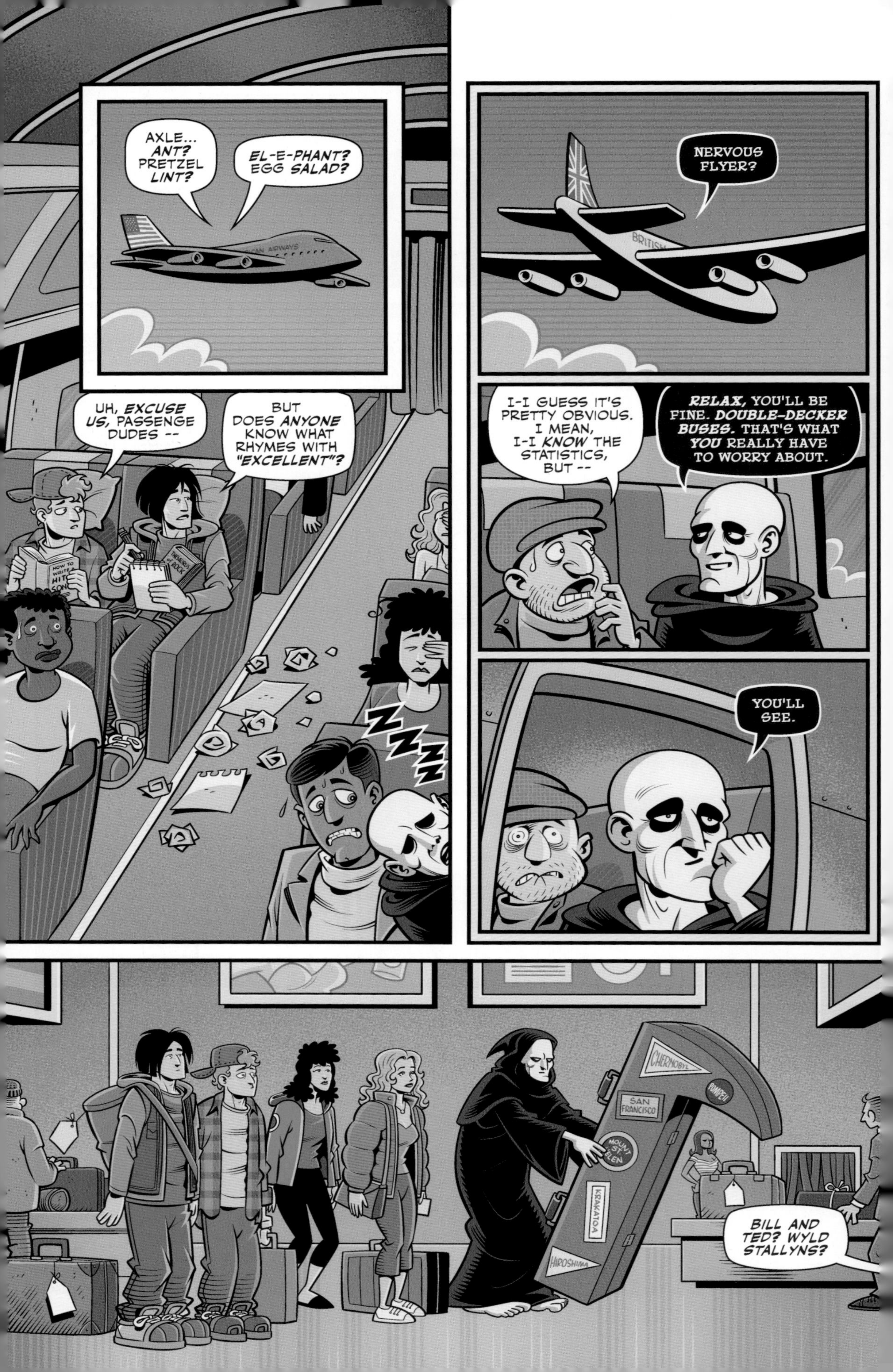
AXLE... ANT? PRETZEL LINT?
EL-E-PHANT? EGG SALAD?
NERVOUS FLYER?
BRITISH
UH, EXCUSE US, PASSENGE DUDES --
BUT DOES ANYONE KNOW WHAT RHYMES WITH "EXCELLENT"?
HOW TO WRITE A HIT SONG
THESAURUS OF ROCK
I-I GUESS IT'S PRETTY OBVIOUS. I MEAN, I-I KNOW THE STATISTICS, BUT --
RELAX, YOU'LL BE FINE. DOUBLE-DECKER BUSES. THAT'S WHAT YOU REALLY HAVE TO WORRY ABOUT.
YOU'LL SEE.
CHERNOBYL
POMPEII
SAN FRANCISCO
MOUNT ST. HELEN
KRAKATOA
HIROSHIMA
BILL AND TED? WYLD STALLYNS?

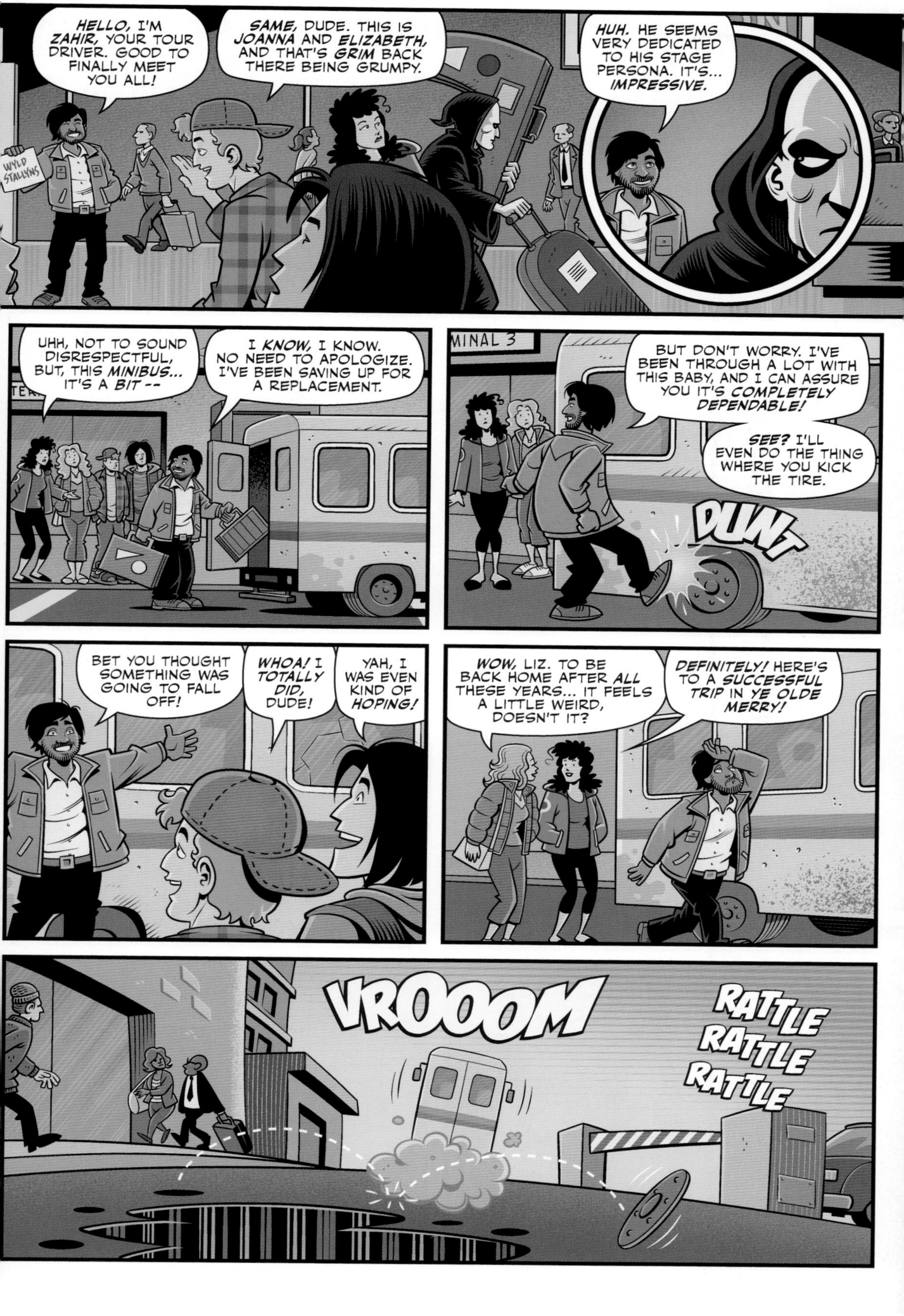

HELLO, I'M ZAHIR, YOUR TOUR DRIVER. GOOD TO FINALLY MEET YOU ALL!
WYLD STALLYNS
SAME, DUDE. THIS IS JOANNA AND ELIZABETH, AND THAT'S GRIM BACK THERE BEING GRUMPY.
HUH. HE SEEMS VERY DEDICATED TO HIS STAGE PERSONA. IT'S... IMPRESSIVE.
UHH, NOT TO SOUND DISRESPECTFUL, BUT, THIS MINIBUS... IT'S A BIT --
I KNOW, I KNOW. NO NEED TO APOLOGIZE. I'VE BEEN SAVING UP FOR A REPLACEMENT.
MINAL 3
BUT DON'T WORRY. I'VE BEEN THROUGH A LOT WITH THIS BABY, AND I CAN ASSURE YOU IT'S COMPLETELY DEPENDABLE!
SEE? I'LL EVEN DO THE THING WHERE YOU KICK THE TIRE.
DUNT
BET YOU THOUGHT SOMETHING WAS GOING TO FALL OFF!
WHOA! I TOTALLY DID, DUDE!
YAH, I WAS EVEN KIND OF HOPING!
WOW, LIZ. TO BE BACK HOME AFTER ALL THESE YEARS... IT FEELS A LITTLE WEIRD, DOESN'T IT?
DEFINITELY! HERE'S TO A SUCCESSFUL TRIP IN YE OLDE MERRY!
VROOOM
RATTLE
RATTLE
RATTLE

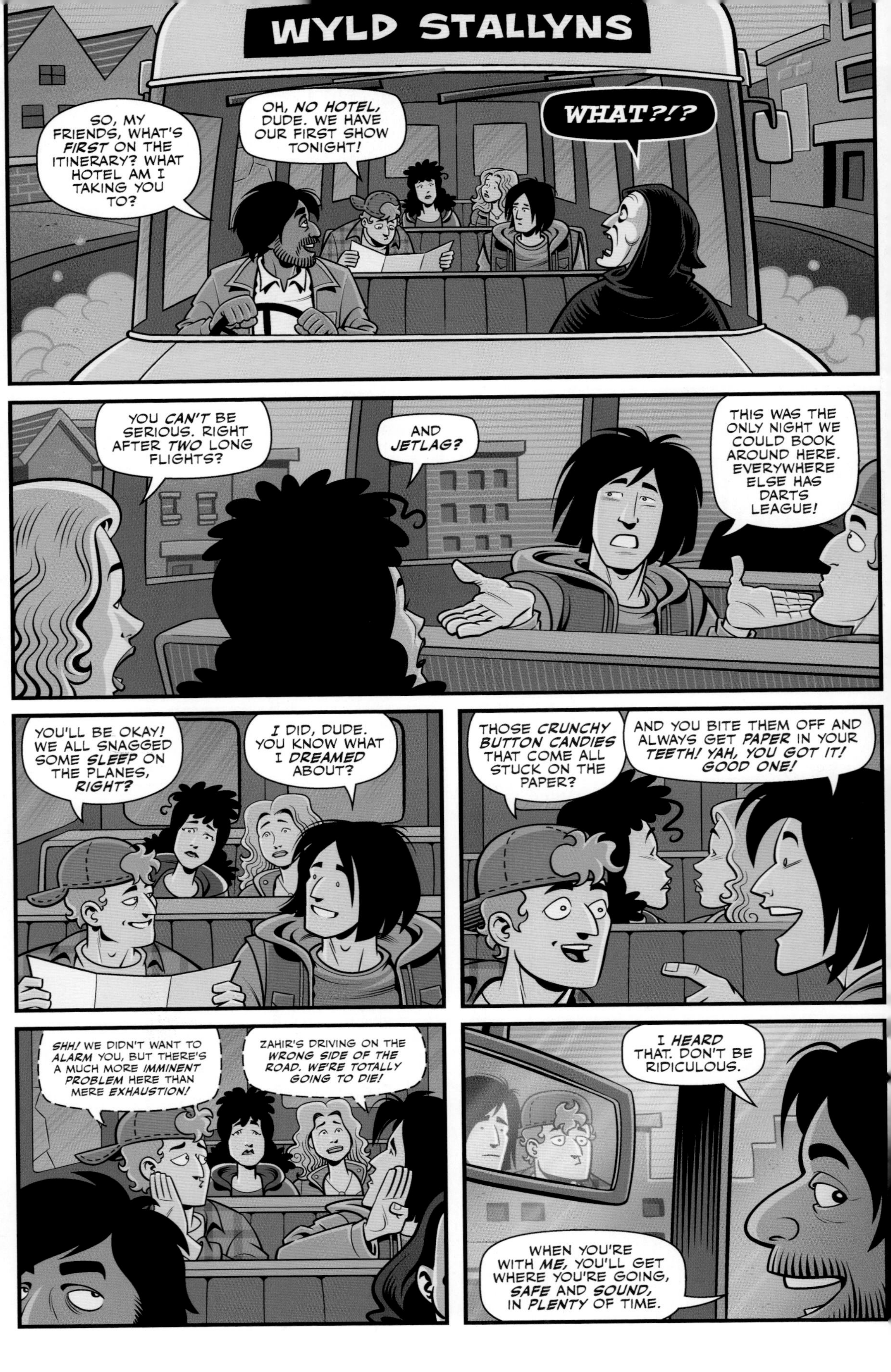
WYLD STALLYNS
SO, MY FRIENDS, WHAT'S *FIRST* ON THE ITINERARY? WHAT HOTEL AM I TAKING YOU TO?
OH, *NO HOTEL,* DUDE. WE HAVE OUR FIRST SHOW TONIGHT!
WHAT?!?
YOU *CAN'T* BE SERIOUS. RIGHT AFTER *TWO* LONG FLIGHTS?
AND *JETLAG?*
THIS WAS THE ONLY NIGHT WE COULD BOOK AROUND HERE. EVERYWHERE ELSE HAS DARTS LEAGUE!
YOU'LL BE OKAY! WE ALL SNAGGED SOME *SLEEP* ON THE PLANES, *RIGHT?*
I DID, DUDE. YOU KNOW WHAT I *DREAMED* ABOUT?
THOSE *CRUNCHY BUTTON CANDIES* THAT COME ALL STUCK ON THE PAPER?
AND YOU BITE THEM OFF AND ALWAYS GET *PAPER* IN YOUR *TEETH! YAH, YOU GOT IT! GOOD ONE!*
SHH! WE DIDN'T WANT TO *ALARM* YOU, BUT THERE'S A MUCH MORE *IMMINENT PROBLEM* HERE THAN MERE *EXHAUSTION!*
ZAHIR'S DRIVING ON THE *WRONG SIDE OF THE ROAD. WE'RE TOTALLY GOING TO DIE!*
I *HEARD* THAT. DON'T BE RIDICULOUS.
WHEN YOU'RE WITH *ME,* YOU'LL GET WHERE YOU'RE GOING, *SAFE* AND *SOUND,* IN *PLENTY* OF TIME.

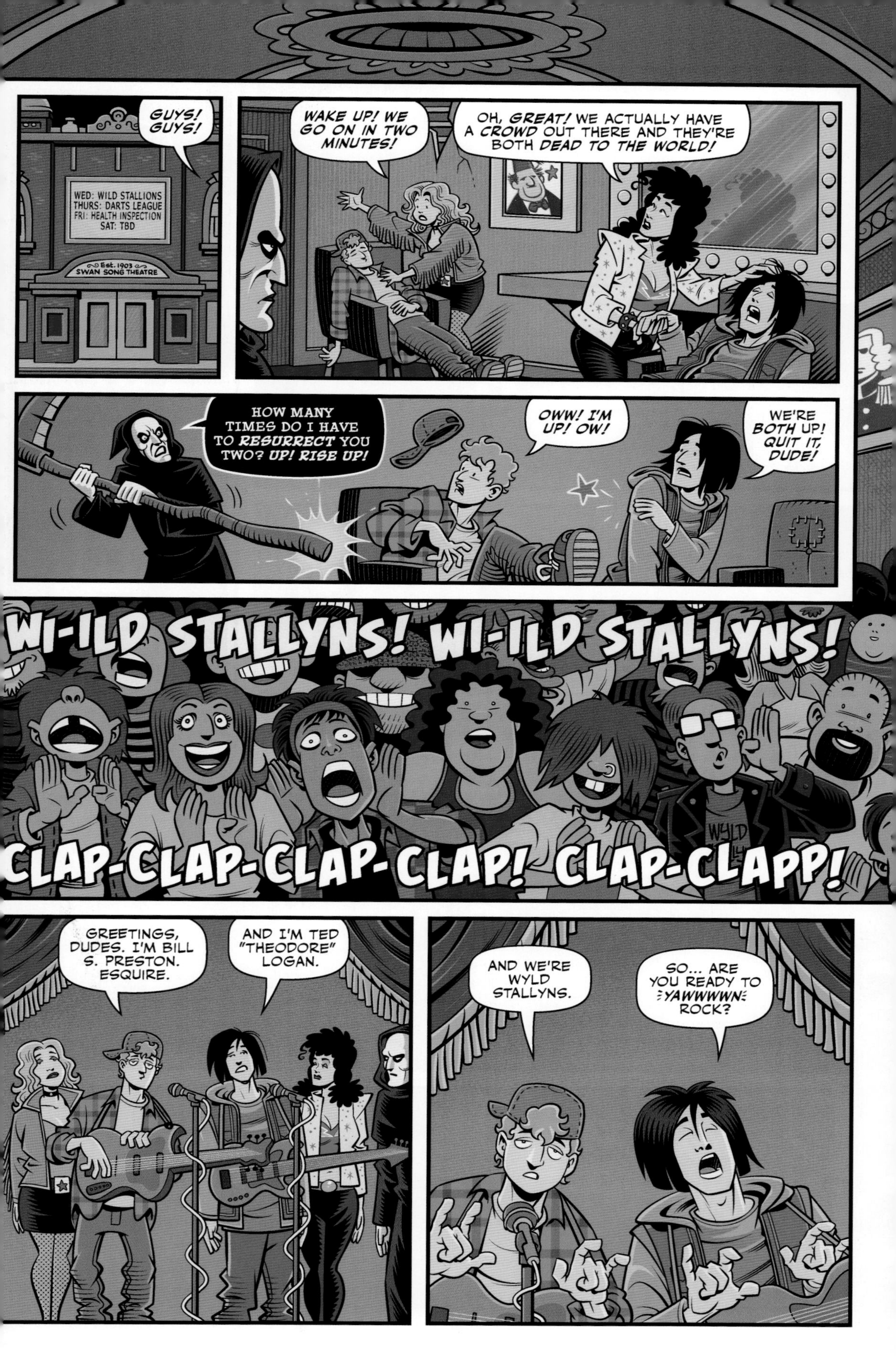
GUYS! GUYS!
WED: WILD STALLIONS
THURS: DARTS LEAGUE
FRI: HEALTH INSPECTION
SAT: TBD
Est. 1903
SWAN SONG THEATRE
WAKE UP! WE GO ON IN TWO MINUTES!
OH, GREAT! WE ACTUALLY HAVE A CROWD OUT THERE AND THEY'RE BOTH DEAD TO THE WORLD!
HOW MANY TIMES DO I HAVE TO RESURRECT YOU TWO? UP! RISE UP!
OWW! I'M UP! OW!
WE'RE BOTH UP! QUIT IT, DUDE!
WI-ILD STALLYNS! WI-ILD STALLYNS!
CLAP-CLAP-CLAP-CLAP! CLAP-CLAPP!
GREETINGS, DUDES. I'M BILL S. PRESTON. ESQUIRE.
AND I'M TED "THEODORE" LOGAN.
AND WE'RE WYLD STALLYNS.
SO... ARE YOU READY TO YAWWWWN ROCK?

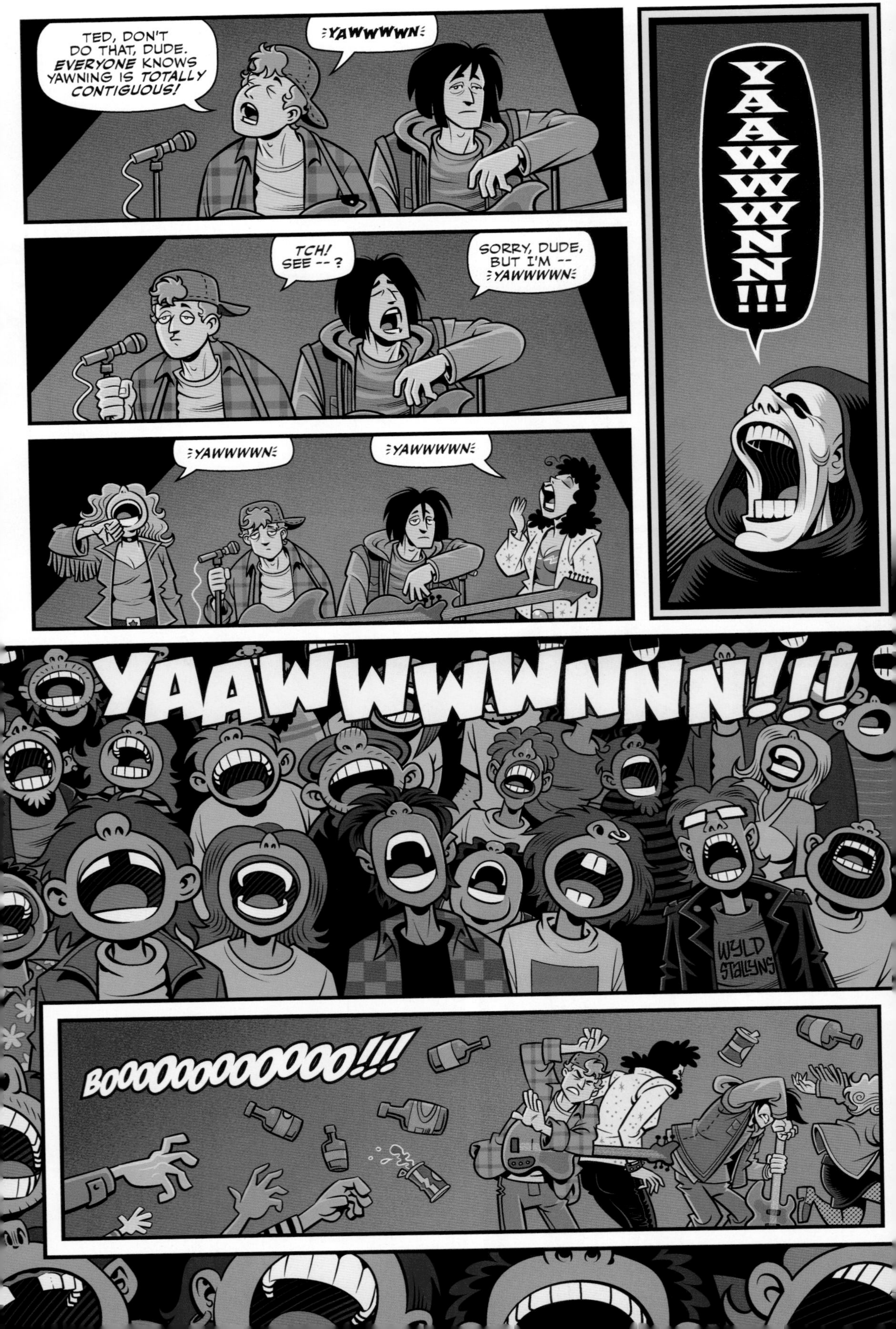

TED, DON'T DO THAT, DUDE. EVERYONE KNOWS YAWNING IS TOTALLY CONTIGUOUS!
YAWWWWN
TCH! SEE -- ?
SORRY, DUDE, BUT I'M -- YAWWWWN
YAWWWWN
YAWWWWN
YAAWWWNN!!!
YAAWWWWNNNN!!!
WYLD STALLYNS
BOOOOOOOOOOOO!!!

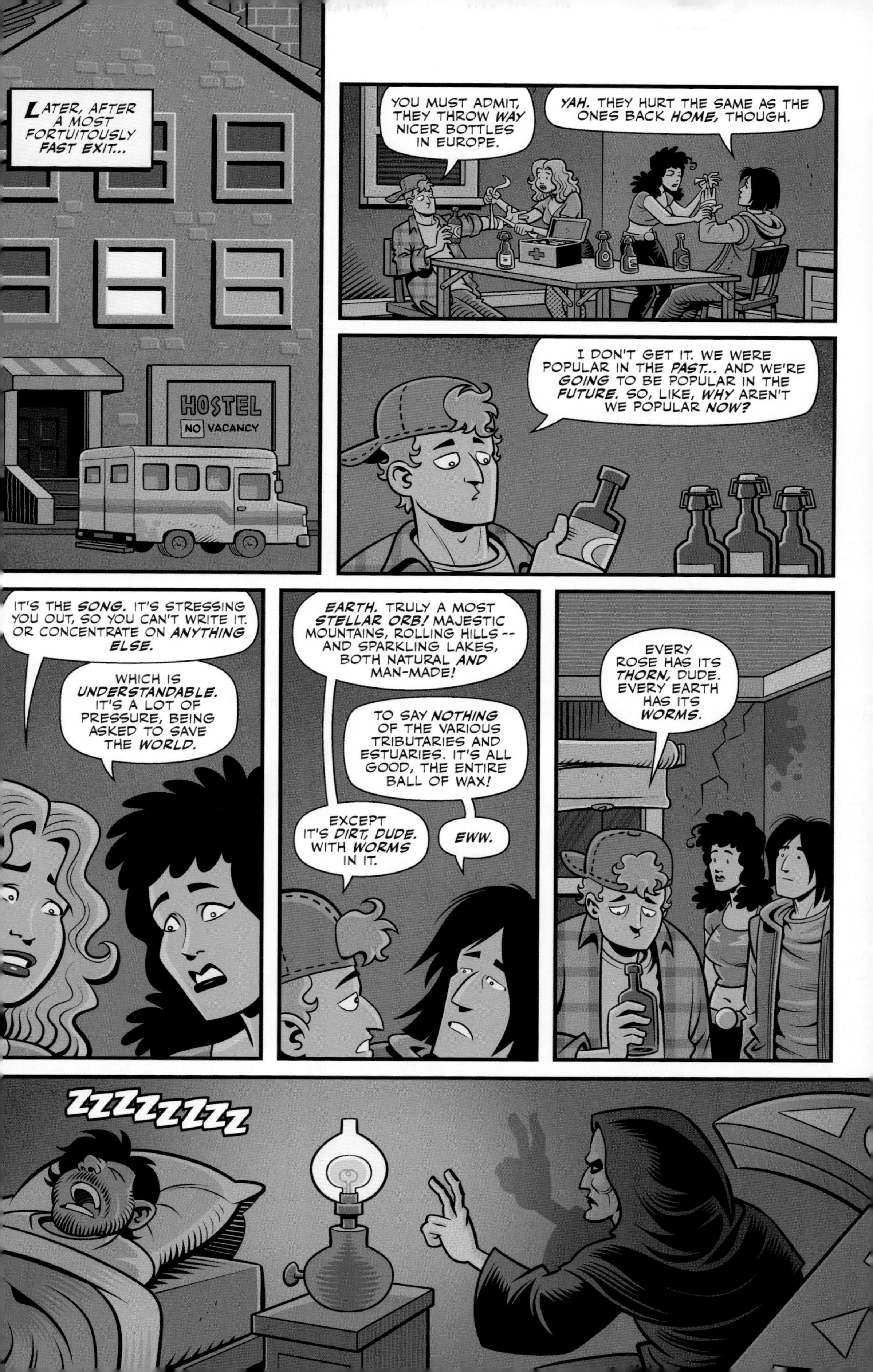
LATER, AFTER A MOST FORTUITOUSLY FAST EXIT...
HOSTEL
NO VACANCY
YOU MUST ADMIT, THEY THROW WAY NICER BOTTLES IN EUROPE.
YAH. THEY HURT THE SAME AS THE ONES BACK HOME, THOUGH.
I DON'T GET IT. WE WERE POPULAR IN THE PAST... AND WE'RE GOING TO BE POPULAR IN THE FUTURE. SO, LIKE, WHY AREN'T WE POPULAR NOW?
IT'S THE SONG. IT'S STRESSING YOU OUT, SO YOU CAN'T WRITE IT. OR CONCENTRATE ON ANYTHING ELSE.
WHICH IS UNDERSTANDABLE. IT'S A LOT OF PRESSURE, BEING ASKED TO SAVE THE WORLD.
EARTH. TRULY A MOST STELLAR ORB! MAJESTIC MOUNTAINS, ROLLING HILLS -- AND SPARKLING LAKES, BOTH NATURAL AND MAN-MADE!
TO SAY NOTHING OF THE VARIOUS TRIBUTARIES AND ESTUARIES. IT'S ALL GOOD, THE ENTIRE BALL OF WAX!
EXCEPT IT'S DIRT, DUDE. WITH WORMS IN IT.
EWW.
EVERY ROSE HAS ITS THORN, DUDE. EVERY EARTH HAS ITS WORMS.
ZZZZZZZZ

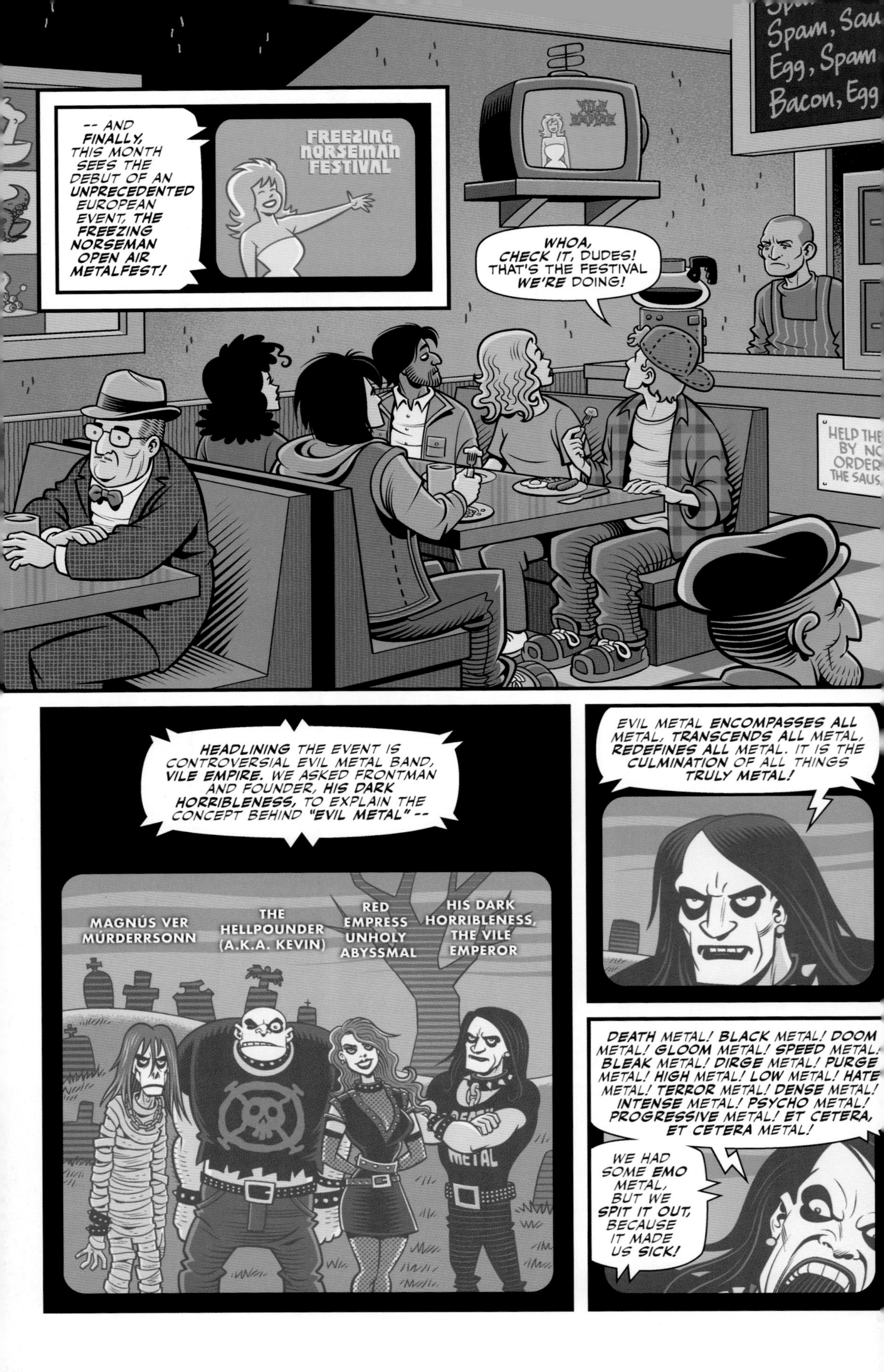

Spam, Sau
Egg, Spam
Bacon, Egg
-- AND FINALLY, THIS MONTH SEES THE DEBUT OF AN UNPRECEDENTED EUROPEAN EVENT, THE FREEZING NORSEMAN OPEN AIR METALFEST!
FREEZING NORSEMAN FESTIVAL
WHOA, CHECK IT, DUDES! THAT'S THE FESTIVAL WE'RE DOING!
HELP THE
BY NO
ORDER
THE SAUS
HEADLINING THE EVENT IS CONTROVERSIAL EVIL METAL BAND, VILE EMPIRE. WE ASKED FRONTMAN AND FOUNDER, HIS DARK HORRIBLENESS, TO EXPLAIN THE CONCEPT BEHIND "EVIL METAL" --
MAGNÚS VER MÚRDERRSONN
THE HELLPOUNDER (A.K.A. KEVIN)
RED EMPRESS UNHOLY ABYSSMAL
HIS DARK HORRIBLENESS, THE VILE EMPEROR
METAL
EVIL METAL ENCOMPASSES ALL METAL, TRANSCENDS ALL METAL, REDEFINES ALL METAL. IT IS THE CULMINATION OF ALL THINGS TRULY METAL!
DEATH METAL! BLACK METAL! DOOM METAL! GLOOM METAL! SPEED METAL! BLEAK METAL! DIRGE METAL! PURGE METAL! HIGH METAL! LOW METAL! HATE METAL! TERROR METAL! DENSE METAL! INTENSE METAL! PSYCHO METAL! PROGRESSIVE METAL! ET CETERA, ET CETERA METAL!
WE HAD SOME EMO METAL, BUT WE SPIT IT OUT, BECAUSE IT MADE US SICK!

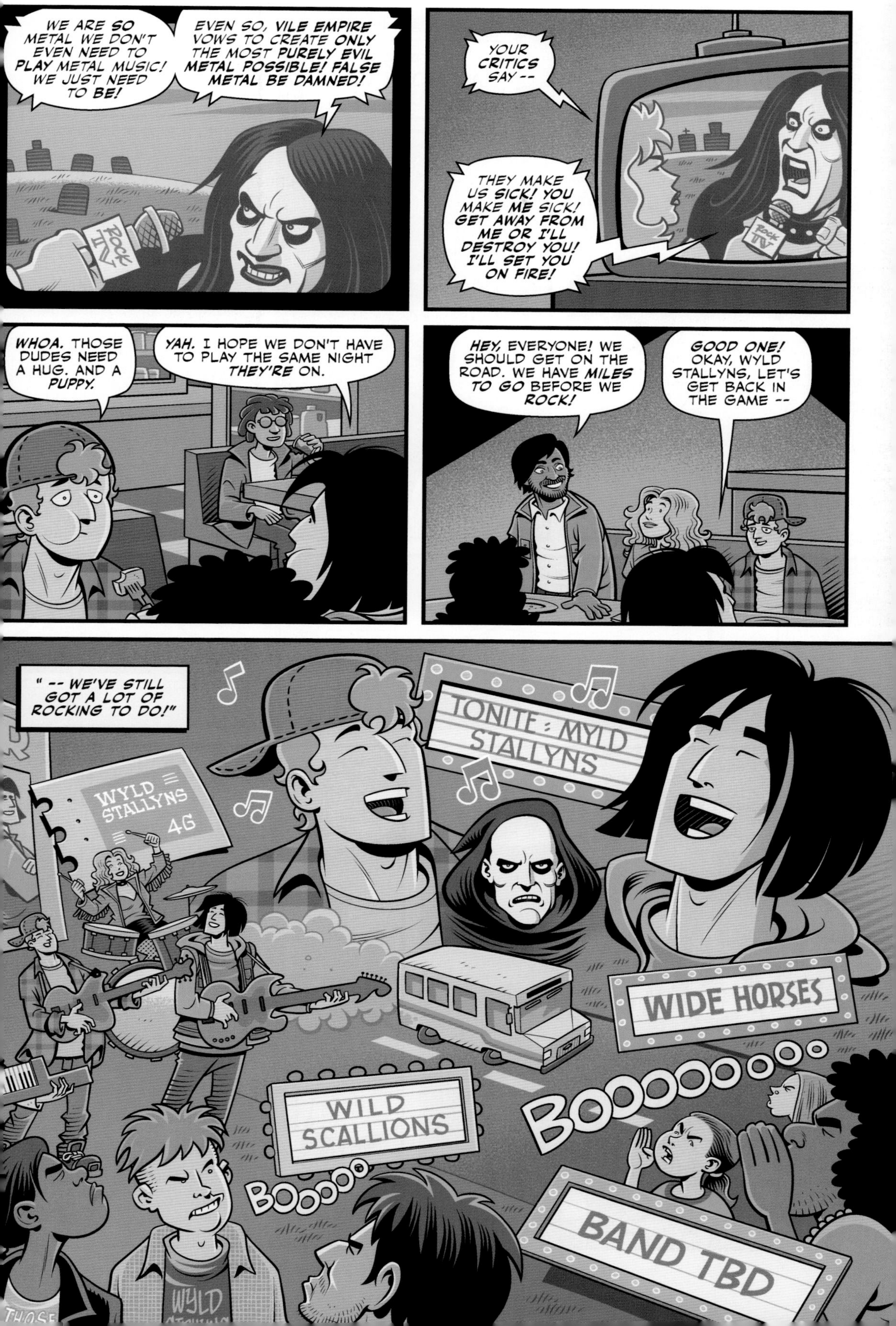
WE ARE SO METAL WE DON'T EVEN NEED TO PLAY METAL MUSIC! WE JUST NEED TO BE!
EVEN SO, VILE EMPIRE VOWS TO CREATE ONLY THE MOST PURELY EVIL METAL POSSIBLE! FALSE METAL BE DAMNED!
ROCK TV
YOUR CRITICS SAY --
THEY MAKE US SICK! YOU MAKE ME SICK! GET AWAY FROM ME OR I'LL DESTROY YOU! I'LL SET YOU ON FIRE!
ROCK TV
WHOA. THOSE DUDES NEED A HUG. AND A PUPPY.
YAH. I HOPE WE DON'T HAVE TO PLAY THE SAME NIGHT THEY'RE ON.
HEY, EVERYONE! WE SHOULD GET ON THE ROAD. WE HAVE MILES TO GO BEFORE WE ROCK!
GOOD ONE! OKAY, WYLD STALLYNS, LET'S GET BACK IN THE GAME --
" -- WE'VE STILL GOT A LOT OF ROCKING TO DO!"
TONITE : WYLD STALLYNS
WYLD STALLYNS 4G
WIDE HORSES
WILD SCALLIONS
BOOOOOOOO
BOOOOO
BAND TBD
WYLD

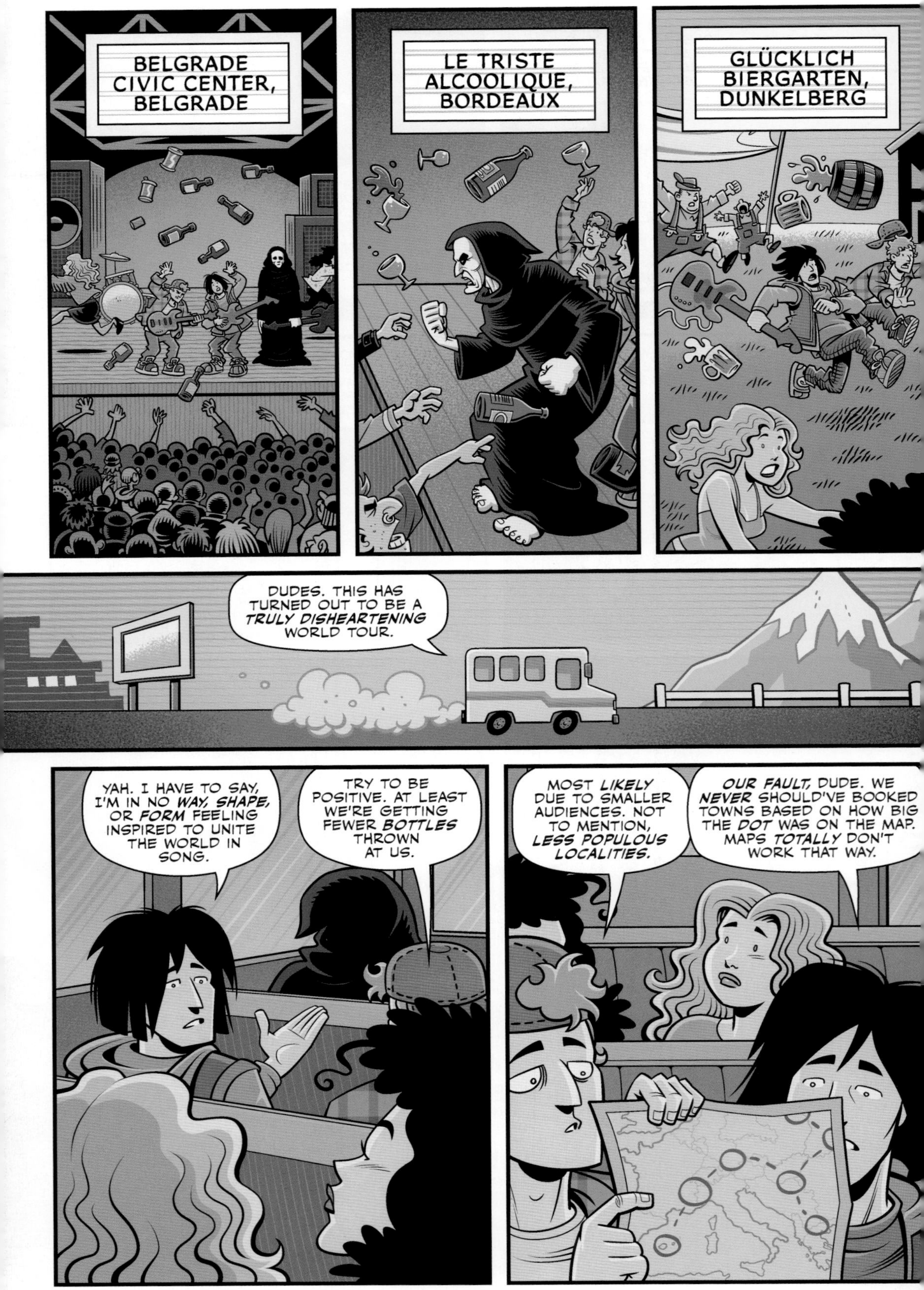
BELGRADE CIVIC CENTER, BELGRADE
LE TRISTE ALCOOLIQUE, BORDEAUX
GLÜCKLICH BIERGARTEN, DUNKELBERG
DUDES. THIS HAS TURNED OUT TO BE A TRULY DISHEARTENING WORLD TOUR.
YAH. I HAVE TO SAY, I'M IN NO WAY, SHAPE, OR FORM FEELING INSPIRED TO UNITE THE WORLD IN SONG.
TRY TO BE POSITIVE. AT LEAST WE'RE GETTING FEWER BOTTLES THROWN AT US.
MOST LIKELY DUE TO SMALLER AUDIENCES. NOT TO MENTION, LESS POPULOUS LOCALITIES.
OUR FAULT, DUDE. WE NEVER SHOULD'VE BOOKED TOWNS BASED ON HOW BIG THE DOT WAS ON THE MAP. MAPS TOTALLY DON'T WORK THAT WAY.

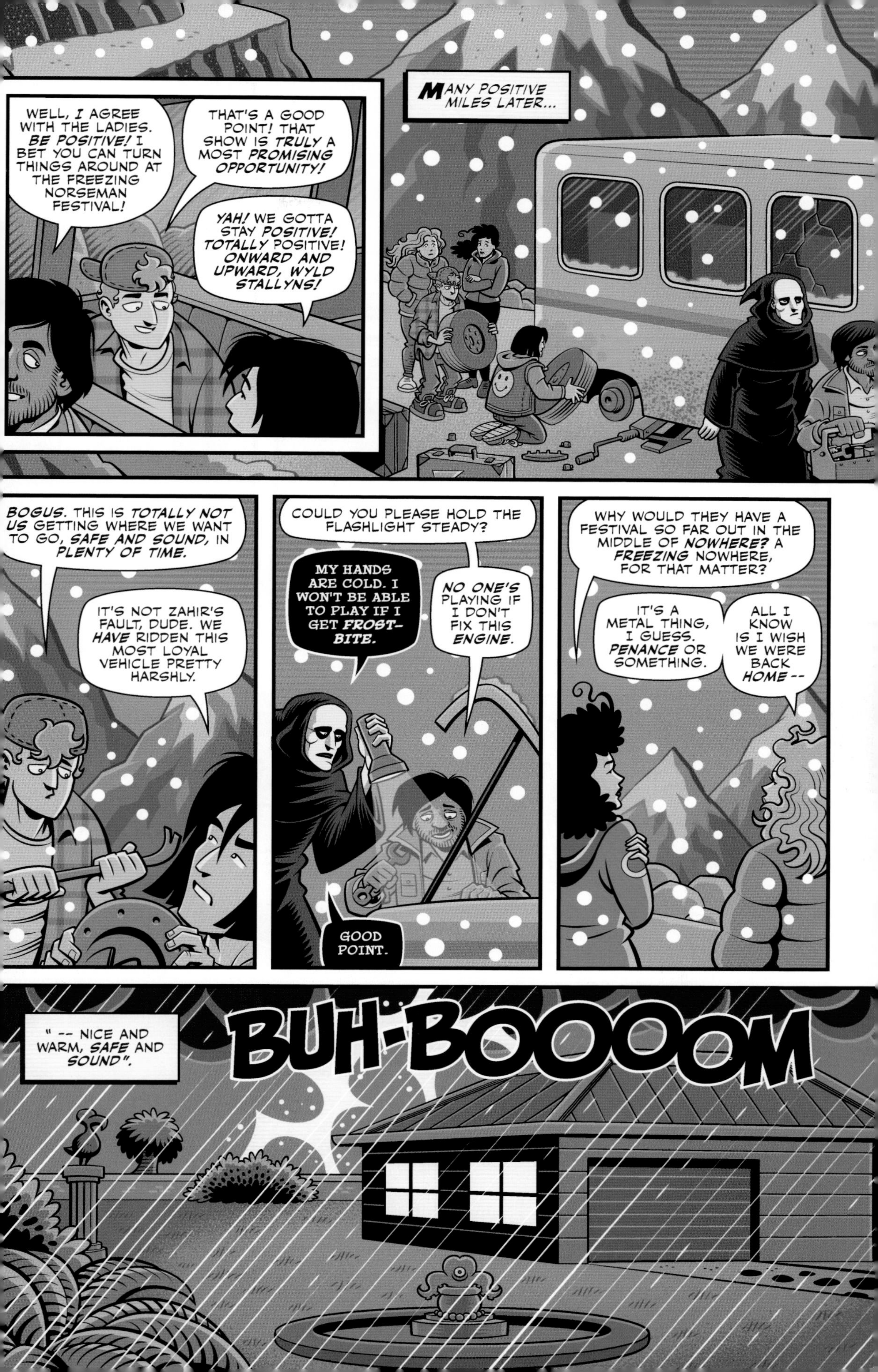

WELL, *I* AGREE WITH THE LADIES. ***BE POSITIVE!*** I BET YOU CAN TURN THINGS AROUND AT THE FREEZING NORSEMAN FESTIVAL!
THAT'S A GOOD POINT! THAT SHOW IS *TRULY* A MOST *PROMISING OPPORTUNITY!*
YAH! WE GOTTA STAY *POSITIVE! TOTALLY* POSITIVE! *ONWARD AND UPWARD, WYLD STALLYNS!*
MANY POSITIVE MILES LATER...
BOGUS. THIS IS *TOTALLY NOT US* GETTING WHERE WE WANT TO GO, *SAFE AND SOUND,* IN *PLENTY OF TIME.*
IT'S NOT ZAHIR'S FAULT, DUDE. WE *HAVE* RIDDEN THIS MOST LOYAL VEHICLE PRETTY HARSHLY.
COULD YOU PLEASE HOLD THE FLASHLIGHT STEADY?
MY HANDS ARE COLD. I WON'T BE ABLE TO PLAY IF I GET *FROST-BITE.*
NO ONE'S PLAYING IF I DON'T FIX THIS *ENGINE.*
GOOD POINT.
WHY WOULD THEY HAVE A FESTIVAL SO FAR OUT IN THE MIDDLE OF *NOWHERE?* A *FREEZING* NOWHERE, FOR THAT MATTER?
IT'S A METAL THING, I GUESS. *PENANCE* OR SOMETHING.
ALL I KNOW IS I WISH WE WERE BACK *HOME --*
" -- NICE AND WARM, *SAFE* AND *SOUND*".
BUH-BOOOOOM

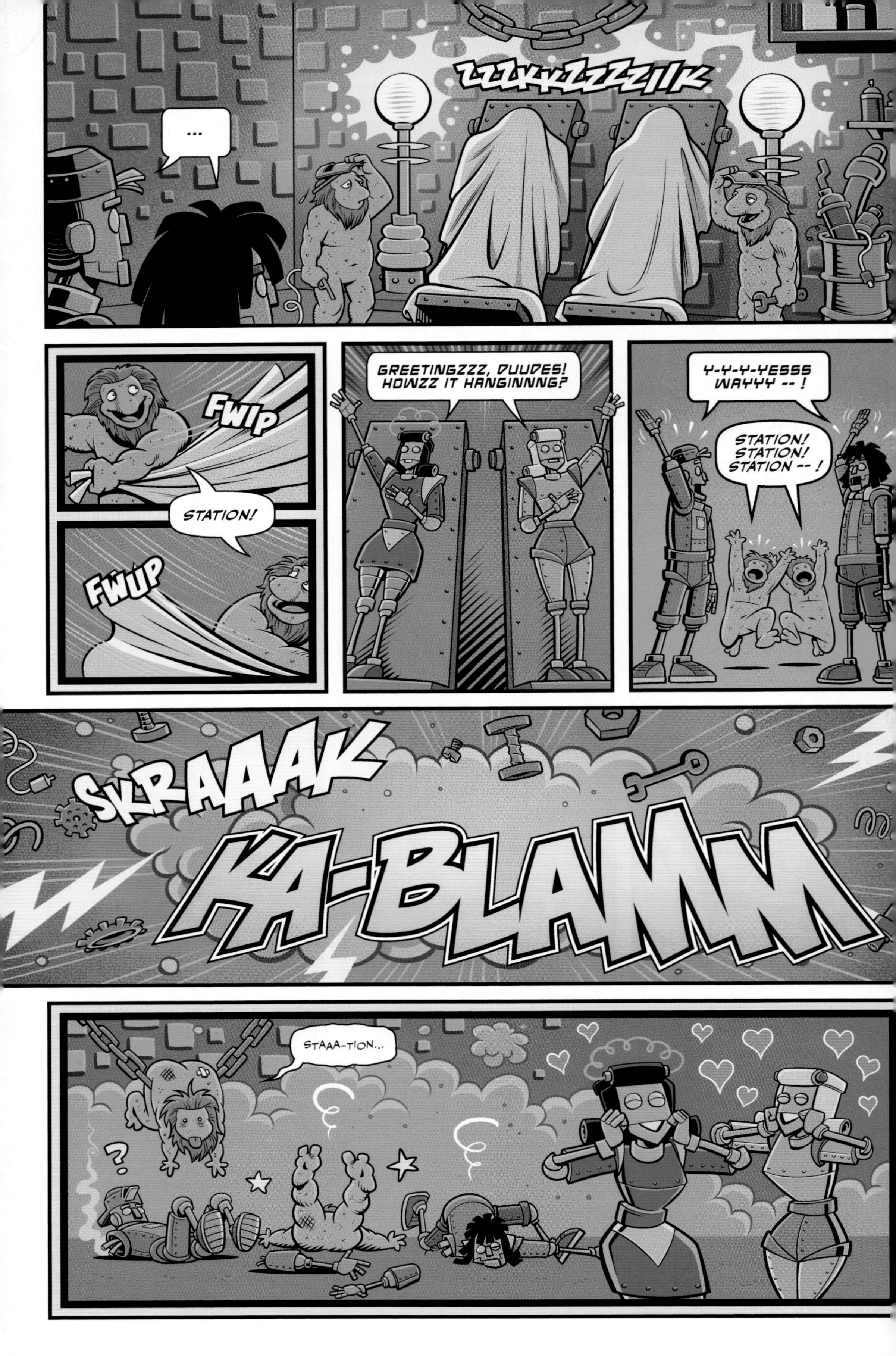

...
ZZZKKZZZZZIIK
FWIP
STATION!
FWUP
GREETINGZZZ, DUUDES! HOWZZ IT HANGINNNG?
Y-Y-Y-YESSS WAYYY -- !
STATION! STATION! STATION -- !
SKRAAAK
KA-BLAMM
STAAA-TION...
?

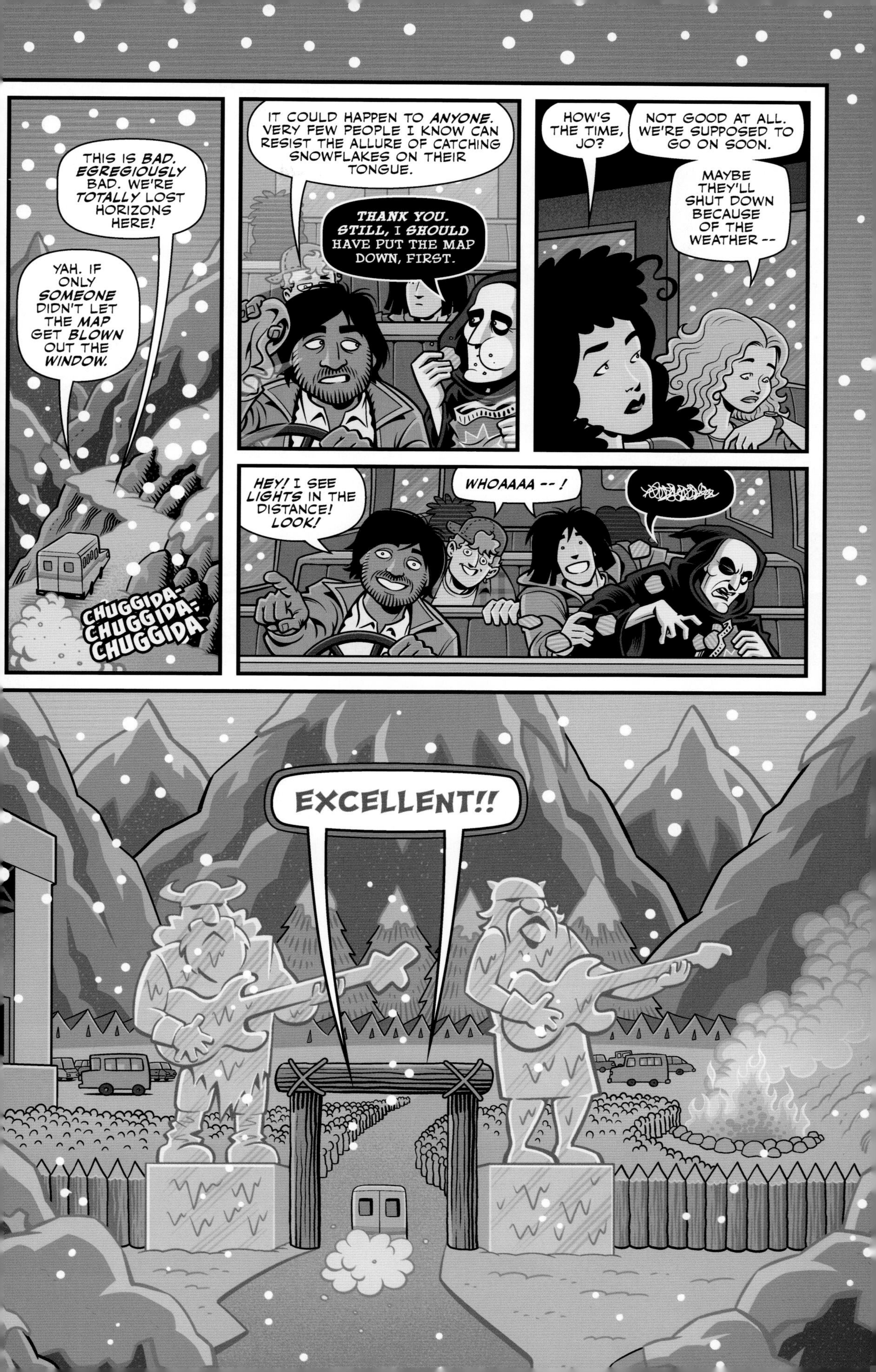

THIS IS BAD. EGREGIOUSLY BAD. WE'RE TOTALLY LOST HORIZONS HERE!
YAH. IF ONLY SOMEONE DIDN'T LET THE MAP GET BLOWN OUT THE WINDOW.
CHUGGIDA-CHUGGIDA-CHUGGIDA
IT COULD HAPPEN TO ANYONE. VERY FEW PEOPLE I KNOW CAN RESIST THE ALLURE OF CATCHING SNOWFLAKES ON THEIR TONGUE.
THANK YOU. STILL, I SHOULD HAVE PUT THE MAP DOWN, FIRST.
HOW'S THE TIME, JO?
NOT GOOD AT ALL. WE'RE SUPPOSED TO GO ON SOON.
MAYBE THEY'LL SHUT DOWN BECAUSE OF THE WEATHER --
HEY! I SEE LIGHTS IN THE DISTANCE! LOOK!
WHOAAAA -- !
EXCELLENT!!

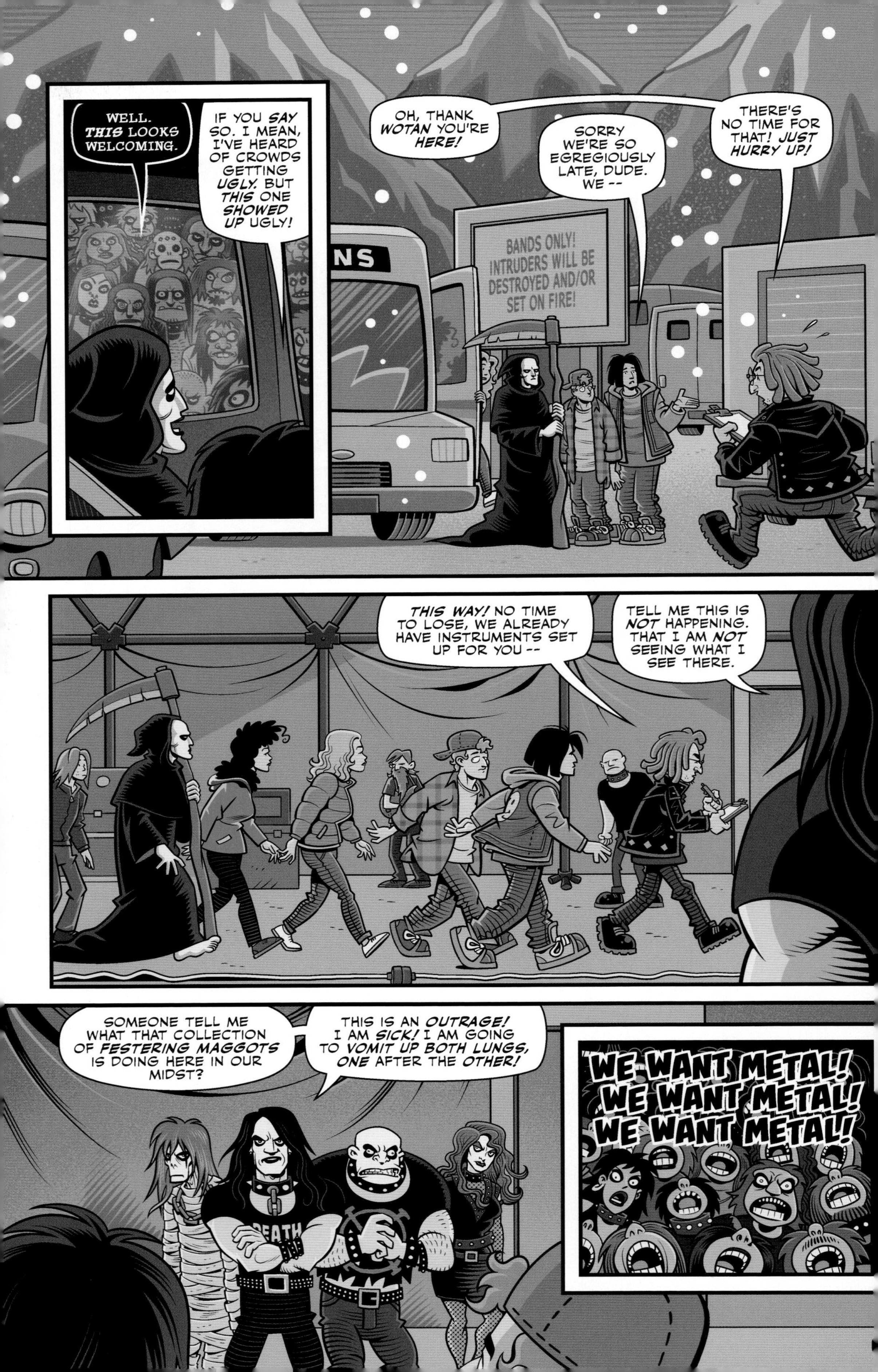

WELL. THIS LOOKS WELCOMING.
IF YOU SAY SO. I MEAN, I'VE HEARD OF CROWDS GETTING UGLY. BUT THIS ONE SHOWED UP UGLY!
OH, THANK WOTAN YOU'RE HERE!
SORRY WE'RE SO EGREGIOUSLY LATE, DUDE. WE --
THERE'S NO TIME FOR THAT! JUST HURRY UP!
BANDS ONLY! INTRUDERS WILL BE DESTROYED AND/OR SET ON FIRE!
THIS WAY! NO TIME TO LOSE, WE ALREADY HAVE INSTRUMENTS SET UP FOR YOU --
TELL ME THIS IS NOT HAPPENING. THAT I AM NOT SEEING WHAT I SEE THERE.
SOMEONE TELL ME WHAT THAT COLLECTION OF FESTERING MAGGOTS IS DOING HERE IN OUR MIDST?
THIS IS AN OUTRAGE! I AM SICK! I AM GOING TO VOMIT UP BOTH LUNGS, ONE AFTER THE OTHER!
"WE WANT METAL! WE WANT METAL! WE WANT METAL!

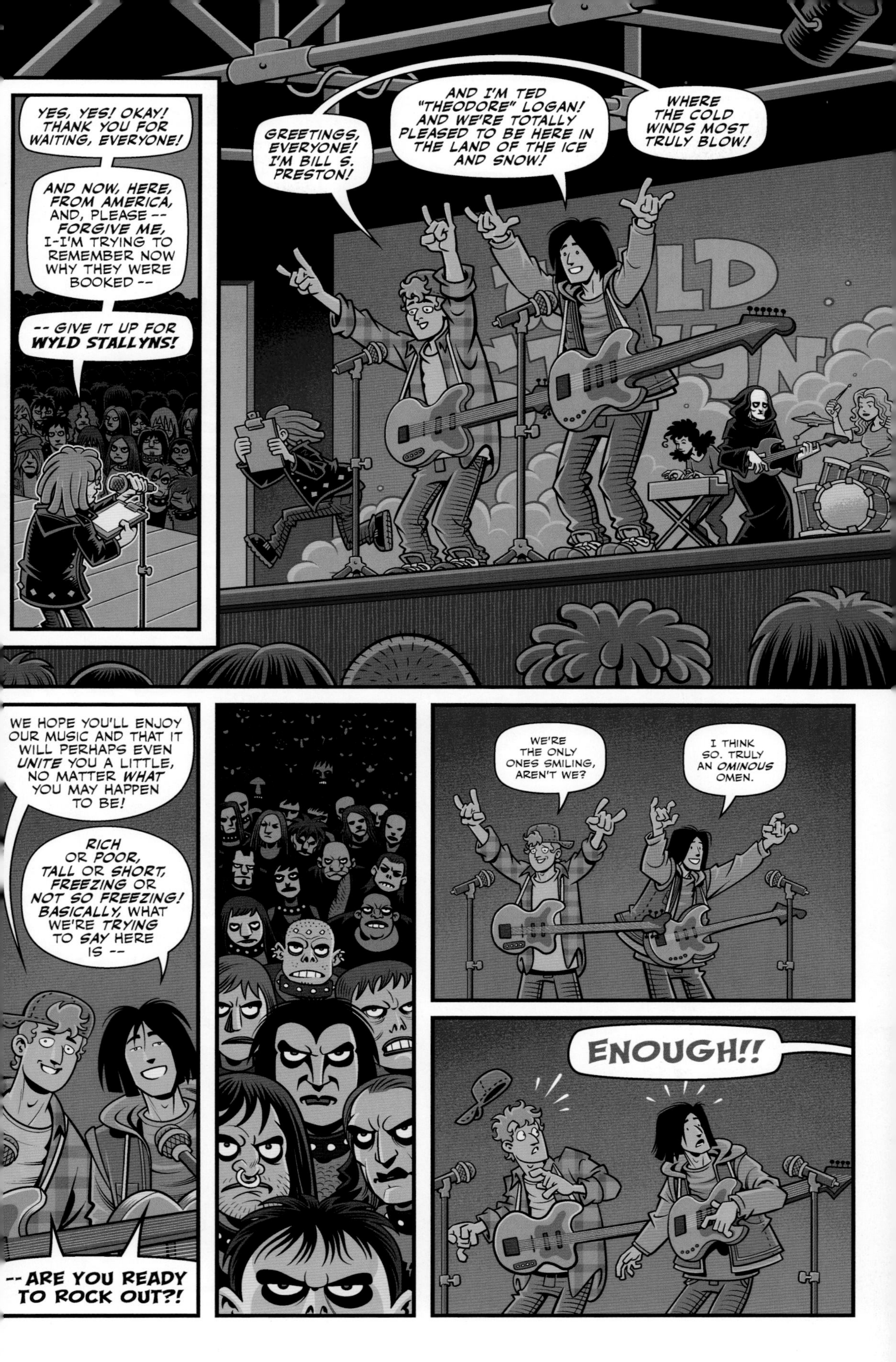

YES, YES! OKAY! THANK YOU FOR WAITING, EVERYONE!
AND NOW, HERE, FROM AMERICA, AND, PLEASE -- FORGIVE ME, I-I'M TRYING TO REMEMBER NOW WHY THEY WERE BOOKED --
-- GIVE IT UP FOR WYLD STALLYNS!
GREETINGS, EVERYONE! I'M BILL S. PRESTON!
AND I'M TED "THEODORE" LOGAN! AND WE'RE TOTALLY PLEASED TO BE HERE IN THE LAND OF THE ICE AND SNOW!
WHERE THE COLD WINDS MOST TRULY BLOW!
WE HOPE YOU'LL ENJOY OUR MUSIC AND THAT IT WILL PERHAPS EVEN UNITE YOU A LITTLE, NO MATTER WHAT YOU MAY HAPPEN TO BE!
RICH OR POOR, TALL OR SHORT, FREEZING OR NOT SO FREEZING! BASICALLY, WHAT WE'RE TRYING TO SAY HERE IS --
-- ARE YOU READY TO ROCK OUT?!
WE'RE THE ONLY ONES SMILING, AREN'T WE?
I THINK SO. TRULY AN OMINOUS OMEN.
ENOUGH!!

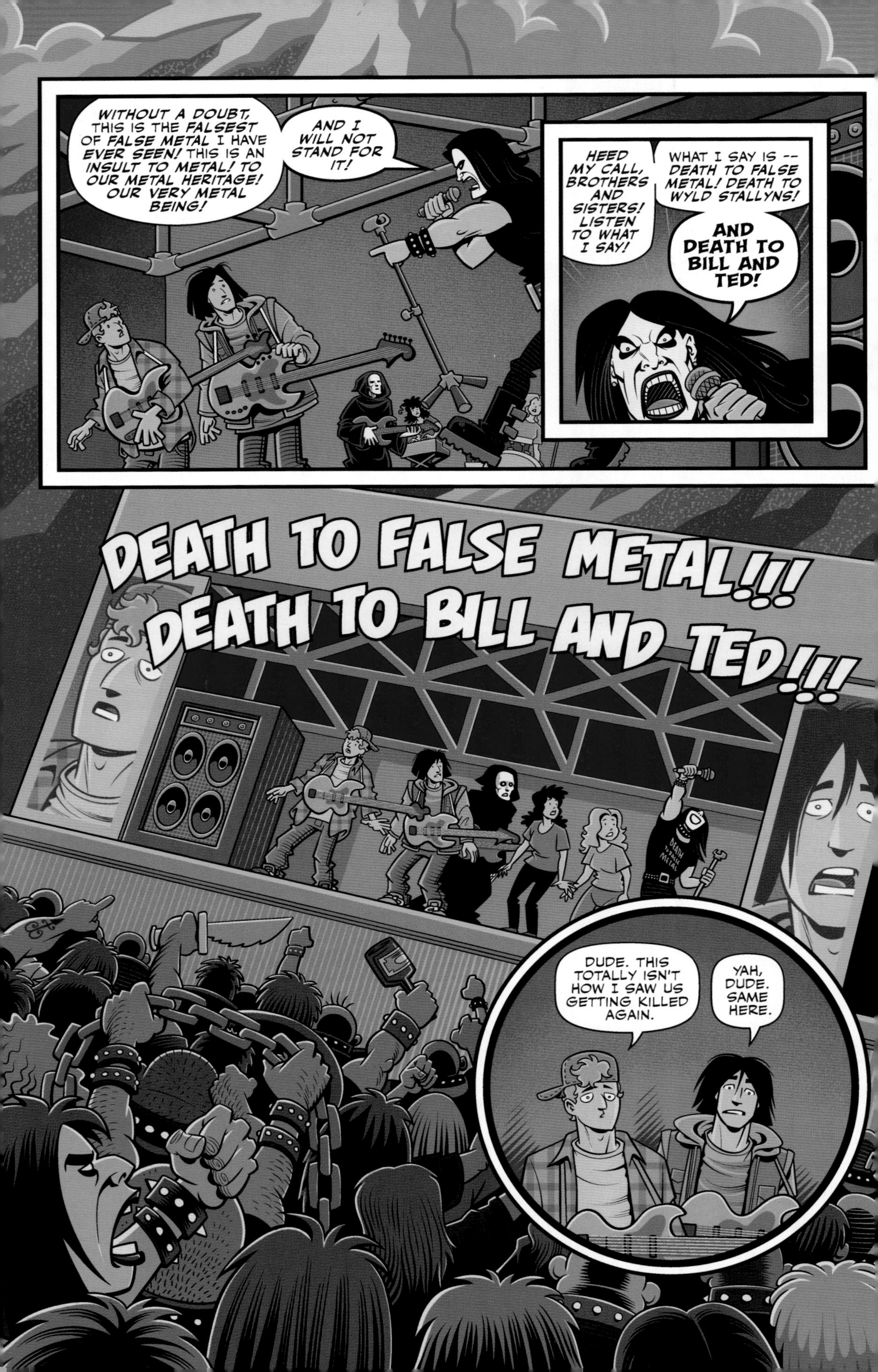
WITHOUT A DOUBT, THIS IS THE FALSEST OF FALSE METAL I HAVE EVER SEEN! THIS IS AN INSULT TO METAL! TO OUR METAL HERITAGE! OUR VERY METAL BEING!
AND I WILL NOT STAND FOR IT!
HEED MY CALL, BROTHERS AND SISTERS! LISTEN TO WHAT I SAY!
WHAT I SAY IS -- DEATH TO FALSE METAL! DEATH TO WYLD STALLYNS!
AND DEATH TO BILL AND TED!
DEATH TO FALSE METAL!!! DEATH TO BILL AND TED!!!
DUDE. THIS TOTALLY ISN'T HOW I SAW US GETTING KILLED AGAIN.
YAH, DUDE. SAME HERE.

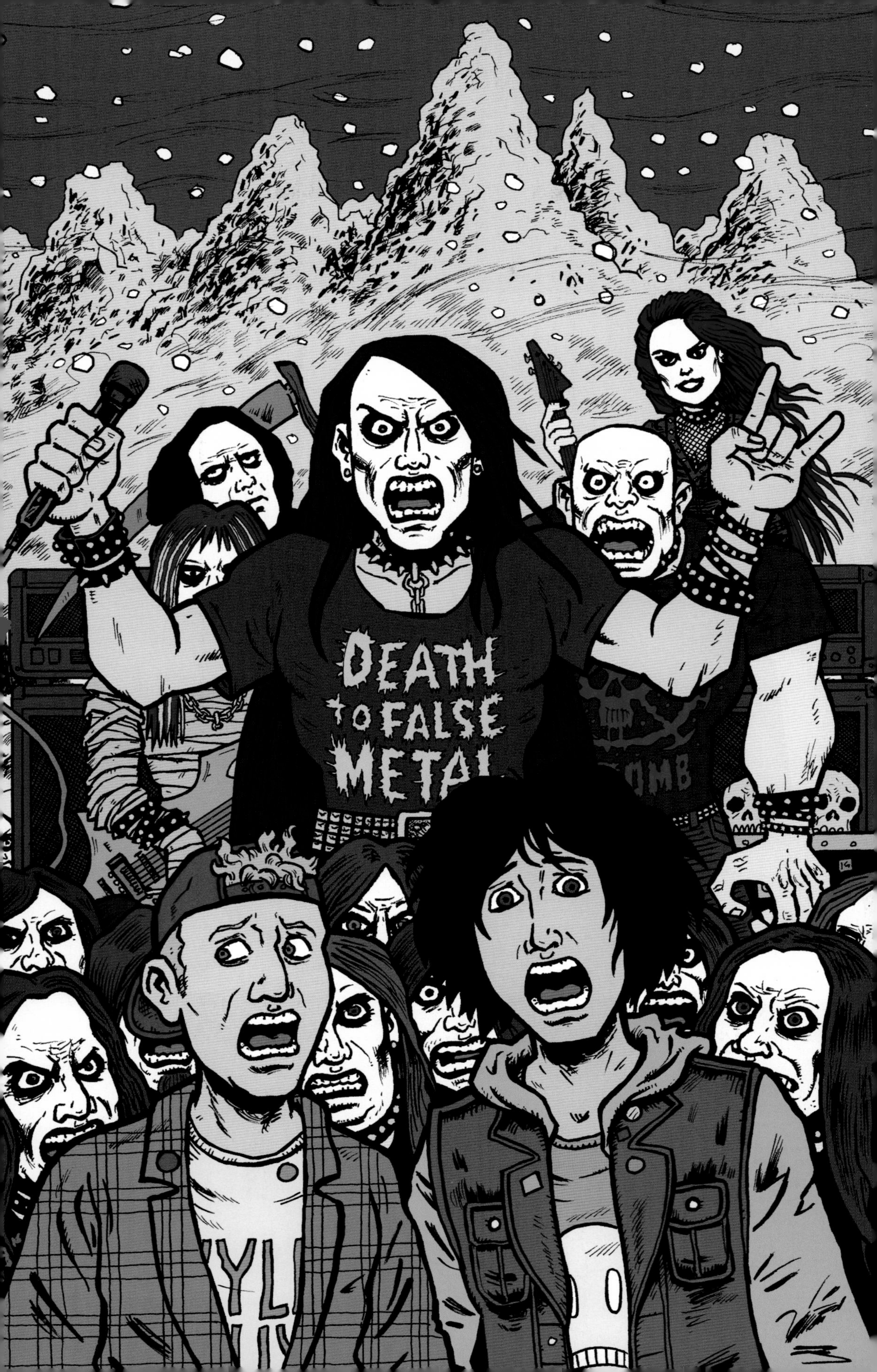
DEATH
to FALSE
METAL

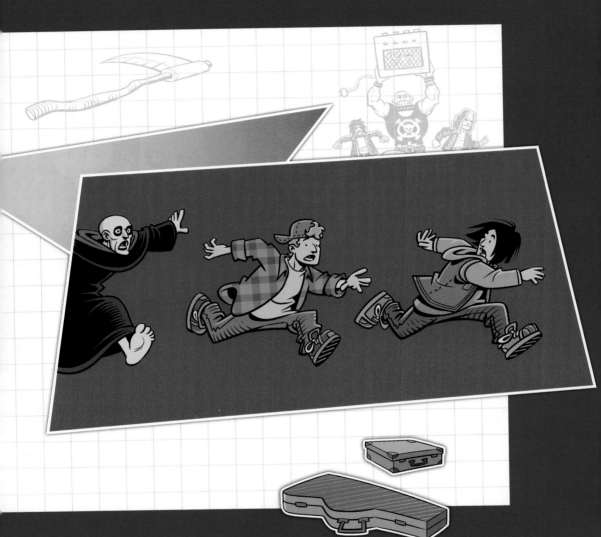

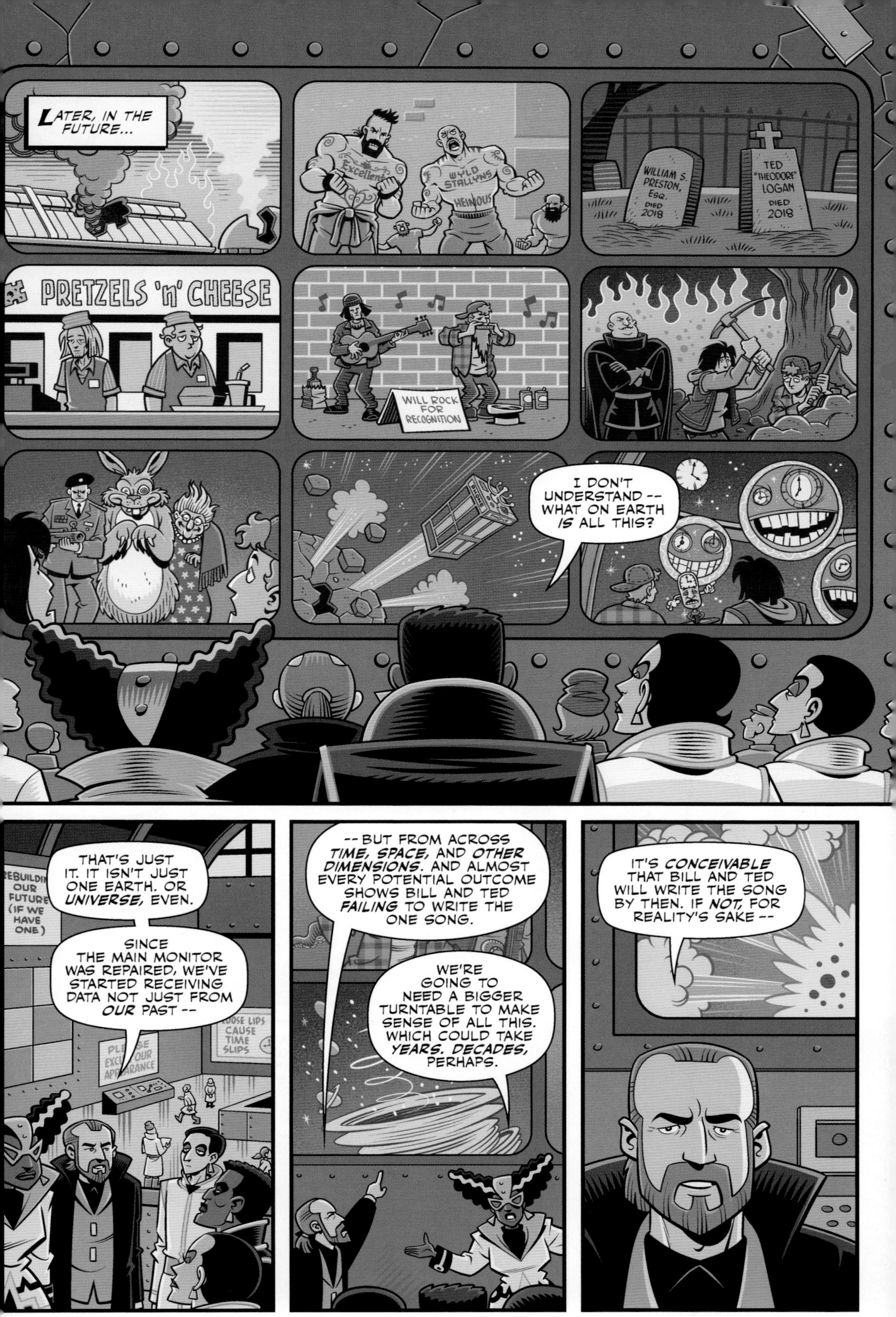
LATER, IN THE FUTURE...
EXCELLENT
WYLD STALLYNS
HEINOUS
WILLIAM S. PRESTON, ESQ. DIED 2018
TED "THEODORE" LOGAN DIED 2018
PRETZELS 'n' CHEESE
WILL ROCK FOR RECOGNITION
I DON'T UNDERSTAND -- WHAT ON EARTH *IS* ALL THIS?
REBUILDING OUR FUTURE (IF WE HAVE ONE)
THAT'S JUST IT. IT ISN'T JUST ONE EARTH. OR *UNIVERSE,* EVEN.
SINCE THE MAIN MONITOR WAS REPAIRED, WE'VE STARTED RECEIVING DATA NOT JUST FROM *OUR* PAST --
LOOSE LIPS CAUSE TIME SLIPS
PLEASE EXCUSE OUR APPEARANCE
-- BUT FROM ACROSS *TIME, SPACE,* AND *OTHER DIMENSIONS.* AND ALMOST EVERY POTENTIAL OUTCOME SHOWS BILL AND TED *FAILING* TO WRITE THE ONE SONG.
WE'RE GOING TO NEED A BIGGER TURNTABLE TO MAKE SENSE OF ALL THIS. WHICH COULD TAKE *YEARS. DECADES,* PERHAPS.
IT'S *CONCEIVABLE* THAT BILL AND TED WILL WRITE THE SONG BY THEN. IF *NOT,* FOR REALITY'S SAKE --

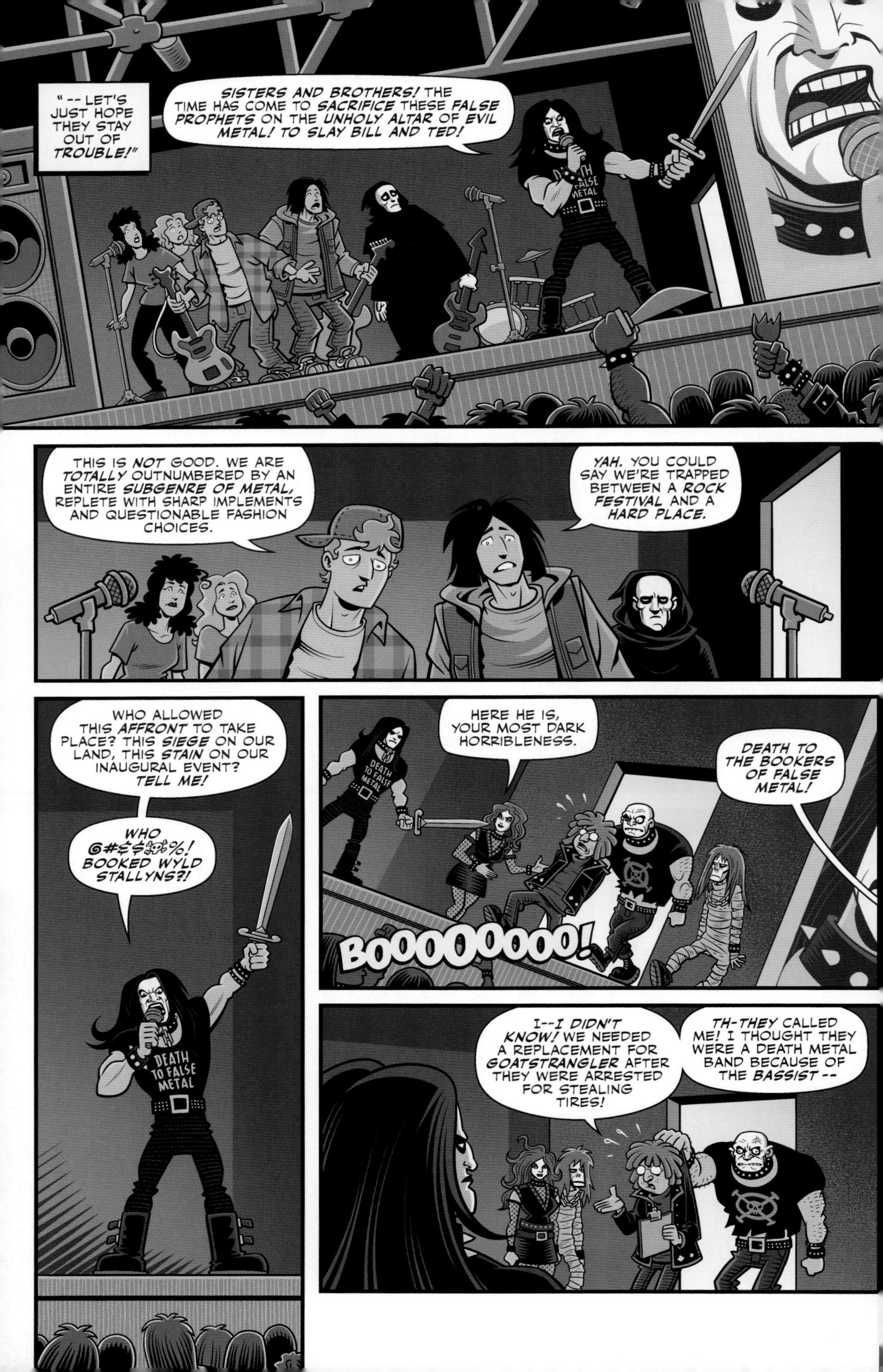
"-- LET'S JUST HOPE THEY STAY OUT OF *TROUBLE!*"
SISTERS AND BROTHERS! THE TIME HAS COME TO *SACRIFICE* THESE *FALSE PROPHETS* ON THE *UNHOLY ALTAR* OF *EVIL METAL! TO SLAY BILL AND TED!*
DEATH TO FALSE METAL
THIS IS *NOT* GOOD. WE ARE *TOTALLY* OUTNUMBERED BY AN ENTIRE *SUBGENRE OF METAL,* REPLETE WITH SHARP IMPLEMENTS AND QUESTIONABLE FASHION CHOICES.
YAH. YOU COULD SAY WE'RE TRAPPED BETWEEN A *ROCK FESTIVAL* AND A *HARD PLACE.*
WHO ALLOWED THIS *AFFRONT* TO TAKE PLACE? THIS *SIEGE* ON OUR LAND, THIS *STAIN* ON OUR INAUGURAL EVENT? *TELL ME!*
WHO @#$$☠%! BOOKED WYLD STALLYNS?!
DEATH TO FALSE METAL
HERE HE IS, YOUR MOST DARK HORRIBLENESS.
DEATH TO FALSE METAL
DEATH TO THE BOOKERS OF FALSE METAL!
BOOOOOOOO!
I--*I DIDN'T KNOW!* WE NEEDED A REPLACEMENT FOR *GOATSTRANGLER* AFTER THEY WERE ARRESTED FOR STEALING TIRES!
TH-THEY CALLED ME! I THOUGHT THEY WERE A DEATH METAL BAND BECAUSE OF THE *BASSIST* --

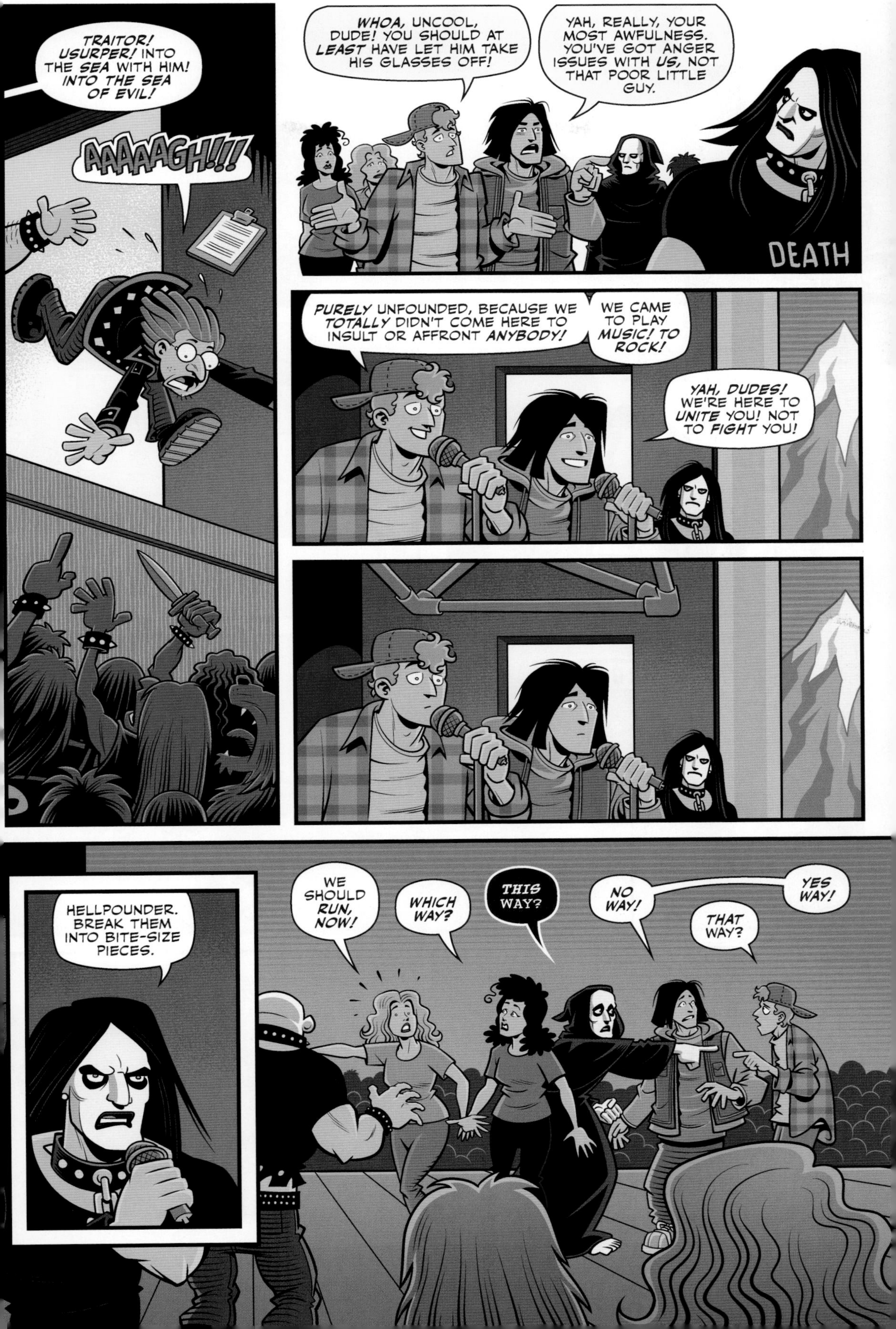
TRAITOR! USURPER! INTO THE SEA WITH HIM! INTO THE SEA OF EVIL!
AAAAAGH!!!
WHOA, UNCOOL, DUDE! YOU SHOULD AT LEAST HAVE LET HIM TAKE HIS GLASSES OFF!
YAH, REALLY, YOUR MOST AWFULNESS. YOU'VE GOT ANGER ISSUES WITH US, NOT THAT POOR LITTLE GUY.
DEATH
PURELY UNFOUNDED, BECAUSE WE TOTALLY DIDN'T COME HERE TO INSULT OR AFFRONT ANYBODY!
WE CAME TO PLAY MUSIC! TO ROCK!
YAH, DUDES! WE'RE HERE TO UNITE YOU! NOT TO FIGHT YOU!
HELLPOUNDER. BREAK THEM INTO BITE-SIZE PIECES.
WE SHOULD RUN, NOW!
WHICH WAY?
THIS WAY?
NO WAY!
THAT WAY?
YES WAY!

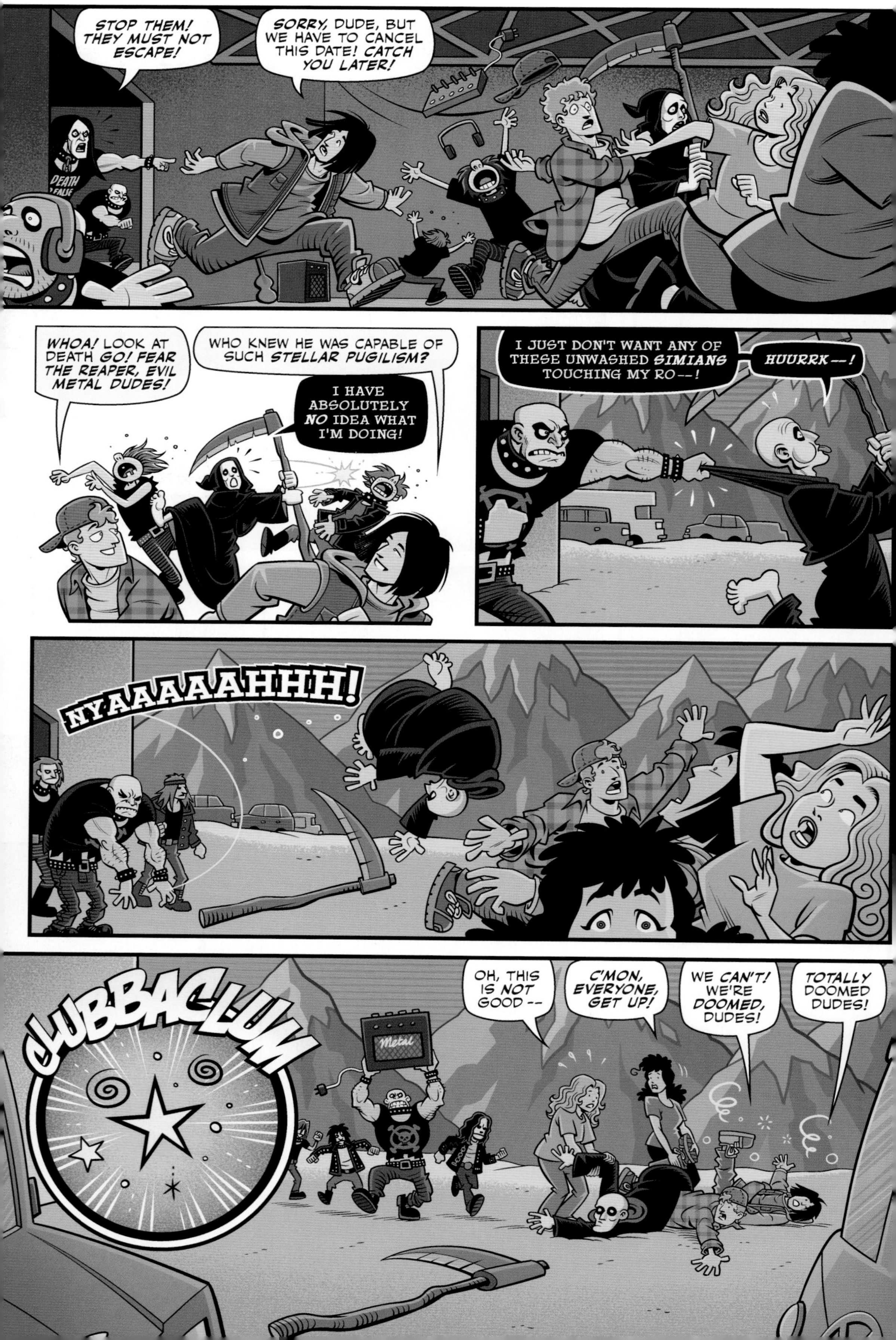

STOP THEM! THEY MUST NOT ESCAPE!
SORRY, DUDE, BUT WE HAVE TO CANCEL THIS DATE! CATCH YOU LATER!
WHOA! LOOK AT DEATH GO! FEAR THE REAPER, EVIL METAL DUDES!
WHO KNEW HE WAS CAPABLE OF SUCH STELLAR PUGILISM?
I HAVE ABSOLUTELY NO IDEA WHAT I'M DOING!
I JUST DON'T WANT ANY OF THESE UNWASHED SIMIANS TOUCHING MY RO--!
HUURRK--!
NYAAAAAAHHH!
CLUBBACLUM
Metal
OH, THIS IS NOT GOOD --
C'MON, EVERYONE, GET UP!
WE CAN'T! WE'RE DOOMED, DUDES!
TOTALLY DOOMED DUDES!

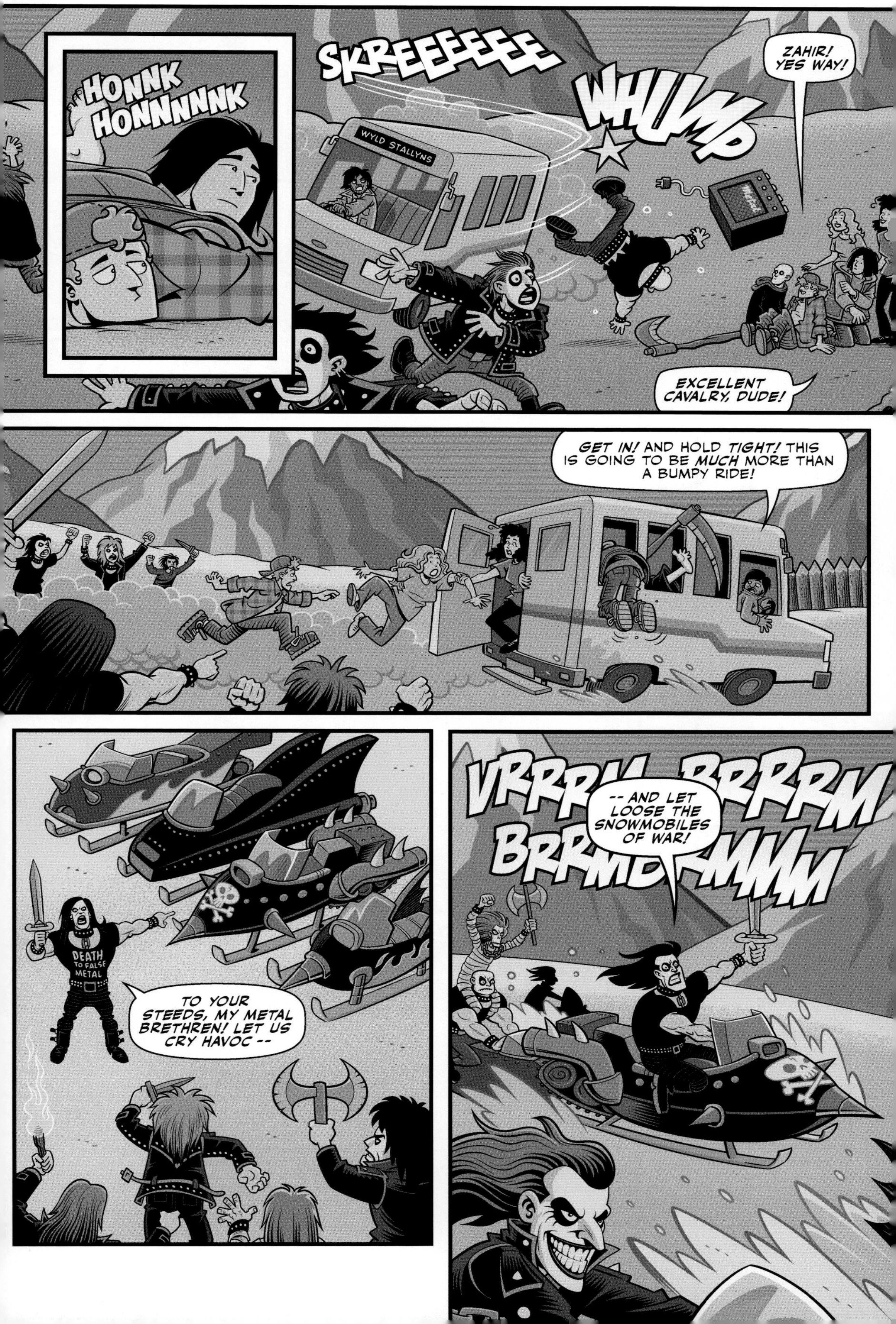
HONNK HONNNNNK
SKREEEEEEE
WYLD STALLYNS
WHUMP
ZAHIR! YES WAY!
EXCELLENT CAVALRY, DUDE!
GET IN! AND HOLD TIGHT! THIS IS GOING TO BE MUCH MORE THAN A BUMPY RIDE!
DEATH TO FALSE METAL
TO YOUR STEEDS, MY METAL BRETHREN! LET US CRY HAVOC --
-- AND LET LOOSE THE SNOWMOBILES OF WAR!

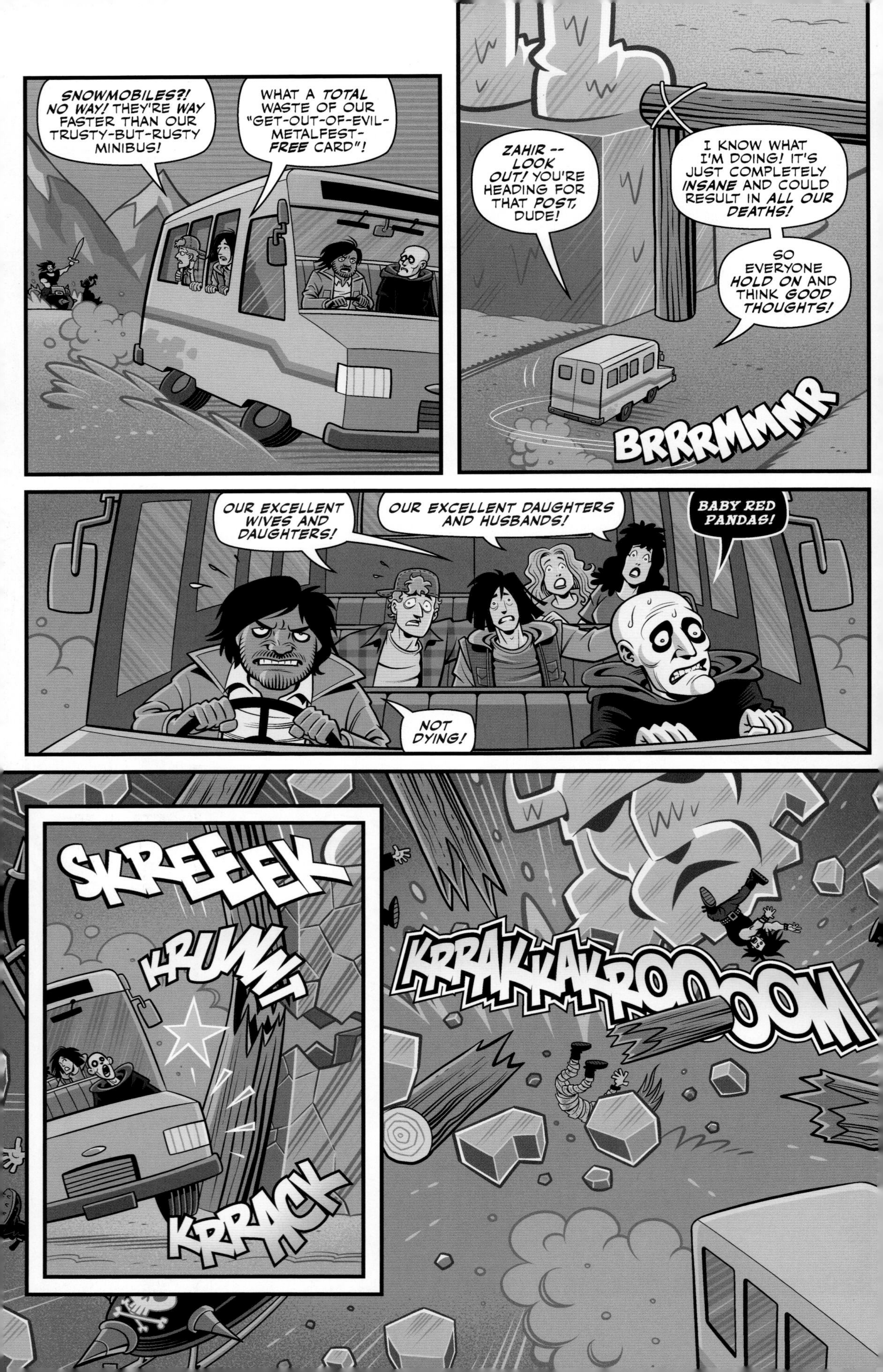
SNOWMOBILES?! NO WAY! THEY'RE WAY FASTER THAN OUR TRUSTY-BUT-RUSTY MINIBUS!
WHAT A TOTAL WASTE OF OUR "GET-OUT-OF-EVIL-METALFEST-FREE CARD"!
ZAHIR -- LOOK OUT! YOU'RE HEADING FOR THAT POST, DUDE!
I KNOW WHAT I'M DOING! IT'S JUST COMPLETELY INSANE AND COULD RESULT IN ALL OUR DEATHS!
SO EVERYONE HOLD ON AND THINK GOOD THOUGHTS!
BRRRMMMR
OUR EXCELLENT WIVES AND DAUGHTERS!
OUR EXCELLENT DAUGHTERS AND HUSBANDS!
BABY RED PANDAS!
NOT DYING!
SKREEEK
KRUNNT
KRRACK
KRRAKKAKROOOOOM

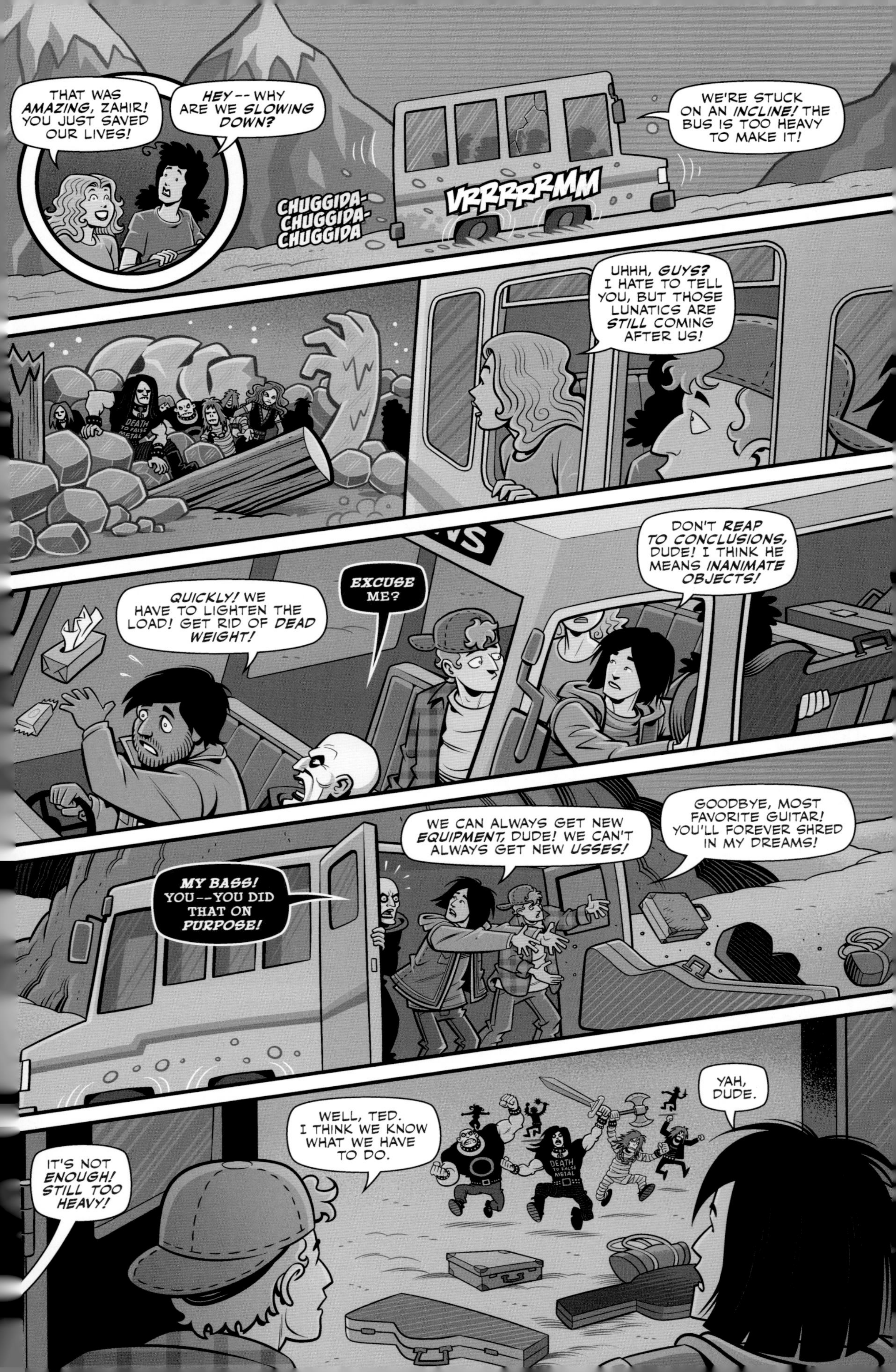
THAT WAS AMAZING, ZAHIR! YOU JUST SAVED OUR LIVES!
HEY--WHY ARE WE SLOWING DOWN?
CHUGGIDA-CHUGGIDA-CHUGGIDA
VRRRRRMM
WE'RE STUCK ON AN INCLINE! THE BUS IS TOO HEAVY TO MAKE IT!
UHHH, GUYS? I HATE TO TELL YOU, BUT THOSE LUNATICS ARE STILL COMING AFTER US!
DEATH TO FALSE METAL
QUICKLY! WE HAVE TO LIGHTEN THE LOAD! GET RID OF DEAD WEIGHT!
EXCUSE ME?
DON'T REAP TO CONCLUSIONS, DUDE! I THINK HE MEANS INANIMATE OBJECTS!
MY BASS! YOU--YOU DID THAT ON PURPOSE!
WE CAN ALWAYS GET NEW EQUIPMENT, DUDE! WE CAN'T ALWAYS GET NEW USSES!
GOODBYE, MOST FAVORITE GUITAR! YOU'LL FOREVER SHRED IN MY DREAMS!
IT'S NOT ENOUGH! STILL TOO HEAVY!
WELL, TED. I THINK WE KNOW WHAT WE HAVE TO DO.
DEATH TO FALSE METAL
YAH, DUDE.

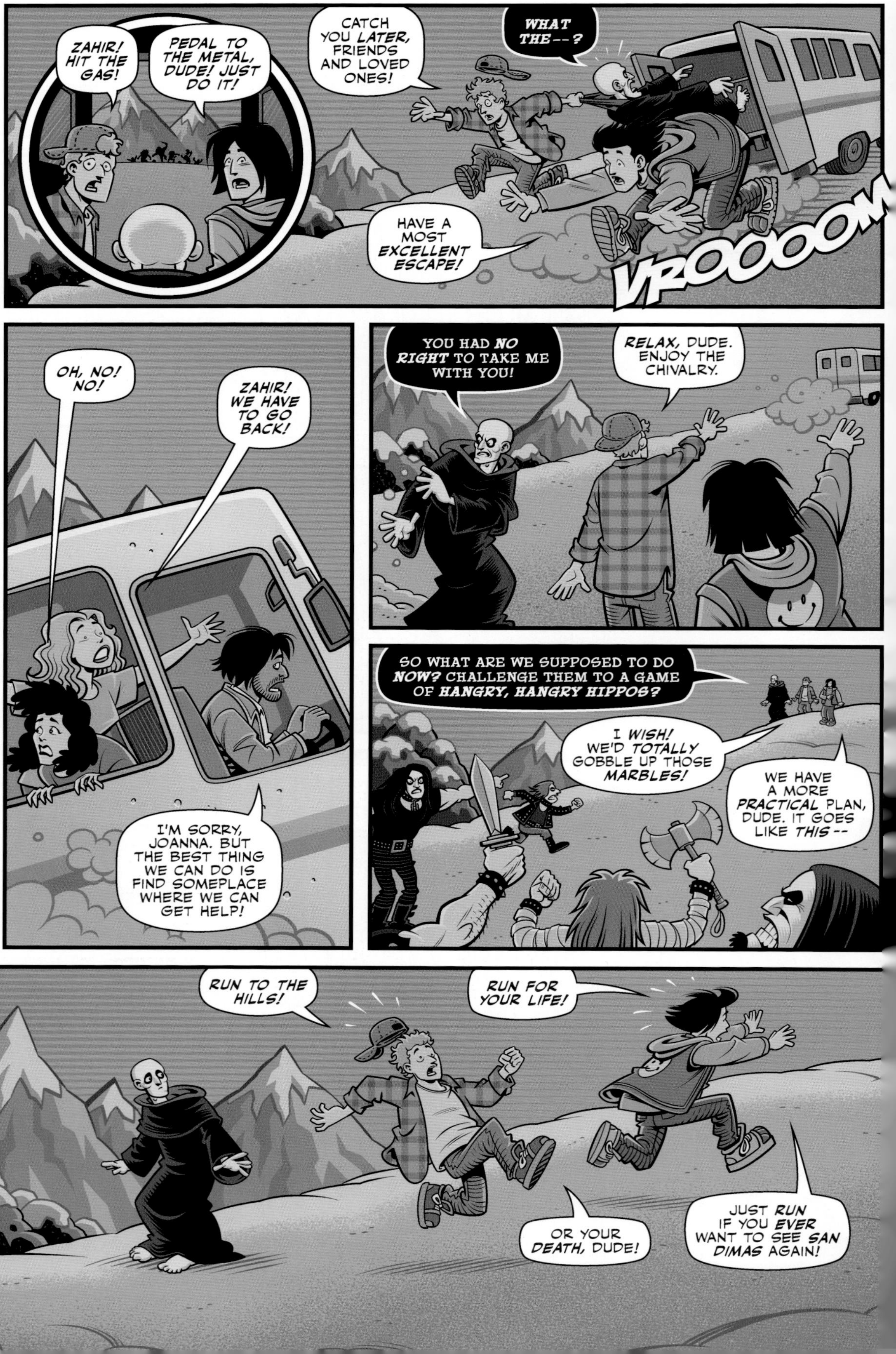
ZAHIR! HIT THE GAS!
PEDAL TO THE METAL, DUDE! JUST DO IT!
CATCH YOU LATER, FRIENDS AND LOVED ONES!
WHAT THE--?
HAVE A MOST EXCELLENT ESCAPE!
VROOOOOM
OH, NO! NO!
ZAHIR! WE HAVE TO GO BACK!
I'M SORRY, JOANNA. BUT THE BEST THING WE CAN DO IS FIND SOMEPLACE WHERE WE CAN GET HELP!
YOU HAD NO RIGHT TO TAKE ME WITH YOU!
RELAX, DUDE. ENJOY THE CHIVALRY.
SO WHAT ARE WE SUPPOSED TO DO NOW? CHALLENGE THEM TO A GAME OF HANGRY, HANGRY HIPPOS?
I WISH! WE'D TOTALLY GOBBLE UP THOSE MARBLES!
WE HAVE A MORE PRACTICAL PLAN, DUDE. IT GOES LIKE THIS--
RUN TO THE HILLS!
RUN FOR YOUR LIFE!
OR YOUR DEATH, DUDE!
JUST RUN IF YOU EVER WANT TO SEE SAN DIMAS AGAIN!

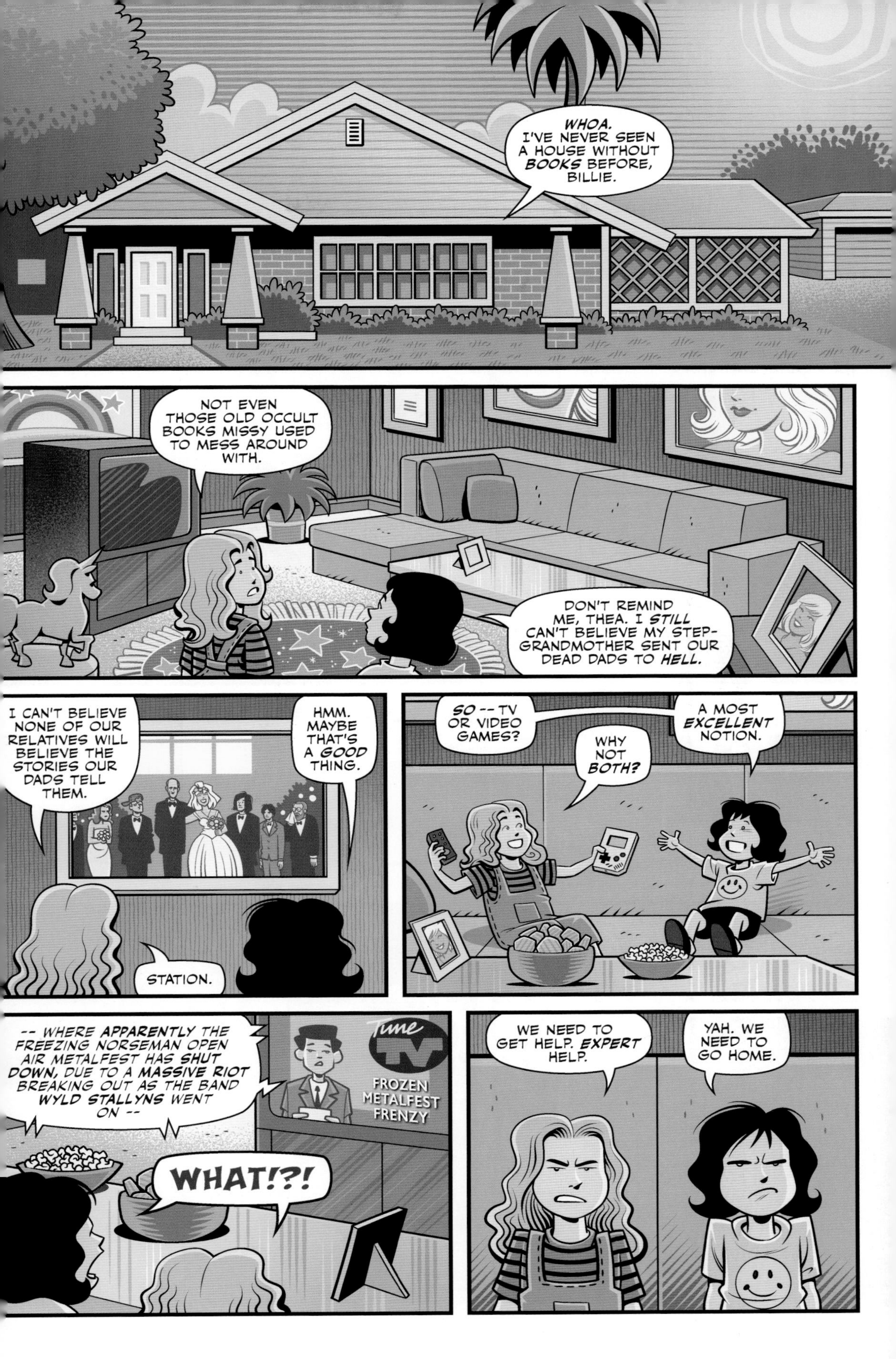
WHOA. I'VE NEVER SEEN A HOUSE WITHOUT BOOKS BEFORE, BILLIE.
NOT EVEN THOSE OLD OCCULT BOOKS MISSY USED TO MESS AROUND WITH.
DON'T REMIND ME, THEA. I STILL CAN'T BELIEVE MY STEP-GRANDMOTHER SENT OUR DEAD DADS TO HELL.
I CAN'T BELIEVE NONE OF OUR RELATIVES WILL BELIEVE THE STORIES OUR DADS TELL THEM.
HMM. MAYBE THAT'S A GOOD THING.
STATION.
SO -- TV OR VIDEO GAMES?
WHY NOT BOTH?
A MOST EXCELLENT NOTION.
-- WHERE APPARENTLY THE FREEZING NORSEMAN OPEN AIR METALFEST HAS SHUT DOWN, DUE TO A MASSIVE RIOT BREAKING OUT AS THE BAND WYLD STALLYNS WENT ON --
Tune TV
FROZEN METALFEST FRENZY
WHAT!?!
WE NEED TO GET HELP. EXPERT HELP.
YAH. WE NEED TO GO HOME.

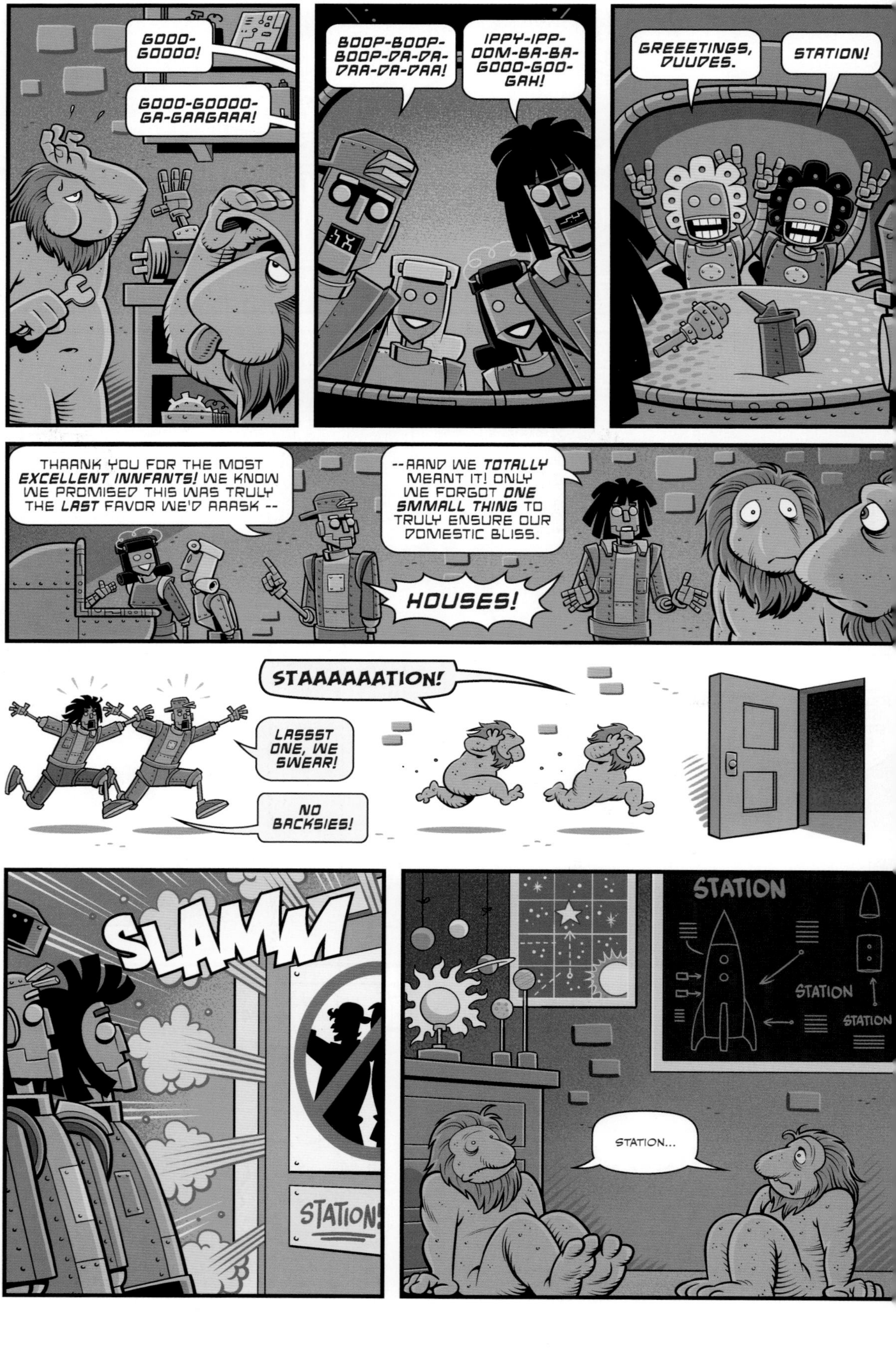
GOOO-GOOOO!
GOOO-GOOOO-GA-GAAGAAA!
BOOP-BOOP-BOOP-DA-DA-DAA-DA-DAA!
IPPY-IPP-OOM-BA-BA-GOOO-GOO-GAH!
GREEETINGS, DUUDES.
STATION!
THAANK YOU FOR THE MOST EXCELLENT INNFANTS! WE KNOW WE PROMISED THIS WAS TRULY THE LAST FAVOR WE'D AAASK --
--AAND WE TOTALLY MEANT IT! ONLY WE FORGOT ONE SMMALL THING TO TRULY ENSURE OUR DOMESTIC BLISS.
HOUSES!
STAAAAAATION!
LASSST ONE, WE SWEAR!
NO BACKSIES!
SLAMM
STATION!
STATION
STATION
STATION
STATION...

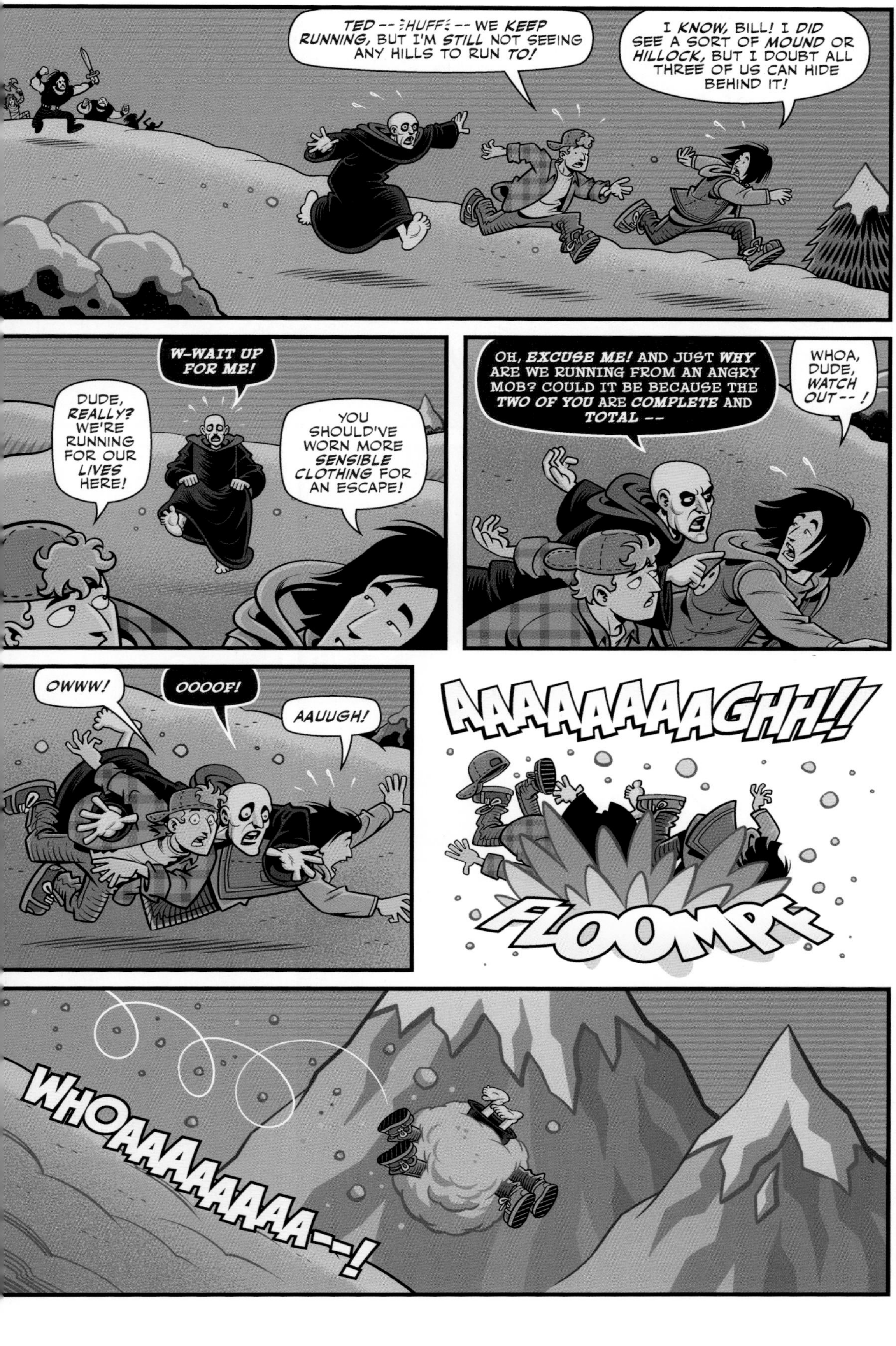

TED -- *HUFF* -- WE KEEP RUNNING, BUT I'M STILL NOT SEEING ANY HILLS TO RUN TO!
I KNOW, BILL! I DID SEE A SORT OF MOUND OR HILLOCK, BUT I DOUBT ALL THREE OF US CAN HIDE BEHIND IT!
W-WAIT UP FOR ME!
DUDE, REALLY? WE'RE RUNNING FOR OUR LIVES HERE!
YOU SHOULD'VE WORN MORE SENSIBLE CLOTHING FOR AN ESCAPE!
OH, EXCUSE ME! AND JUST WHY ARE WE RUNNING FROM AN ANGRY MOB? COULD IT BE BECAUSE THE TWO OF YOU ARE COMPLETE AND TOTAL --
WHOA, DUDE, WATCH OUT -- !
OWWW!
OOOOF!
AAUUGH!
AAAAAAAAAGHH!!
FLOOMPF
WHOAAAAAAAAAA--!

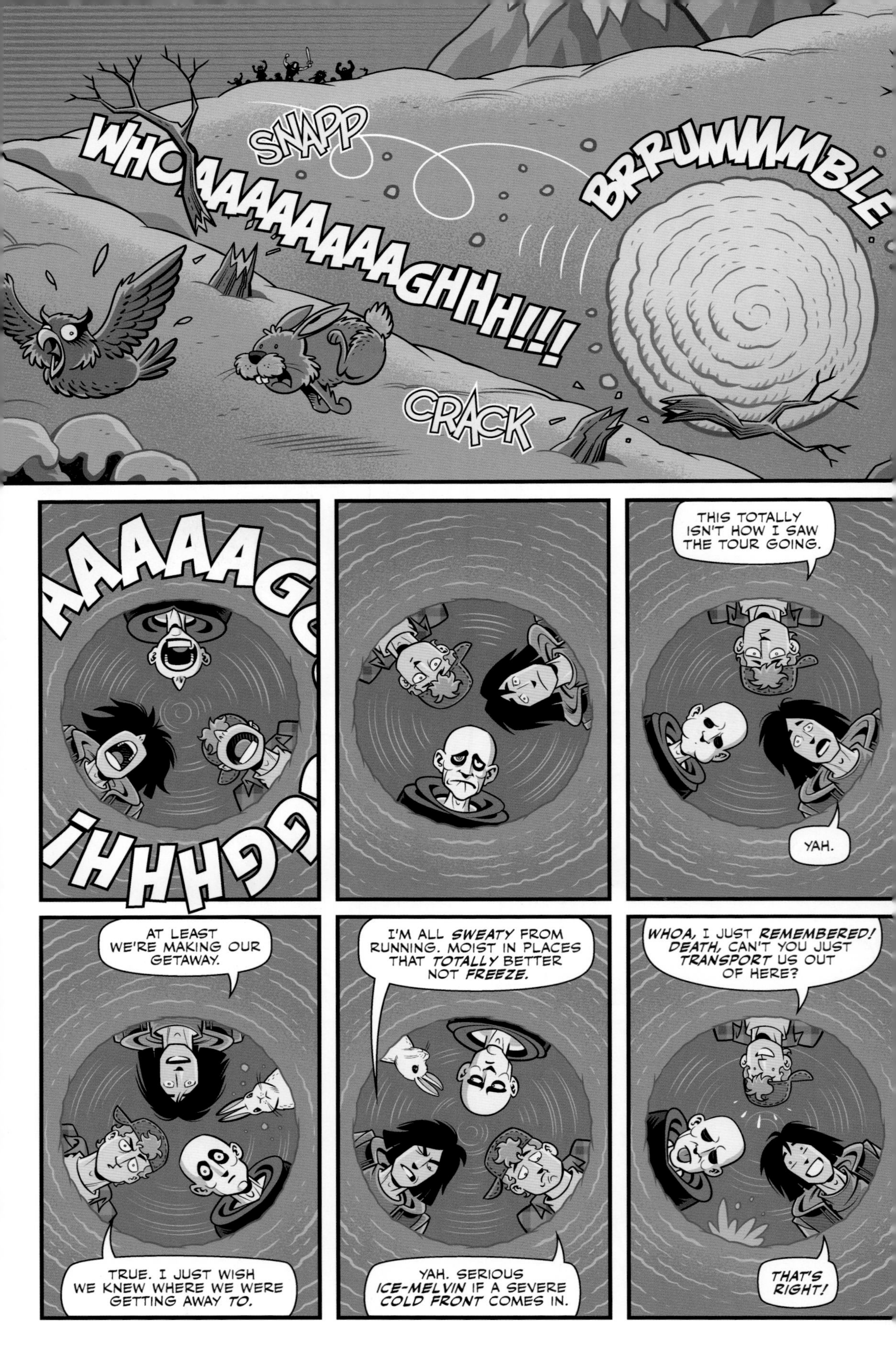

SNAPP
WHOAAAAAAAAAAAAGHHH!!!
BRRUMMMBLE
CRACK
AAAAAG
GGHHH!
THIS TOTALLY ISN'T HOW I SAW THE TOUR GOING.
YAH.
AT LEAST WE'RE MAKING OUR GETAWAY.
TRUE. I JUST WISH WE KNEW WHERE WE WERE GETTING AWAY *TO.*
I'M ALL *SWEATY* FROM RUNNING. MOIST IN PLACES THAT *TOTALLY* BETTER NOT *FREEZE.*
YAH. SERIOUS *ICE-MELVIN* IF A SEVERE *COLD FRONT* COMES IN.
WHOA, I JUST *REMEMBERED! DEATH,* CAN'T YOU JUST *TRANSPORT* US OUT OF HERE?
THAT'S RIGHT!

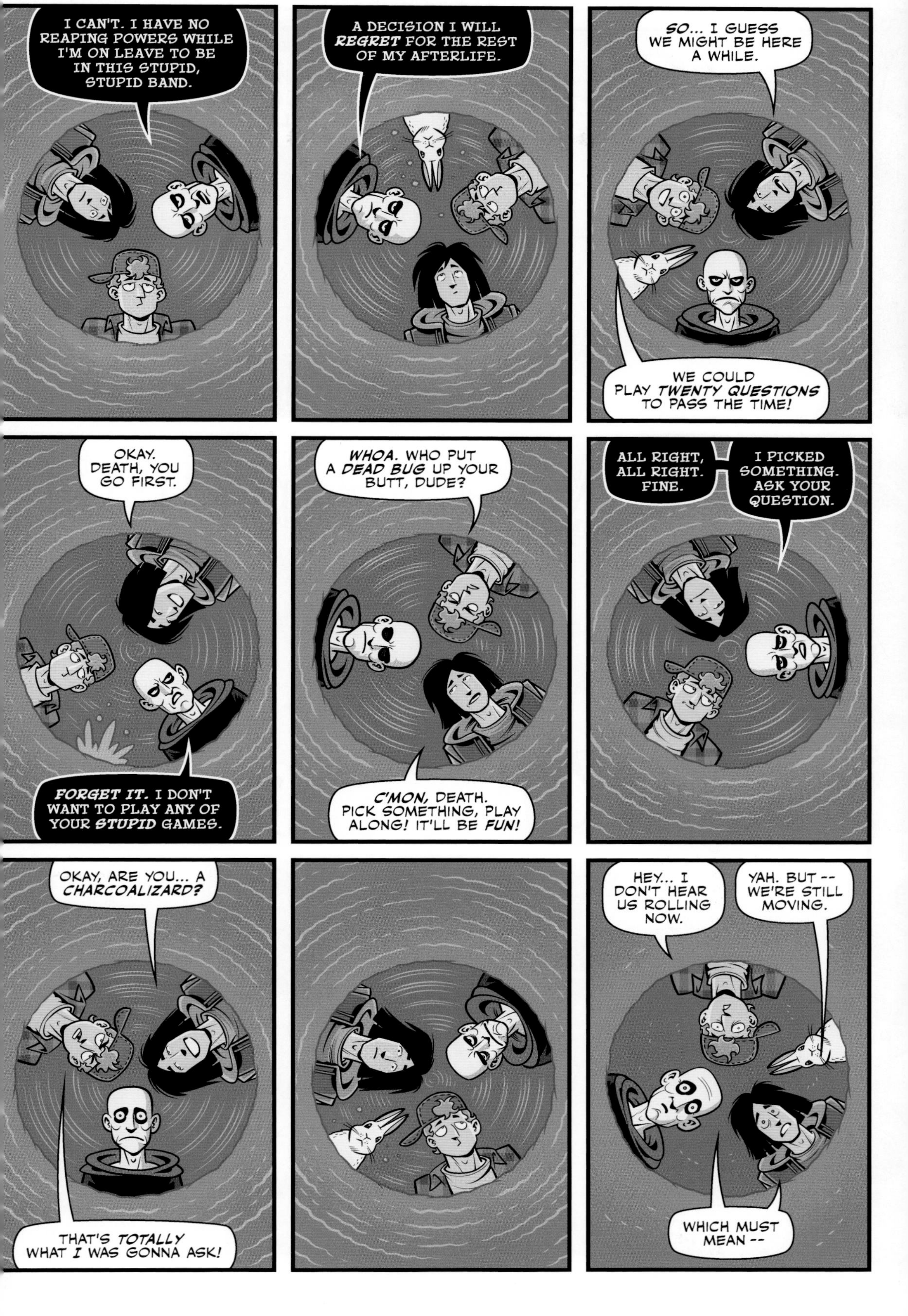
I CAN'T. I HAVE NO REAPING POWERS WHILE I'M ON LEAVE TO BE IN THIS STUPID, STUPID BAND.
A DECISION I WILL *REGRET* FOR THE REST OF MY AFTERLIFE.
SO... I GUESS WE MIGHT BE HERE A WHILE.
WE COULD PLAY *TWENTY QUESTIONS* TO PASS THE TIME!
OKAY. DEATH, YOU GO FIRST.
FORGET IT. I DON'T WANT TO PLAY ANY OF YOUR *STUPID* GAMES.
WHOA. WHO PUT A *DEAD BUG* UP YOUR BUTT, DUDE?
C'MON, DEATH. PICK SOMETHING, PLAY ALONG! IT'LL BE *FUN!*
ALL RIGHT, ALL RIGHT. FINE.
I PICKED SOMETHING. ASK YOUR QUESTION.
OKAY, ARE YOU... A *CHARCOALIZARD?*
THAT'S *TOTALLY* WHAT *I* WAS GONNA ASK!
HEY... I DON'T HEAR US ROLLING NOW.
YAH. BUT -- WE'RE STILL MOVING.
WHICH MUST MEAN --

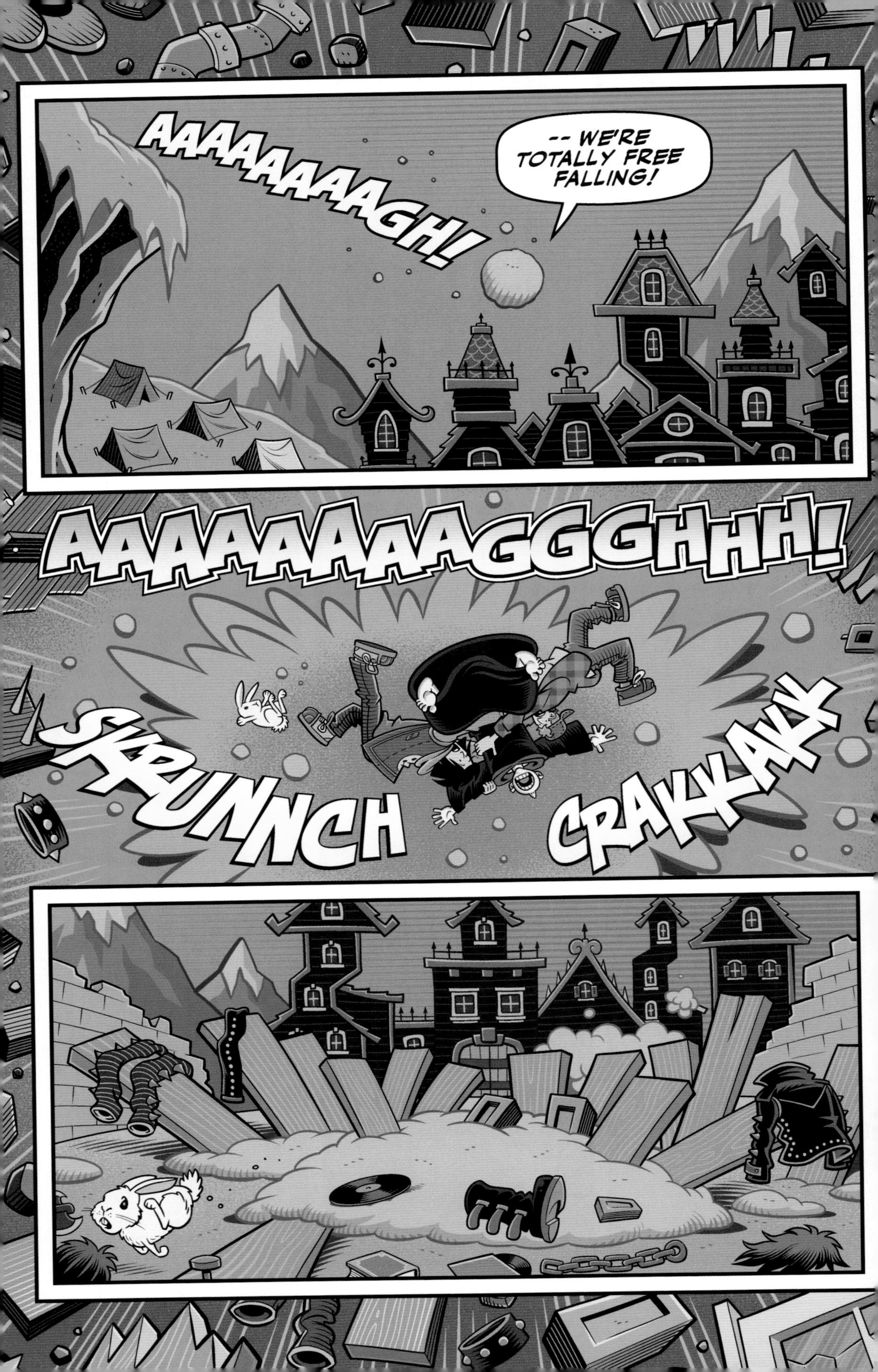
AAAAAAAAAGH!
-- WE'RE TOTALLY FREE FALLING!
AAAAAAAAAGGGHHH!
SKRUNNCH
CRAKKAKK

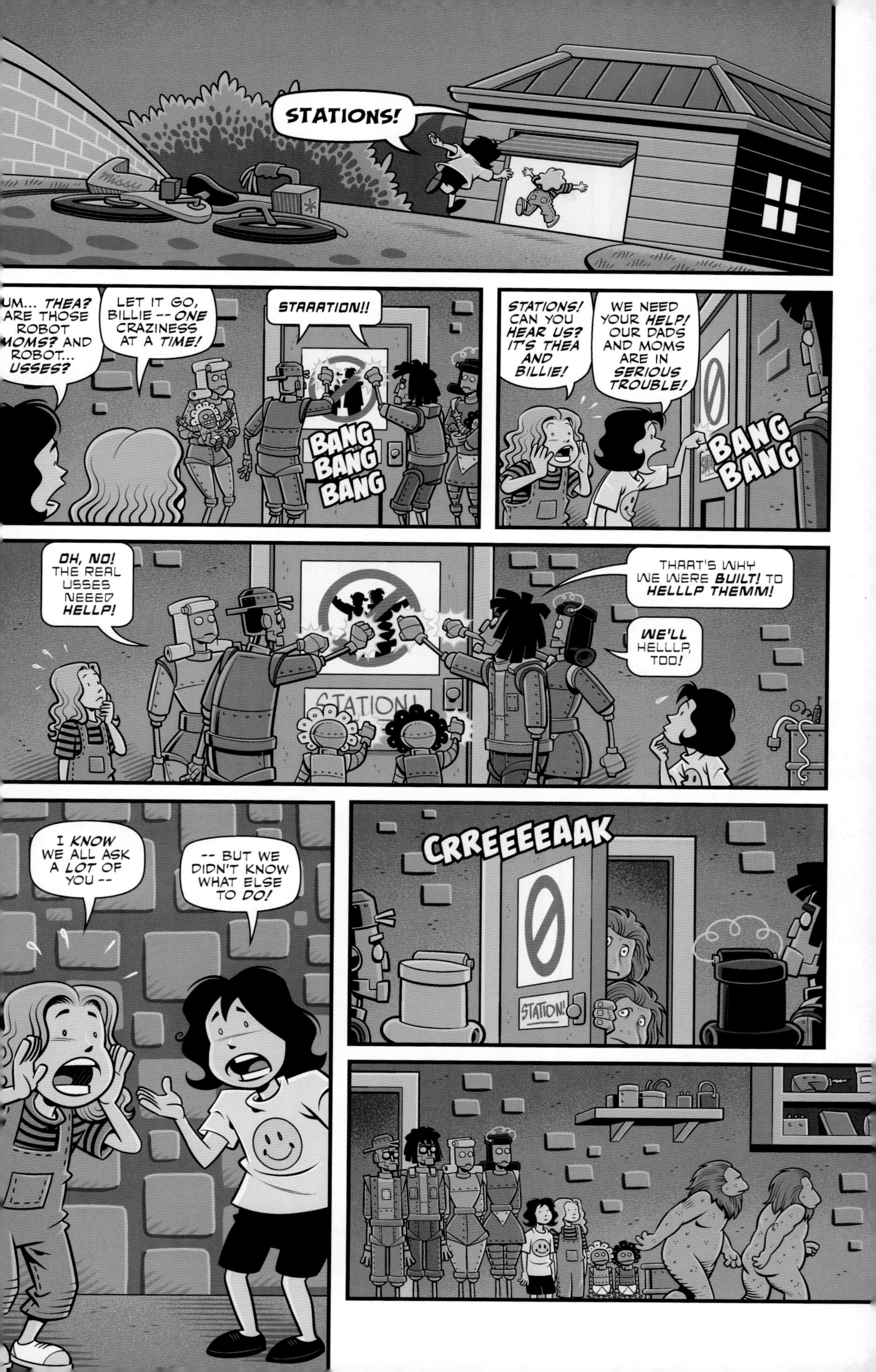

STATIONS!
UM... THEA? ARE THOSE ROBOT MOMS? AND ROBOT... USSES?
LET IT GO, BILLIE -- ONE CRAZINESS AT A TIME!
STAAATION!!
BANG BANG BANG
STATIONS! CAN YOU HEAR US? IT'S THEA AND BILLIE!
WE NEED YOUR HELP! OUR DADS AND MOMS ARE IN SERIOUS TROUBLE!
BANG BANG
OH, NO! THE REAL USSES NEEED HELLP!
THAAT'S WHY WE WERE BUILT! TO HELLLP THEMM!
WE'LL HELLLP, TOO!
STATION!
I KNOW WE ALL ASK A LOT OF YOU --
-- BUT WE DIDN'T KNOW WHAT ELSE TO DO!
CRREEEEAAK
STATION!

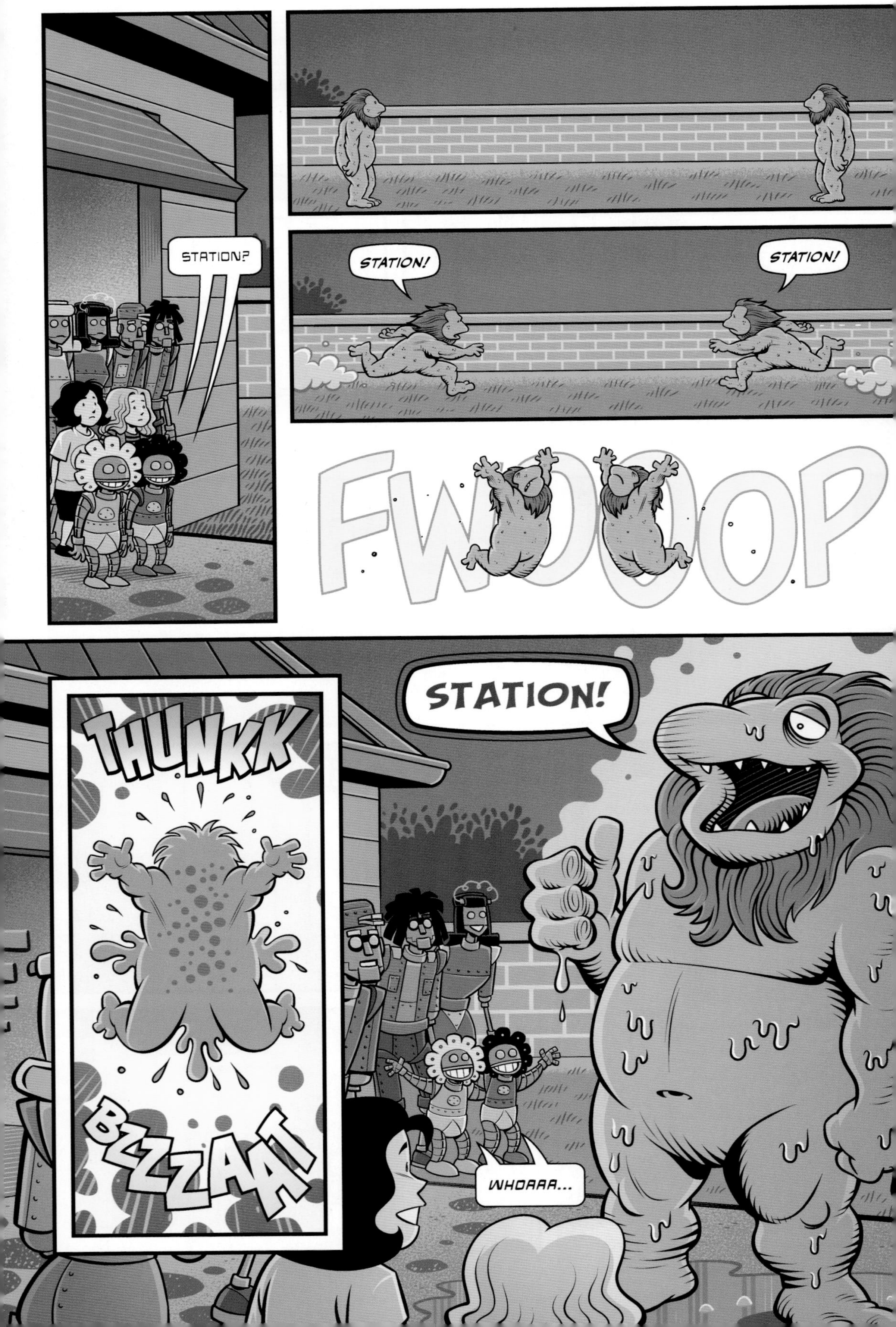
STATION?
STATION!
STATION!
FWOOOP
THUNKK
BZZZAAT
STATION!
WHOAAA...

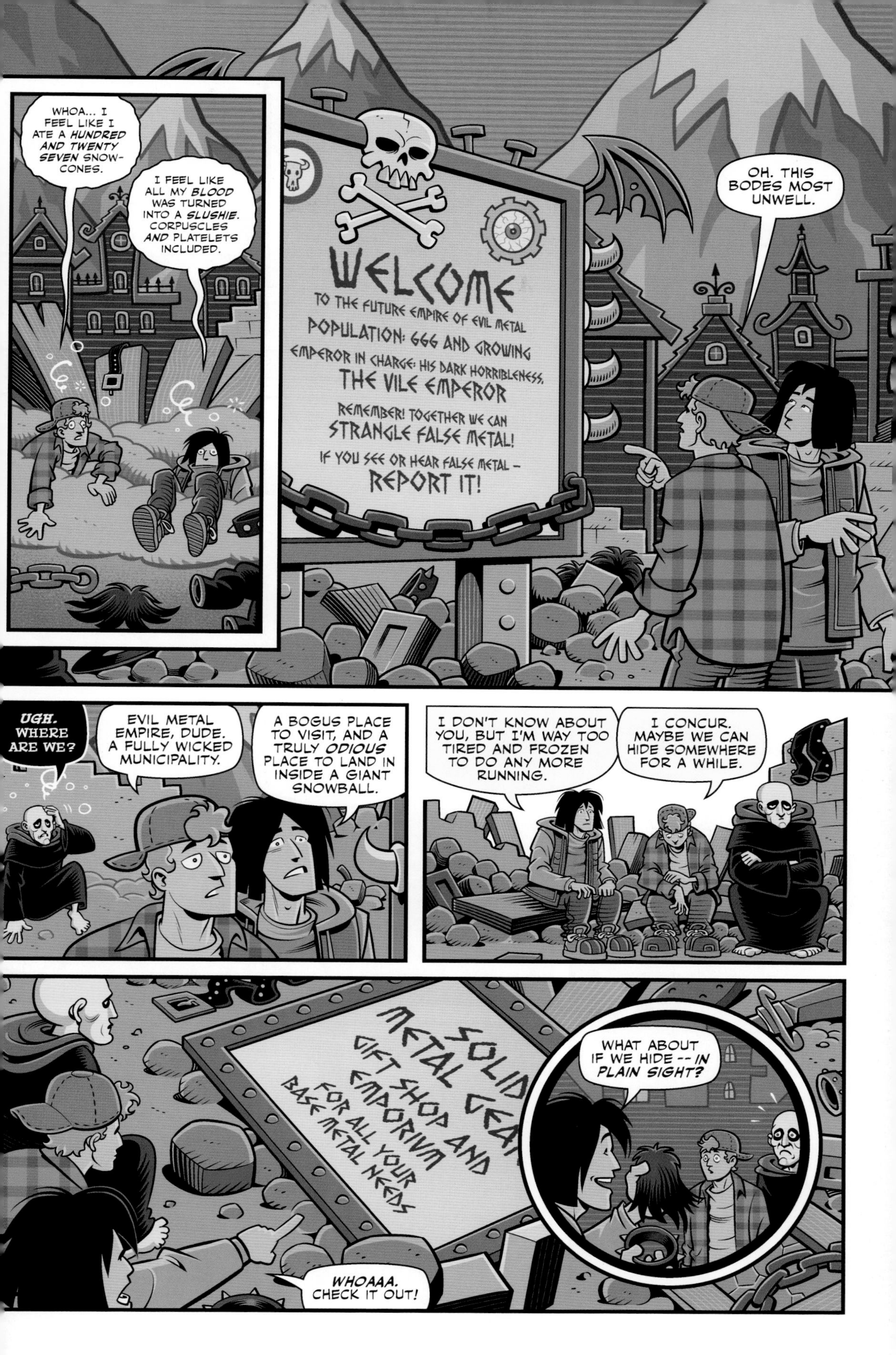

WHOA... I FEEL LIKE I ATE A HUNDRED AND TWENTY SEVEN SNOW-CONES.
I FEEL LIKE ALL MY BLOOD WAS TURNED INTO A SLUSHIE. CORPUSCLES AND PLATELETS INCLUDED.
WELCOME
TO THE FUTURE EMPIRE OF EVIL METAL
POPULATION: 666 AND GROWING
EMPEROR IN CHARGE: HIS DARK HORRIBLENESS, THE VILE EMPEROR
REMEMBER! TOGETHER WE CAN STRANGLE FALSE METAL!
IF YOU SEE OR HEAR FALSE METAL – REPORT IT!
OH. THIS BODES MOST UNWELL.
UGH. WHERE ARE WE?
EVIL METAL EMPIRE, DUDE. A FULLY WICKED MUNICIPALITY.
A BOGUS PLACE TO VISIT, AND A TRULY ODIOUS PLACE TO LAND IN INSIDE A GIANT SNOWBALL.
I DON'T KNOW ABOUT YOU, BUT I'M WAY TOO TIRED AND FROZEN TO DO ANY MORE RUNNING.
I CONCUR. MAYBE WE CAN HIDE SOMEWHERE FOR A WHILE.
SOLID METAL GEA
GIFT SHOP AND EMPORIUM
FOR ALL YOUR BASE METAL NEEDS
WHOAAA. CHECK IT OUT!
WHAT ABOUT IF WE HIDE -- IN PLAIN SIGHT?

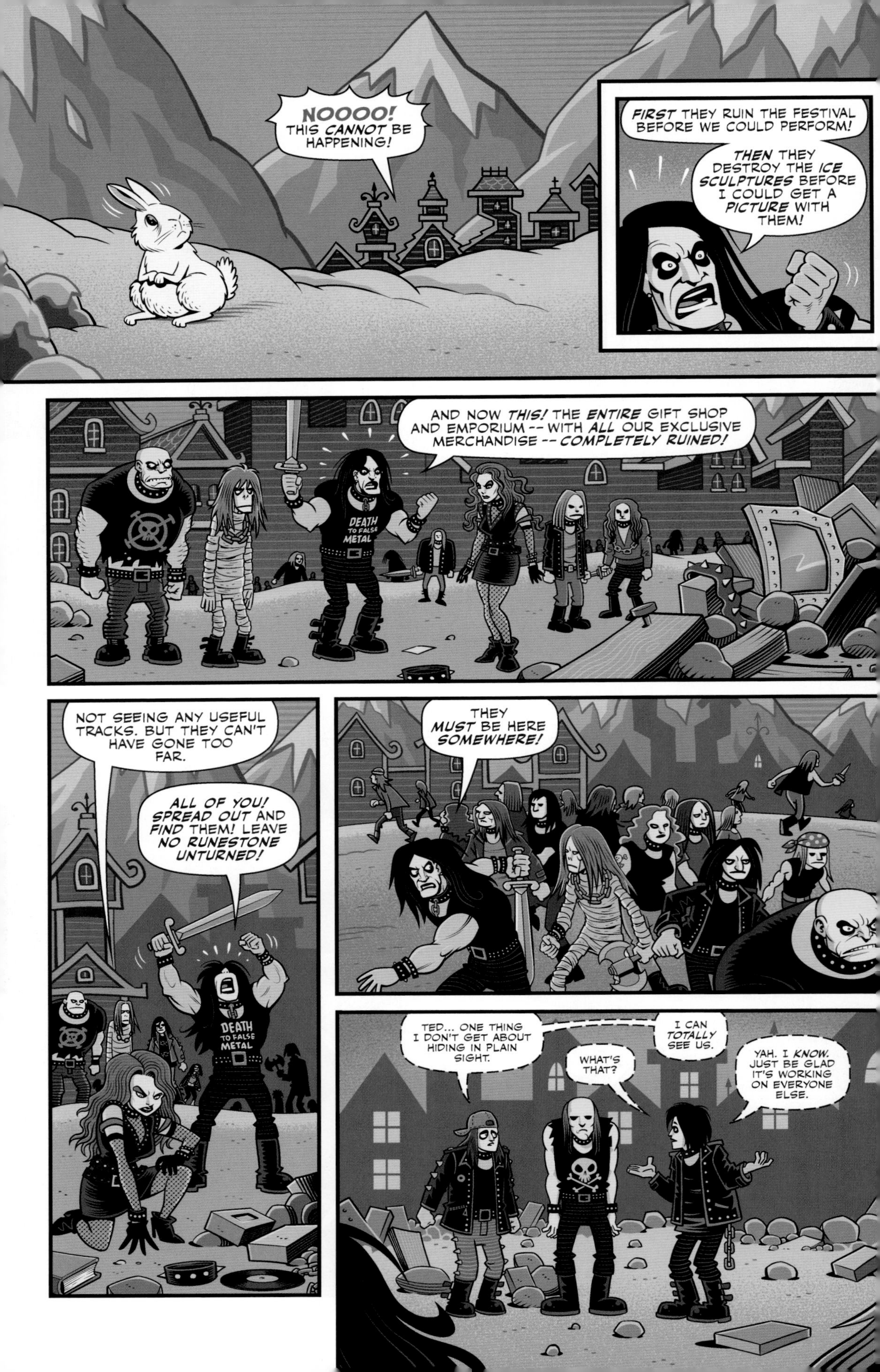
NOOOO! THIS CANNOT BE HAPPENING!
FIRST THEY RUIN THE FESTIVAL BEFORE WE COULD PERFORM!
THEN THEY DESTROY THE ICE SCULPTURES BEFORE I COULD GET A PICTURE WITH THEM!
AND NOW THIS! THE ENTIRE GIFT SHOP AND EMPORIUM -- WITH ALL OUR EXCLUSIVE MERCHANDISE -- COMPLETELY RUINED!
DEATH TO FALSE METAL
NOT SEEING ANY USEFUL TRACKS. BUT THEY CAN'T HAVE GONE TOO FAR.
ALL OF YOU! SPREAD OUT AND FIND THEM! LEAVE NO RUNESTONE UNTURNED!
DEATH TO FALSE METAL
THEY MUST BE HERE SOMEWHERE!
TED... ONE THING I DON'T GET ABOUT HIDING IN PLAIN SIGHT.
I CAN TOTALLY SEE US.
WHAT'S THAT?
YAH. I KNOW. JUST BE GLAD IT'S WORKING ON EVERYONE ELSE.

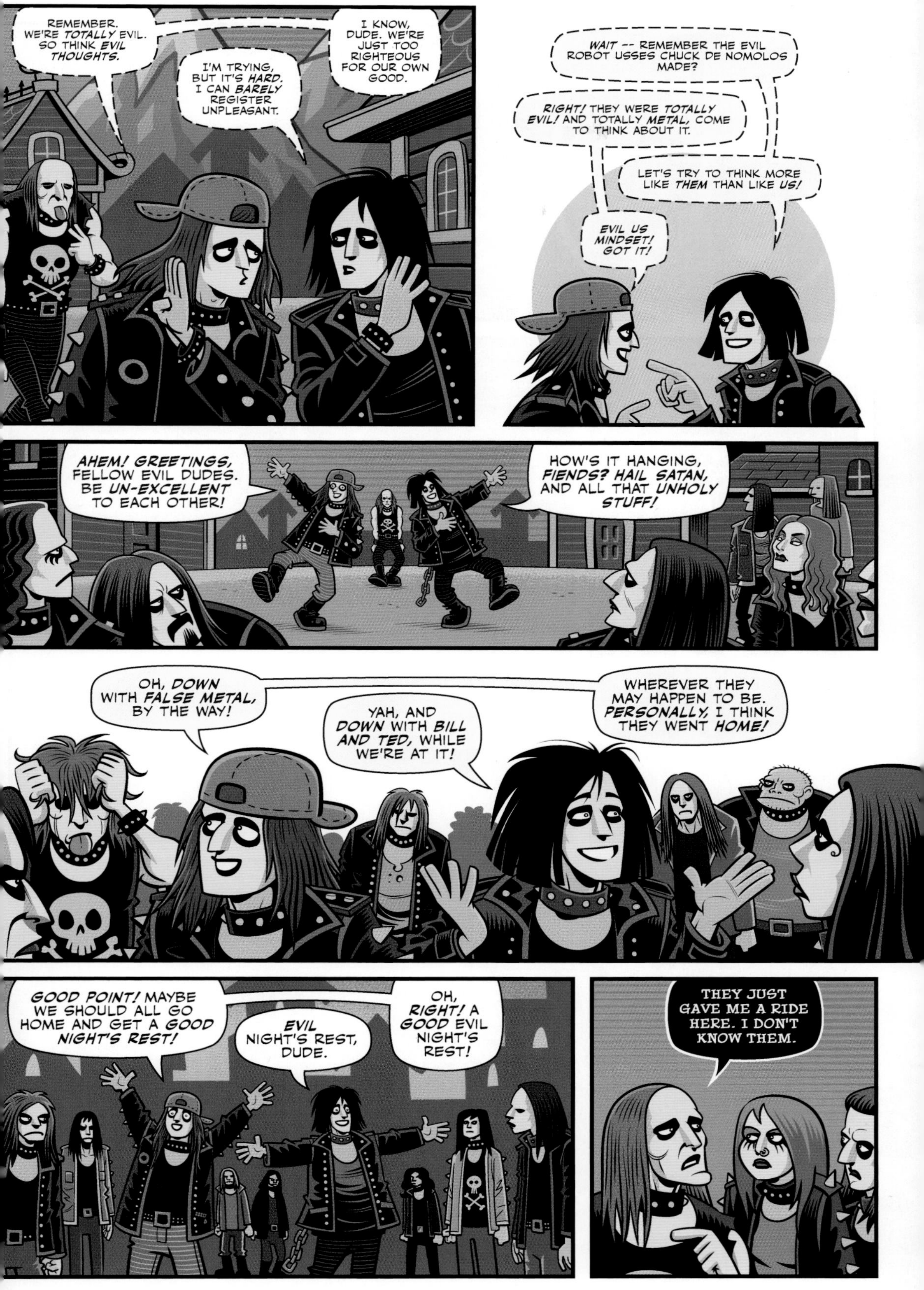
REMEMBER. WE'RE TOTALLY EVIL. SO THINK EVIL THOUGHTS.
I'M TRYING, BUT IT'S HARD. I CAN BARELY REGISTER UNPLEASANT.
I KNOW, DUDE. WE'RE JUST TOO RIGHTEOUS FOR OUR OWN GOOD.
WAIT -- REMEMBER THE EVIL ROBOT USSES CHUCK DE NOMOLOS MADE?
RIGHT! THEY WERE TOTALLY EVIL! AND TOTALLY METAL, COME TO THINK ABOUT IT.
LET'S TRY TO THINK MORE LIKE THEM THAN LIKE US!
EVIL US MINDSET! GOT IT!
AHEM! GREETINGS, FELLOW EVIL DUDES. BE UN-EXCELLENT TO EACH OTHER!
HOW'S IT HANGING, FIENDS? HAIL SATAN, AND ALL THAT UNHOLY STUFF!
OH, DOWN WITH FALSE METAL, BY THE WAY!
YAH, AND DOWN WITH BILL AND TED, WHILE WE'RE AT IT!
WHEREVER THEY MAY HAPPEN TO BE. PERSONALLY, I THINK THEY WENT HOME!
GOOD POINT! MAYBE WE SHOULD ALL GO HOME AND GET A GOOD NIGHT'S REST!
EVIL NIGHT'S REST, DUDE.
OH, RIGHT! A GOOD EVIL NIGHT'S REST!
THEY JUST GAVE ME A RIDE HERE. I DON'T KNOW THEM.

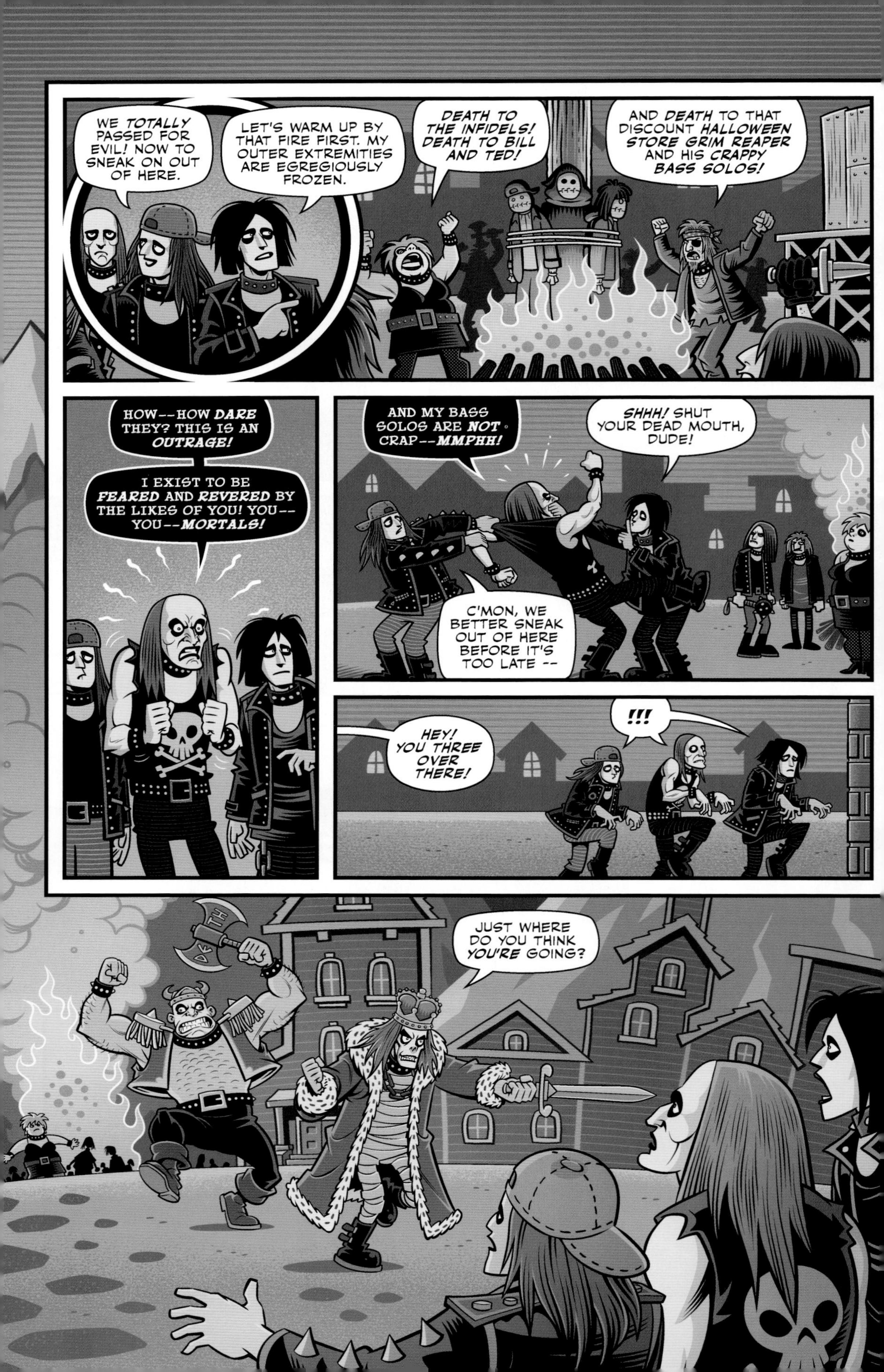
WE TOTALLY PASSED FOR EVIL! NOW TO SNEAK ON OUT OF HERE.
LET'S WARM UP BY THAT FIRE FIRST. MY OUTER EXTREMITIES ARE EGREGIOUSLY FROZEN.
DEATH TO THE INFIDELS! DEATH TO BILL AND TED!
AND DEATH TO THAT DISCOUNT HALLOWEEN STORE GRIM REAPER AND HIS CRAPPY BASS SOLOS!
HOW--HOW DARE THEY? THIS IS AN OUTRAGE!
I EXIST TO BE FEARED AND REVERED BY THE LIKES OF YOU! YOU-- YOU--MORTALS!
AND MY BASS SOLOS ARE NOT CRAP--MMPHH!
SHHH! SHUT YOUR DEAD MOUTH, DUDE!
C'MON, WE BETTER SNEAK OUT OF HERE BEFORE IT'S TOO LATE --
HEY! YOU THREE OVER THERE!
!!!
JUST WHERE DO YOU THINK YOU'RE GOING?

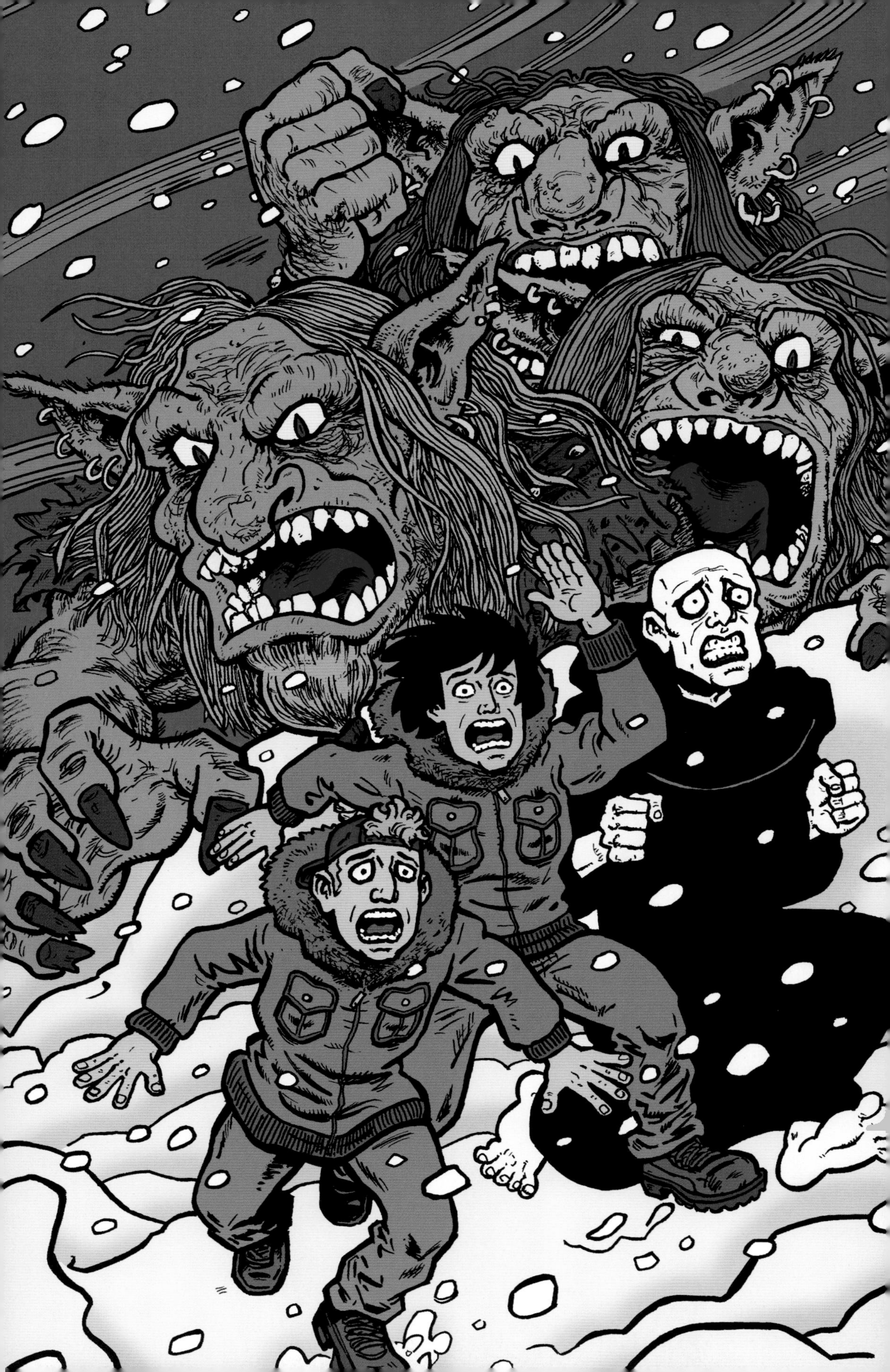

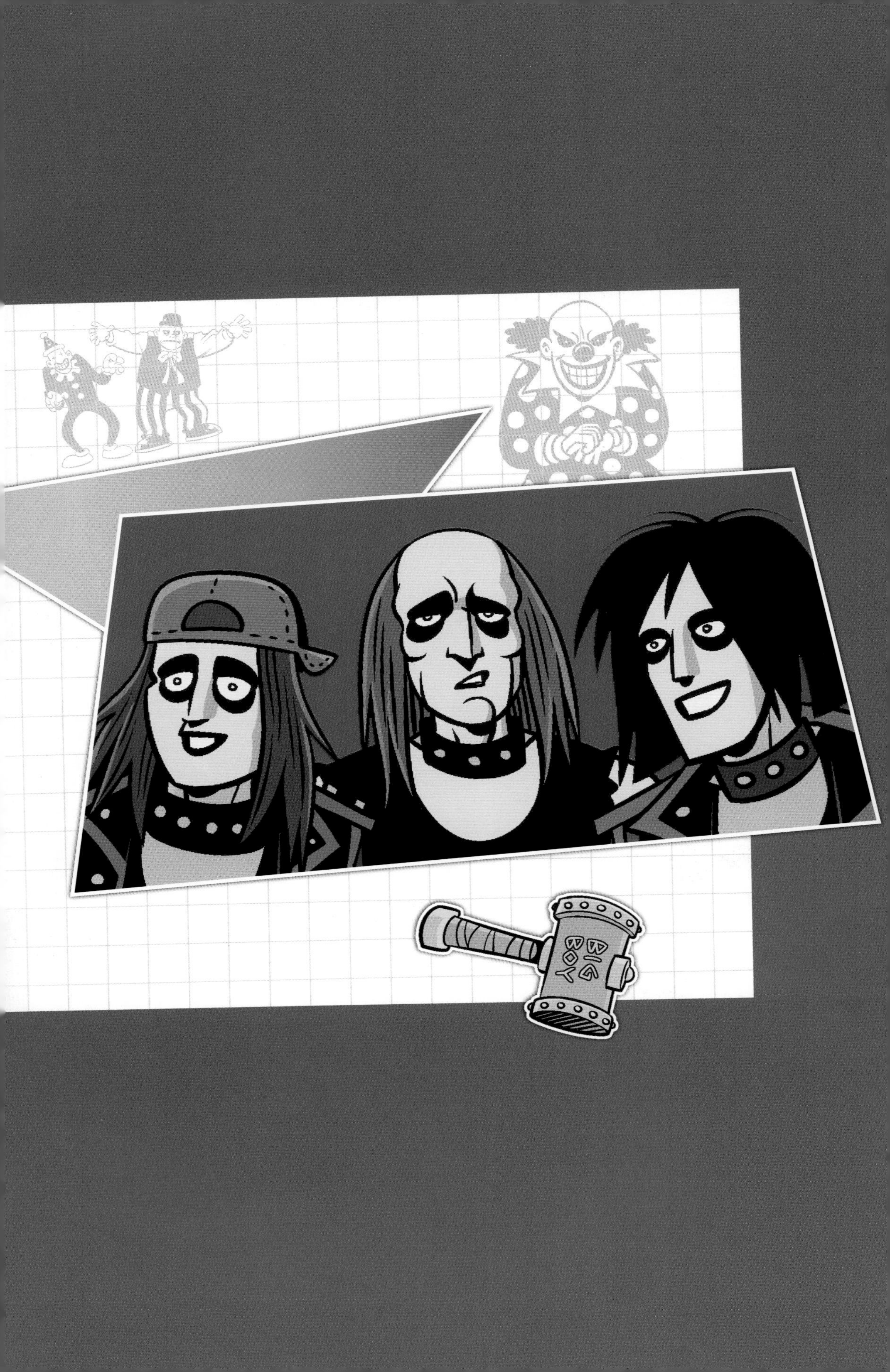
BIG BOY

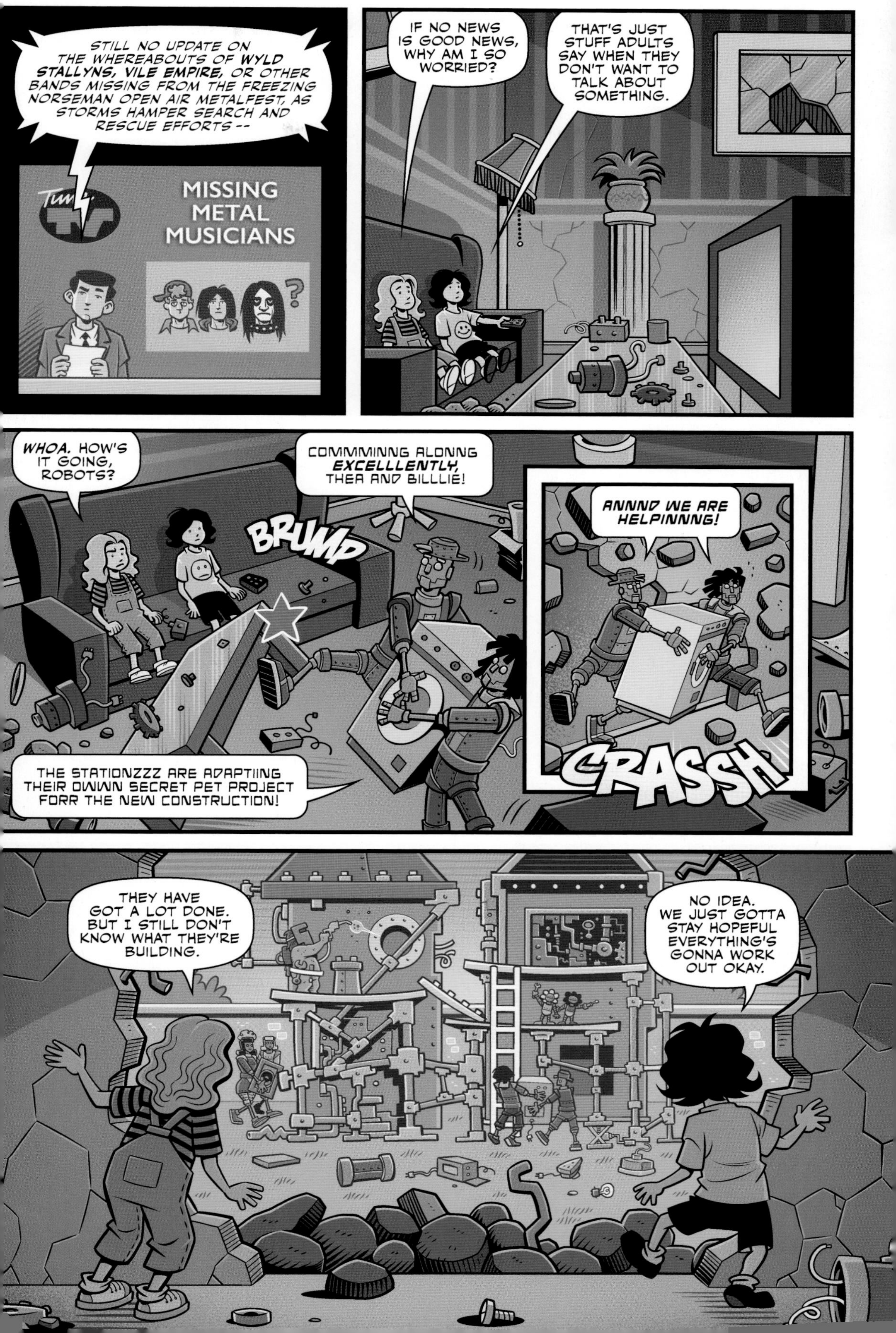

STILL NO UPDATE ON THE WHEREABOUTS OF **WYLD STALLYNS, VILE EMPIRE,** OR OTHER BANDS MISSING FROM THE FREEZING NORSEMAN OPEN AIR METALFEST, AS STORMS HAMPER SEARCH AND RESCUE EFFORTS --
MISSING METAL MUSICIANS
IF NO NEWS IS GOOD NEWS, WHY AM I SO WORRIED?
THAT'S JUST STUFF ADULTS SAY WHEN THEY DON'T WANT TO TALK ABOUT SOMETHING.
WHOA. HOW'S IT GOING, ROBOTS?
COMMMINNG ALONNG *EXCELLLENTLY,* THEA AND BILLLIE!
BRUMP
ANNND WE ARE HELPINNNG!
THE STATIONZZZ ARE ADAPTIING THEIR OWWN SECRET PET PROJECT FORR THE NEW CONSTRUCTION!
CRASSH
THEY HAVE GOT A LOT DONE. BUT I STILL DON'T KNOW WHAT THEY'RE BUILDING.
NO IDEA. WE JUST GOTTA STAY HOPEFUL EVERYTHING'S GONNA WORK OUT OKAY.

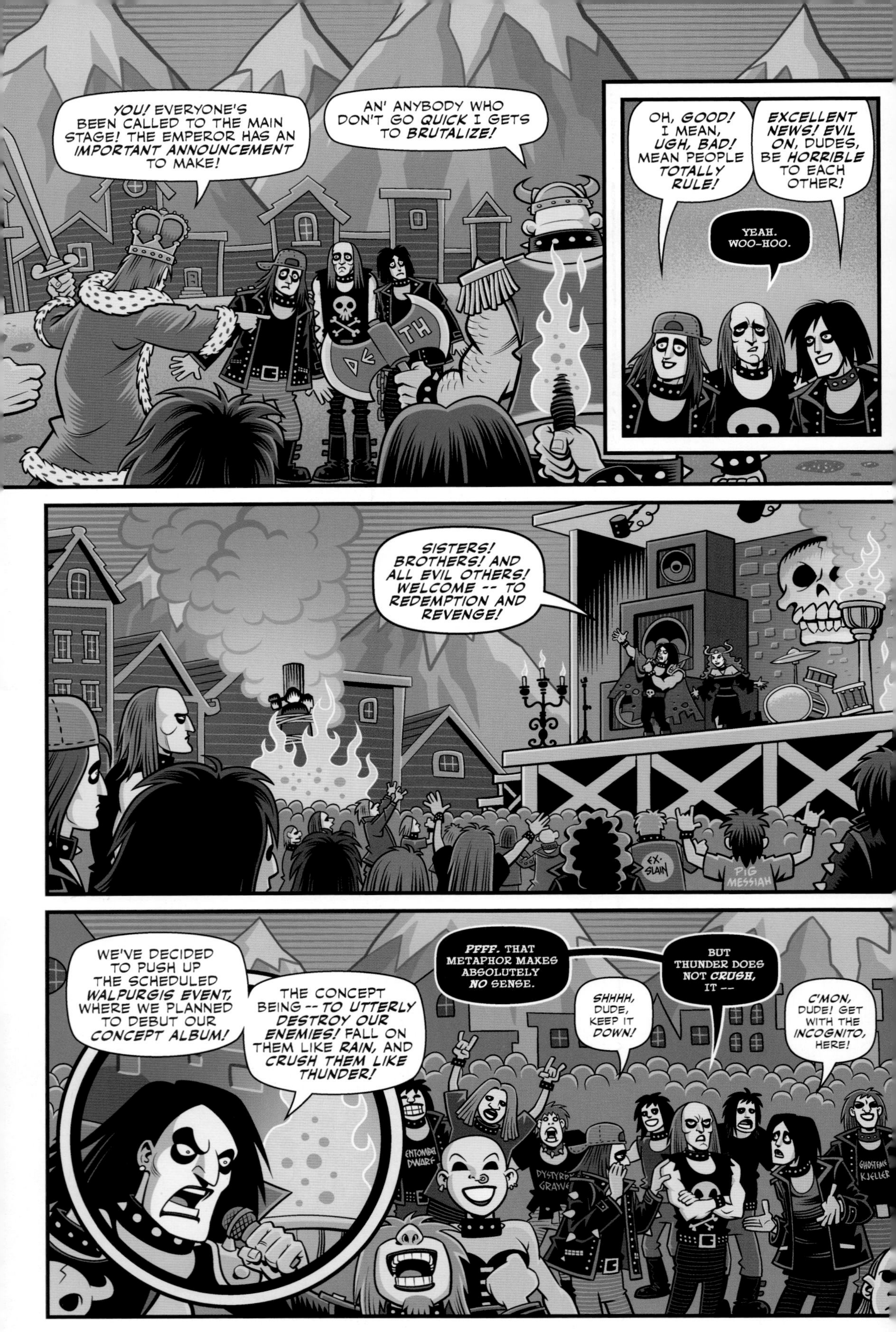
YOU! EVERYONE'S BEEN CALLED TO THE MAIN STAGE! THE EMPEROR HAS AN IMPORTANT ANNOUNCEMENT TO MAKE!
AN' ANYBODY WHO DON'T GO QUICK I GETS TO BRUTALIZE!
OH, GOOD! I MEAN, UGH, BAD! MEAN PEOPLE TOTALLY RULE!
EXCELLENT NEWS! EVIL ON, DUDES, BE HORRIBLE TO EACH OTHER!
YEAH. WOO-HOO.
SISTERS! BROTHERS! AND ALL EVIL OTHERS! WELCOME -- TO REDEMPTION AND REVENGE!
PIG MESSIAH
WE'VE DECIDED TO PUSH UP THE SCHEDULED WALPURGIS EVENT, WHERE WE PLANNED TO DEBUT OUR CONCEPT ALBUM!
THE CONCEPT BEING -- TO UTTERLY DESTROY OUR ENEMIES! FALL ON THEM LIKE RAIN, AND CRUSH THEM LIKE THUNDER!
PFFF. THAT METAPHOR MAKES ABSOLUTELY NO SENSE.
BUT THUNDER DOES NOT CRUSH, IT --
SHHHH, DUDE, KEEP IT DOWN!
C'MON, DUDE! GET WITH THE INCOGNITO, HERE!

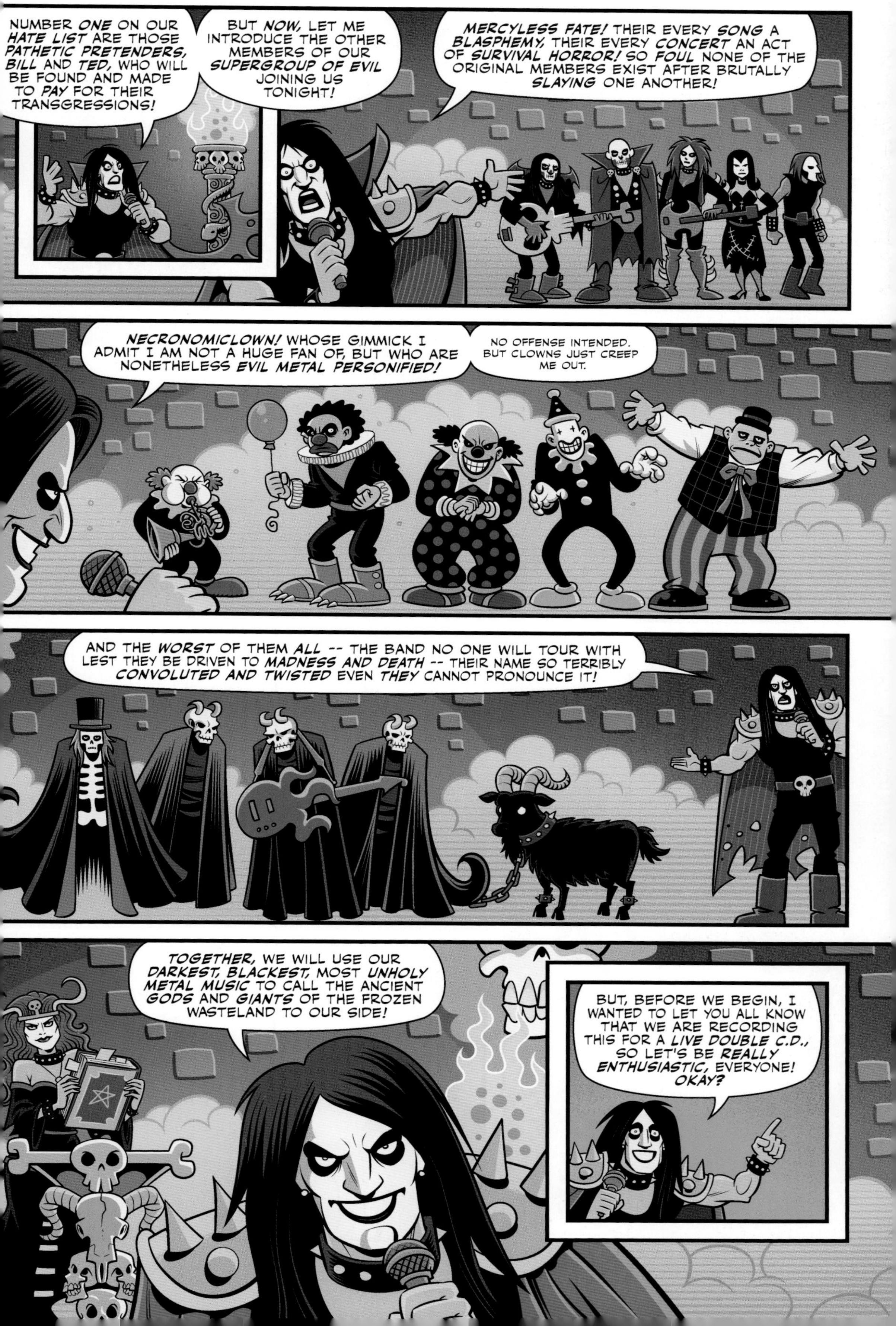
NUMBER ONE ON OUR HATE LIST ARE THOSE PATHETIC PRETENDERS, BILL AND TED, WHO WILL BE FOUND AND MADE TO PAY FOR THEIR TRANSGRESSIONS!
BUT NOW, LET ME INTRODUCE THE OTHER MEMBERS OF OUR SUPERGROUP OF EVIL JOINING US TONIGHT!
MERCYLESS FATE! THEIR EVERY SONG A BLASPHEMY, THEIR EVERY CONCERT AN ACT OF SURVIVAL HORROR! SO FOUL NONE OF THE ORIGINAL MEMBERS EXIST AFTER BRUTALLY SLAYING ONE ANOTHER!
NECRONOMICLOWN! WHOSE GIMMICK I ADMIT I AM NOT A HUGE FAN OF, BUT WHO ARE NONETHELESS EVIL METAL PERSONIFIED!
NO OFFENSE INTENDED. BUT CLOWNS JUST CREEP ME OUT.
AND THE WORST OF THEM ALL -- THE BAND NO ONE WILL TOUR WITH LEST THEY BE DRIVEN TO MADNESS AND DEATH -- THEIR NAME SO TERRIBLY CONVOLUTED AND TWISTED EVEN THEY CANNOT PRONOUNCE IT!
TOGETHER, WE WILL USE OUR DARKEST, BLACKEST, MOST UNHOLY METAL MUSIC TO CALL THE ANCIENT GODS AND GIANTS OF THE FROZEN WASTELAND TO OUR SIDE!
BUT, BEFORE WE BEGIN, I WANTED TO LET YOU ALL KNOW THAT WE ARE RECORDING THIS FOR A LIVE DOUBLE C.D., SO LET'S BE REALLY ENTHUSIASTIC, EVERYONE! OKAY?

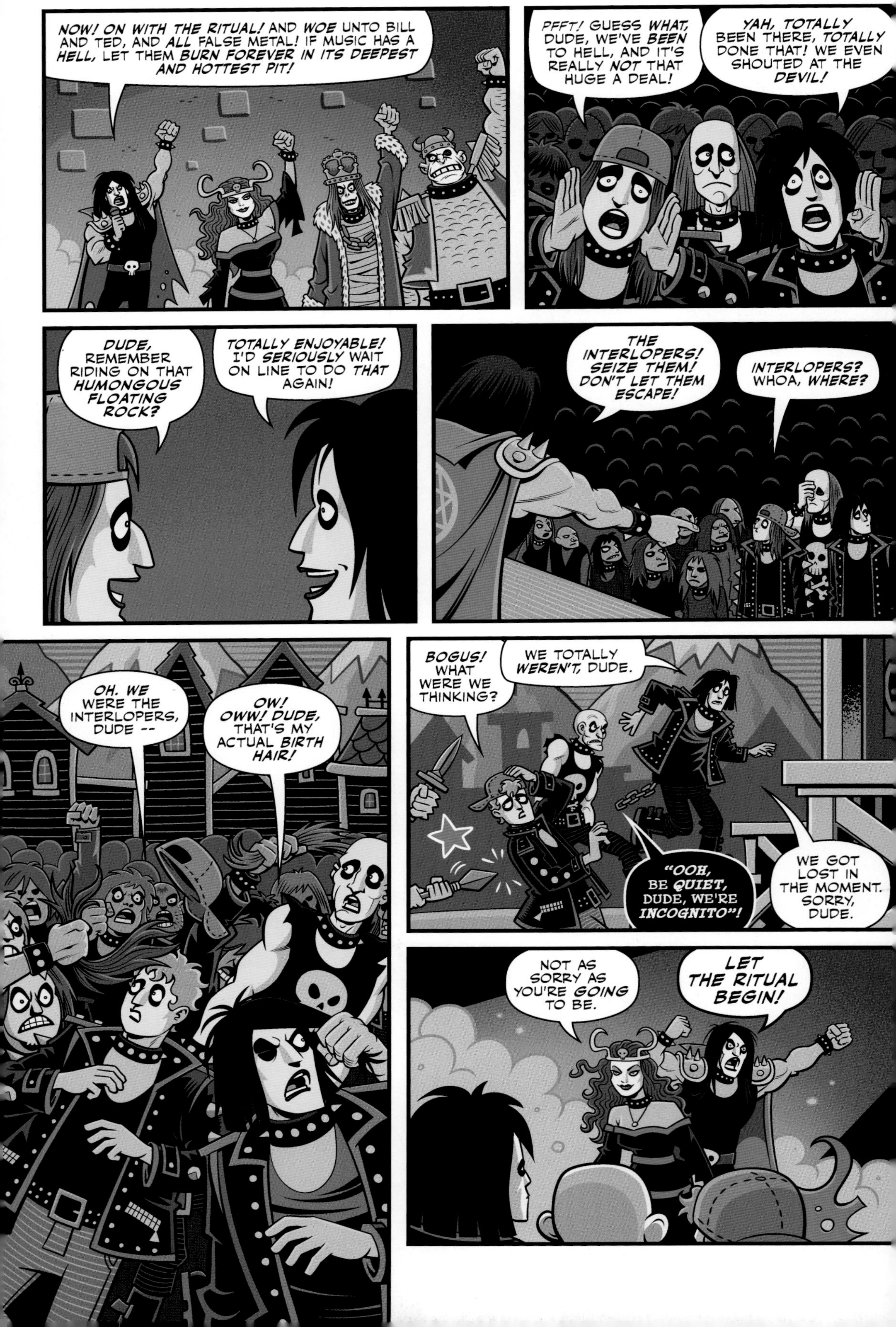
NOW! ON WITH THE RITUAL! AND WOE UNTO BILL AND TED, AND ALL FALSE METAL! IF MUSIC HAS A HELL, LET THEM BURN FOREVER IN ITS DEEPEST AND HOTTEST PIT!
PFFT! GUESS WHAT, DUDE, WE'VE BEEN TO HELL, AND IT'S REALLY NOT THAT HUGE A DEAL!
YAH, TOTALLY BEEN THERE, TOTALLY DONE THAT! WE EVEN SHOUTED AT THE DEVIL!
DUDE, REMEMBER RIDING ON THAT HUMONGOUS FLOATING ROCK?
TOTALLY ENJOYABLE! I'D SERIOUSLY WAIT ON LINE TO DO THAT AGAIN!
THE INTERLOPERS! SEIZE THEM! DON'T LET THEM ESCAPE!
INTERLOPERS? WHOA, WHERE?
OH. WE WERE THE INTERLOPERS, DUDE --
OW! OWW! DUDE, THAT'S MY ACTUAL BIRTH HAIR!
BOGUS! WHAT WERE WE THINKING?
WE TOTALLY WEREN'T, DUDE.
"OOH, BE QUIET, DUDE, WE'RE INCOGNITO"!
WE GOT LOST IN THE MOMENT. SORRY, DUDE.
NOT AS SORRY AS YOU'RE GOING TO BE.
LET THE RITUAL BEGIN!

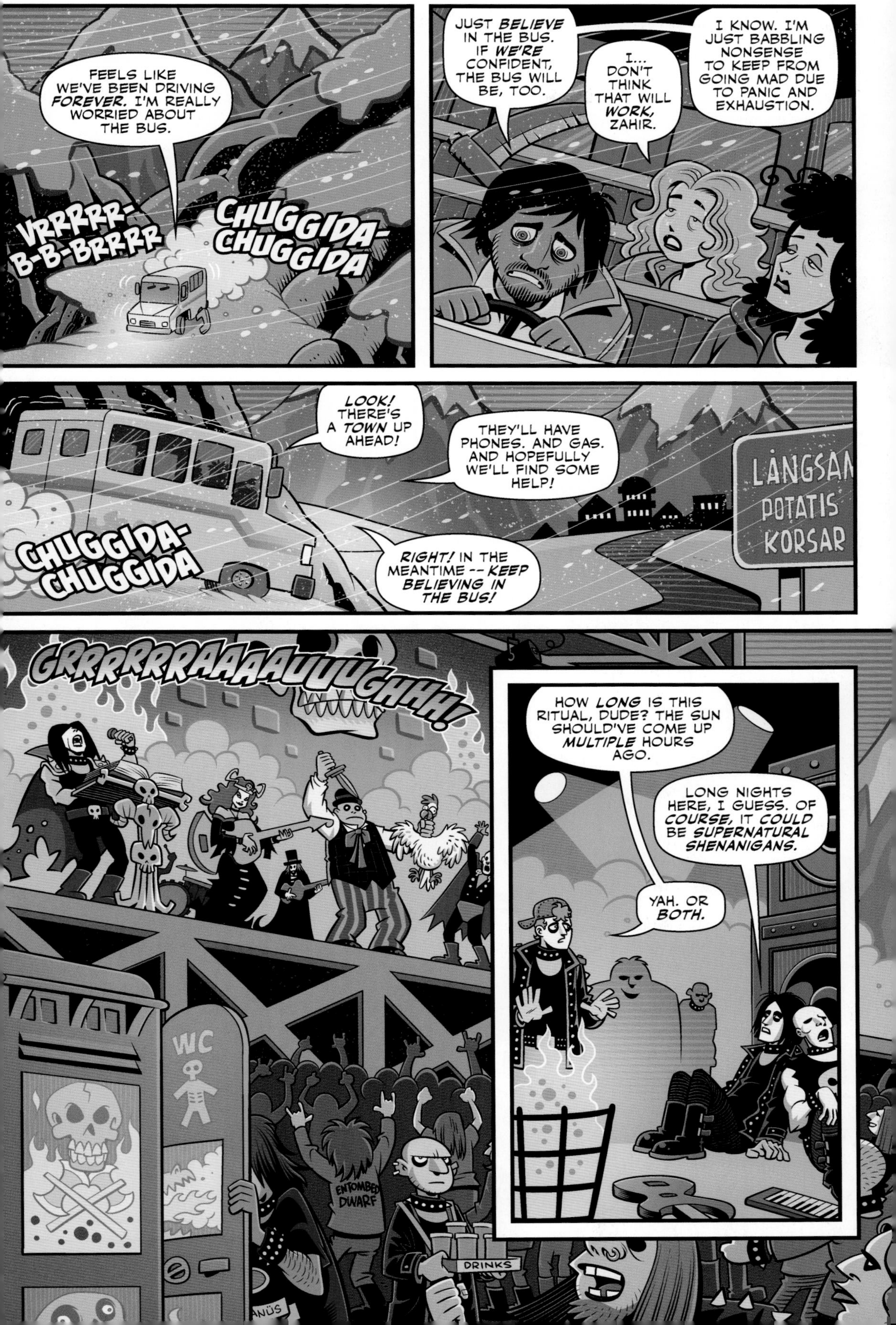
FEELS LIKE WE'VE BEEN DRIVING *FOREVER.* I'M REALLY WORRIED ABOUT THE BUS.
VRRRRR-B-B-BRRRR
CHUGGIDA-CHUGGIDA
JUST *BELIEVE* IN THE BUS. IF *WE'RE* CONFIDENT, THE BUS WILL BE, TOO.
I... DON'T THINK THAT WILL *WORK,* ZAHIR.
I KNOW. I'M JUST BABBLING NONSENSE TO KEEP FROM GOING MAD DUE TO PANIC AND EXHAUSTION.
LOOK! THERE'S A *TOWN* UP AHEAD!
THEY'LL HAVE PHONES. AND GAS. AND HOPEFULLY WE'LL FIND SOME HELP!
LÅNGSAM POTATIS KORSAR
CHUGGIDA-CHUGGIDA
RIGHT! IN THE MEANTIME -- *KEEP BELIEVING IN THE BUS!*
GRRRRRRAAAAUUUGHHH!
HOW *LONG* IS THIS RITUAL, DUDE? THE SUN SHOULD'VE COME UP *MULTIPLE* HOURS AGO.
LONG NIGHTS HERE, I GUESS. OF *COURSE,* IT *COULD* BE *SUPERNATURAL SHENANIGANS.*
YAH. OR *BOTH.*
WC
ENTOMBED DWARF
DRINKS

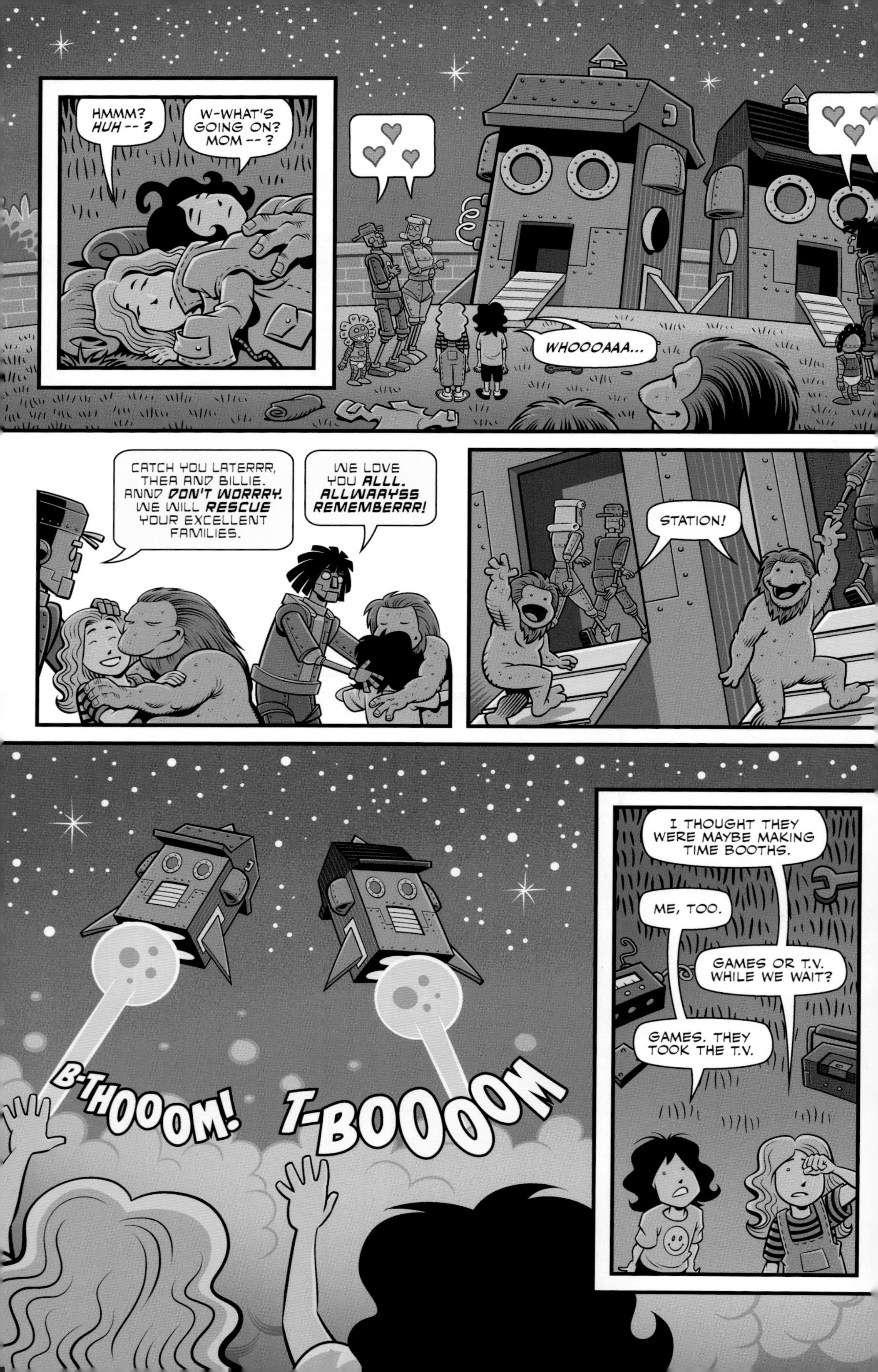
HMMM? HUH -- ?
W-WHAT'S GOING ON? MOM -- ?
WHOOOAAA...
CATCH YOU LATERRR, THEA AND BILLIE. ANND DON'T WORRRY. WE WILL RESCUE YOUR EXCELLENT FAMILIES.
WE LOVE YOU ALLL. ALLWAAYSS REMEMBERRR!
STATION!
B-THOOOM!
T-BOOOOOM
I THOUGHT THEY WERE MAYBE MAKING TIME BOOTHS.
ME, TOO.
GAMES OR T.V. WHILE WE WAIT?
GAMES. THEY TOOK THE T.V.

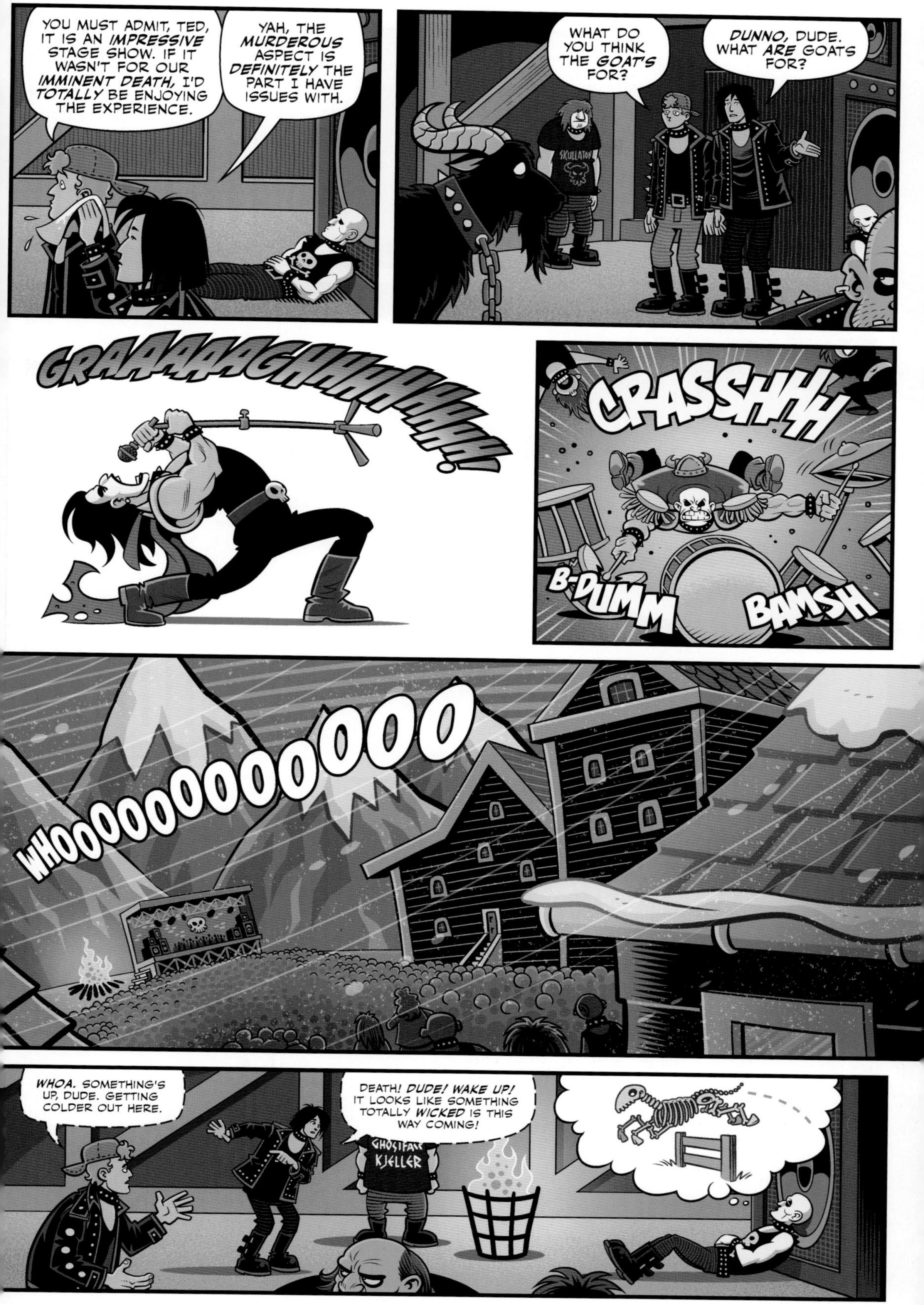

YOU MUST ADMIT, TED, IT IS AN IMPRESSIVE STAGE SHOW. IF IT WASN'T FOR OUR IMMINENT DEATH, I'D TOTALLY BE ENJOYING THE EXPERIENCE.
YAH, THE MURDEROUS ASPECT IS DEFINITELY THE PART I HAVE ISSUES WITH.
WHAT DO YOU THINK THE GOAT'S FOR?
DUNNO, DUDE. WHAT ARE GOATS FOR?
SKULLATOR
GRAAAAAGHHHHHHHH!
CRASSHHH
B-DUMM
BAMSH
WHOOOOOOOOOOOOO
WHOA. SOMETHING'S UP, DUDE. GETTING COLDER OUT HERE.
DEATH! DUDE! WAKE UP! IT LOOKS LIKE SOMETHING TOTALLY WICKED IS THIS WAY COMING!
GHOSTFACE KJELLER

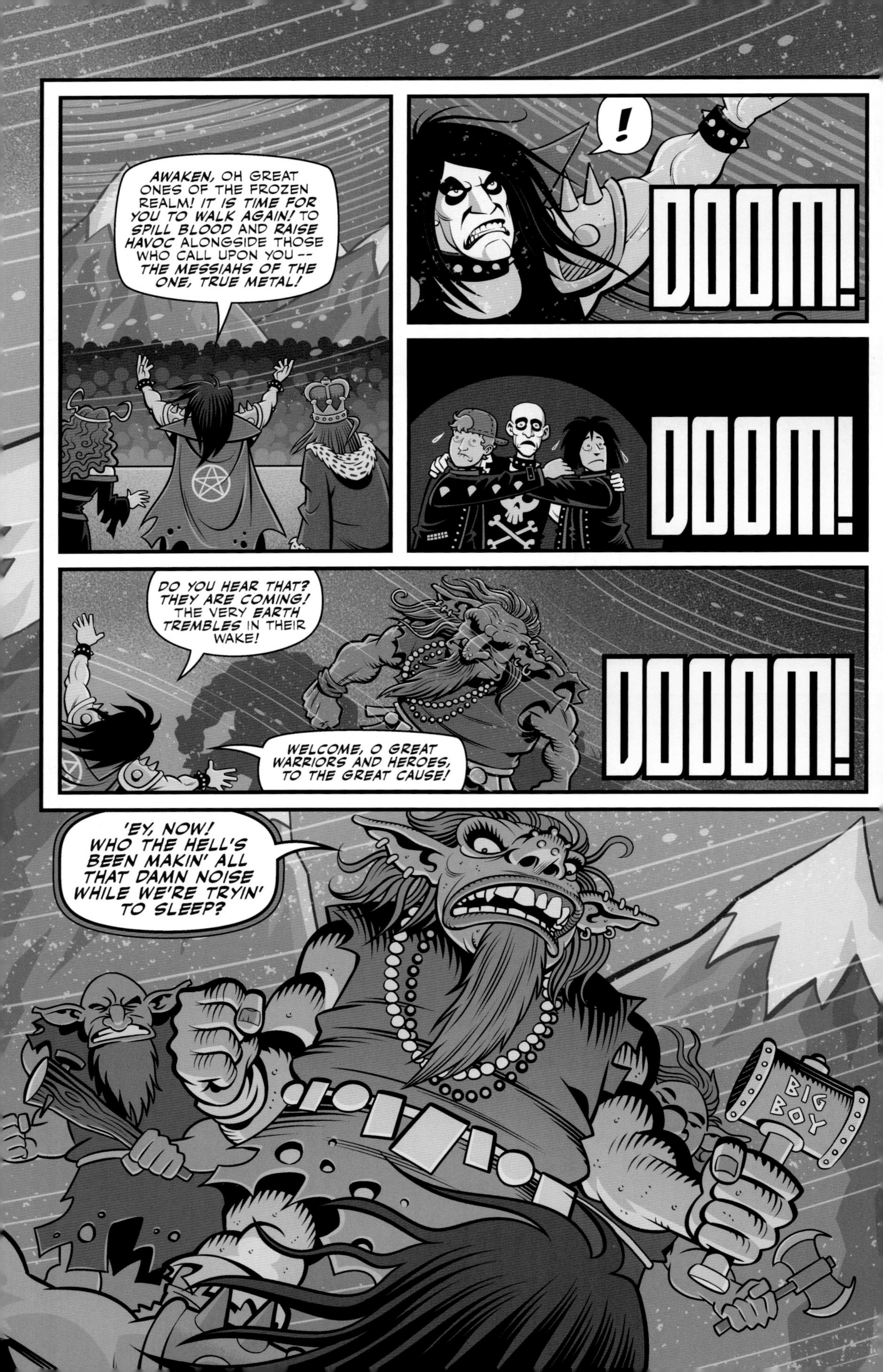
AWAKEN, OH GREAT ONES OF THE FROZEN REALM! IT IS TIME FOR YOU TO WALK AGAIN! TO SPILL BLOOD AND RAISE HAVOC ALONGSIDE THOSE WHO CALL UPON YOU -- THE MESSIAHS OF THE ONE, TRUE METAL!
!
DOOM!
DOOM!
DO YOU HEAR THAT? THEY ARE COMING! THE VERY EARTH TREMBLES IN THEIR WAKE!
DOOOM!
WELCOME, O GREAT WARRIORS AND HEROES, TO THE GREAT CAUSE!
'EY, NOW! WHO THE HELL'S BEEN MAKIN' ALL THAT DAMN NOISE WHILE WE'RE TRYIN' TO SLEEP?
BIG BOY

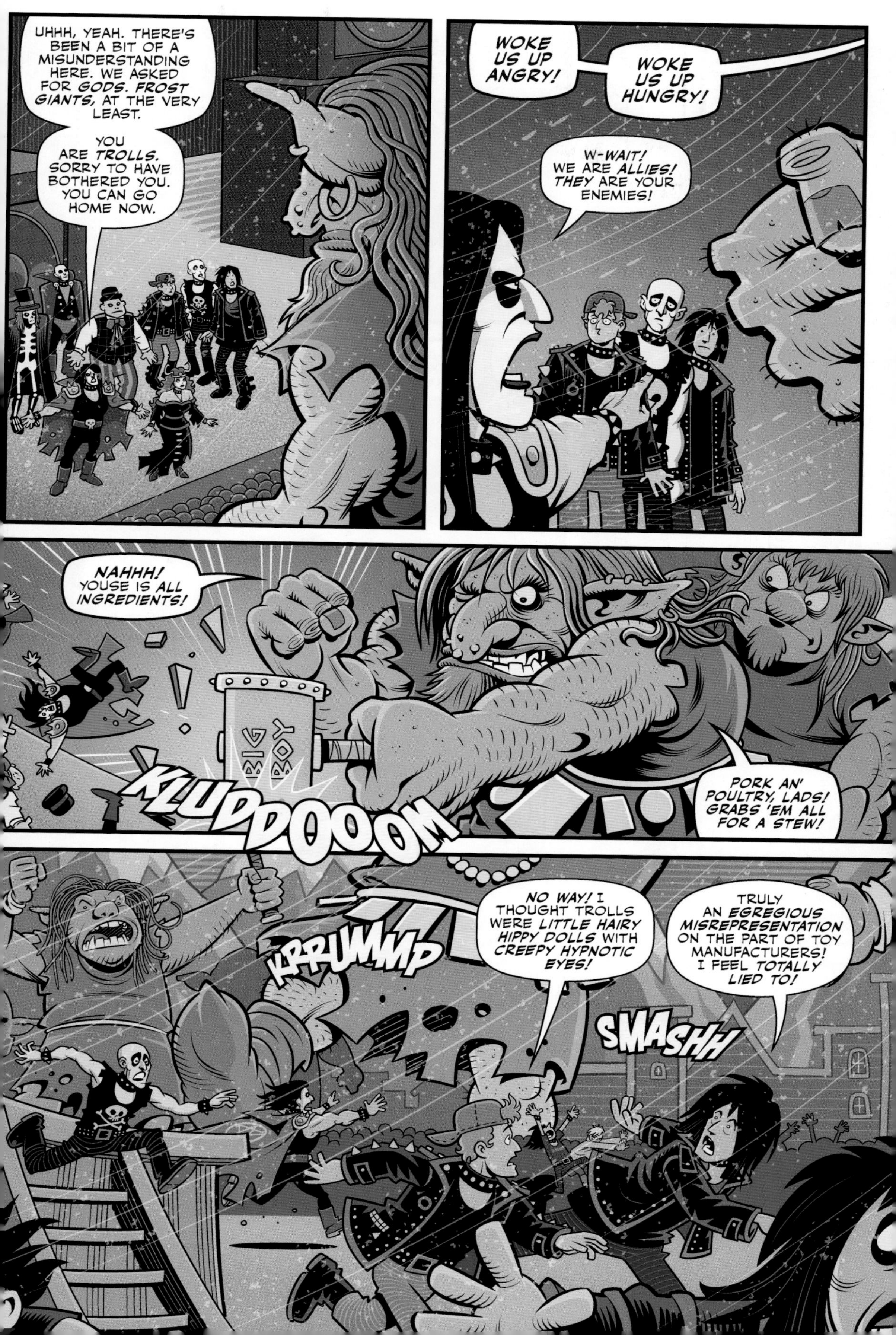
UHHH, YEAH. THERE'S BEEN A BIT OF A MISUNDERSTANDING HERE. WE ASKED FOR *GODS*. *FROST GIANTS*, AT THE VERY LEAST.
YOU ARE *TROLLS*. SORRY TO HAVE BOTHERED YOU. YOU CAN GO HOME NOW.
WOKE US UP ANGRY!
WOKE US UP HUNGRY!
W-WAIT! WE ARE ALLIES! THEY ARE YOUR ENEMIES!
NAHHH! YOUSE IS *ALL INGREDIENTS!*
BIG BOY
KLUDDOOOM
PORK AN' POULTRY, LADS! GRABS 'EM ALL FOR A STEW!
KRRUMMP
NO WAY! I THOUGHT TROLLS WERE *LITTLE HAIRY HIPPY DOLLS* WITH CREEPY HYPNOTIC EYES!
TRULY AN *EGREGIOUS MISREPRESENTATION* ON THE PART OF TOY MANUFACTURERS! I FEEL *TOTALLY* LIED TO!
SMASHH

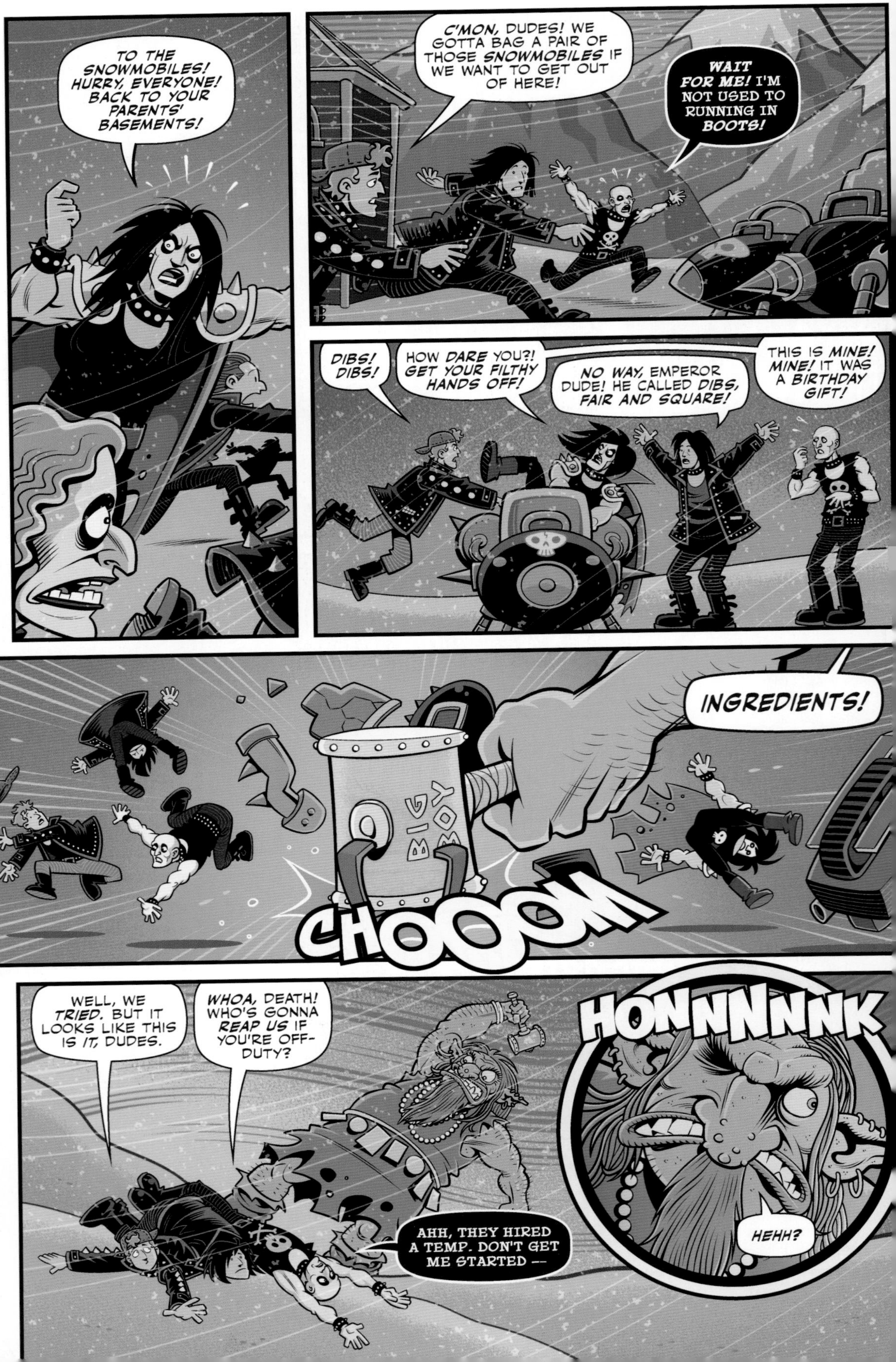
TO THE SNOWMOBILES! HURRY, EVERYONE! BACK TO YOUR PARENTS' BASEMENTS!
C'MON, DUDES! WE GOTTA BAG A PAIR OF THOSE SNOWMOBILES IF WE WANT TO GET OUT OF HERE!
WAIT FOR ME! I'M NOT USED TO RUNNING IN BOOTS!
DIBS! DIBS!
HOW DARE YOU?! GET YOUR FILTHY HANDS OFF!
NO WAY, EMPEROR DUDE! HE CALLED DIBS, FAIR AND SQUARE!
THIS IS MINE! MINE! IT WAS A BIRTHDAY GIFT!
INGREDIENTS!
BIG YOM
CHOOOOM
WELL, WE TRIED. BUT IT LOOKS LIKE THIS IS IT, DUDES.
WHOA, DEATH! WHO'S GONNA REAP US IF YOU'RE OFF-DUTY?
HONNNNNK
AHH, THEY HIRED A TEMP. DON'T GET ME STARTED --
HEHH?

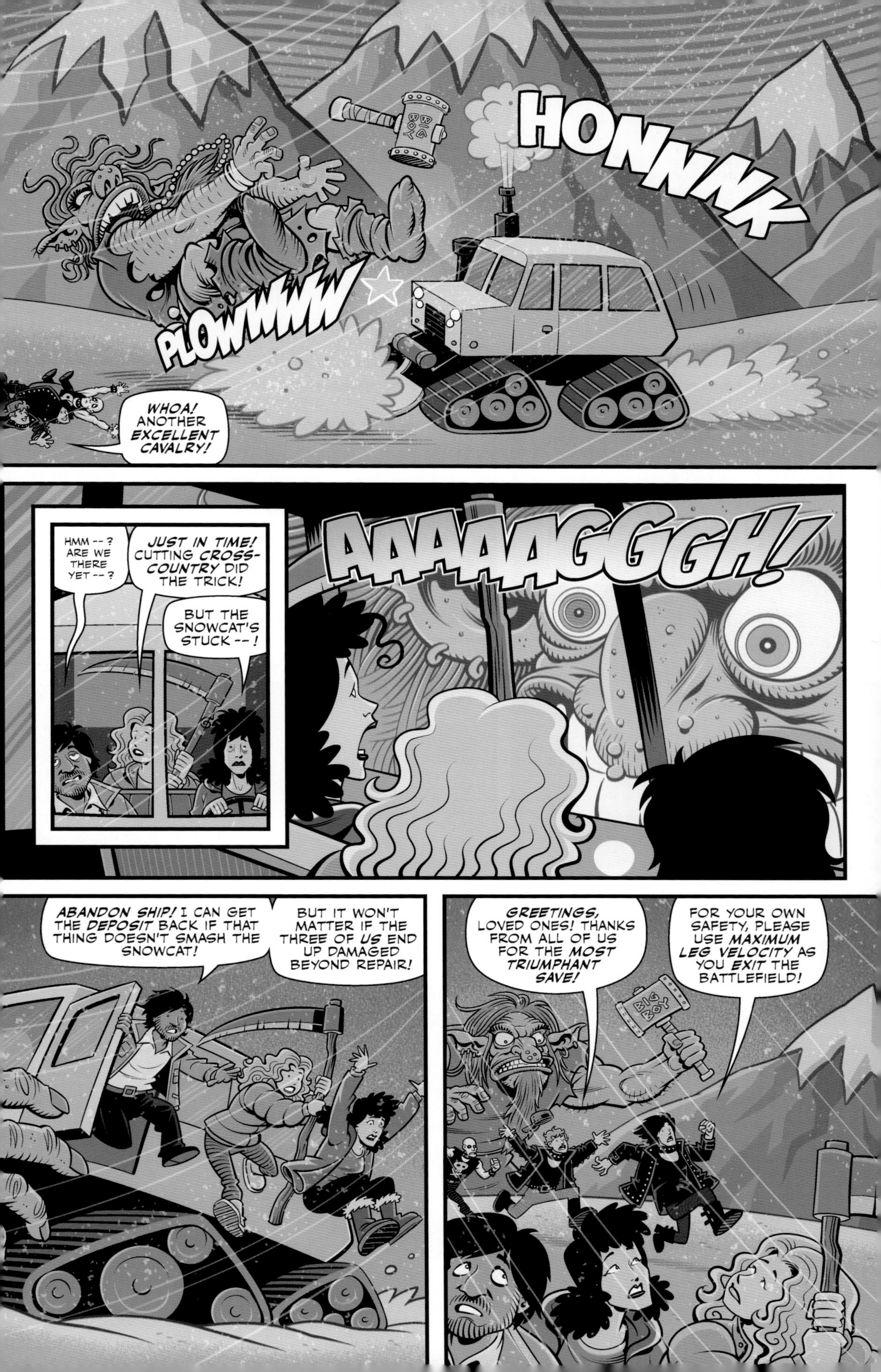
HONNNNK
PLOWWWW
WHOA! ANOTHER EXCELLENT CAVALRY!
HMM -- ? ARE WE THERE YET -- ?
JUST IN TIME! CUTTING CROSS-COUNTRY DID THE TRICK!
BUT THE SNOWCAT'S STUCK -- !
AAAAAGGGH!
ABANDON SHIP! I CAN GET THE DEPOSIT BACK IF THAT THING DOESN'T SMASH THE SNOWCAT!
BUT IT WON'T MATTER IF THE THREE OF US END UP DAMAGED BEYOND REPAIR!
GREETINGS, LOVED ONES! THANKS FROM ALL OF US FOR THE MOST TRIUMPHANT SAVE!
FOR YOUR OWN SAFETY, PLEASE USE MAXIMUM LEG VELOCITY AS YOU EXIT THE BATTLEFIELD!

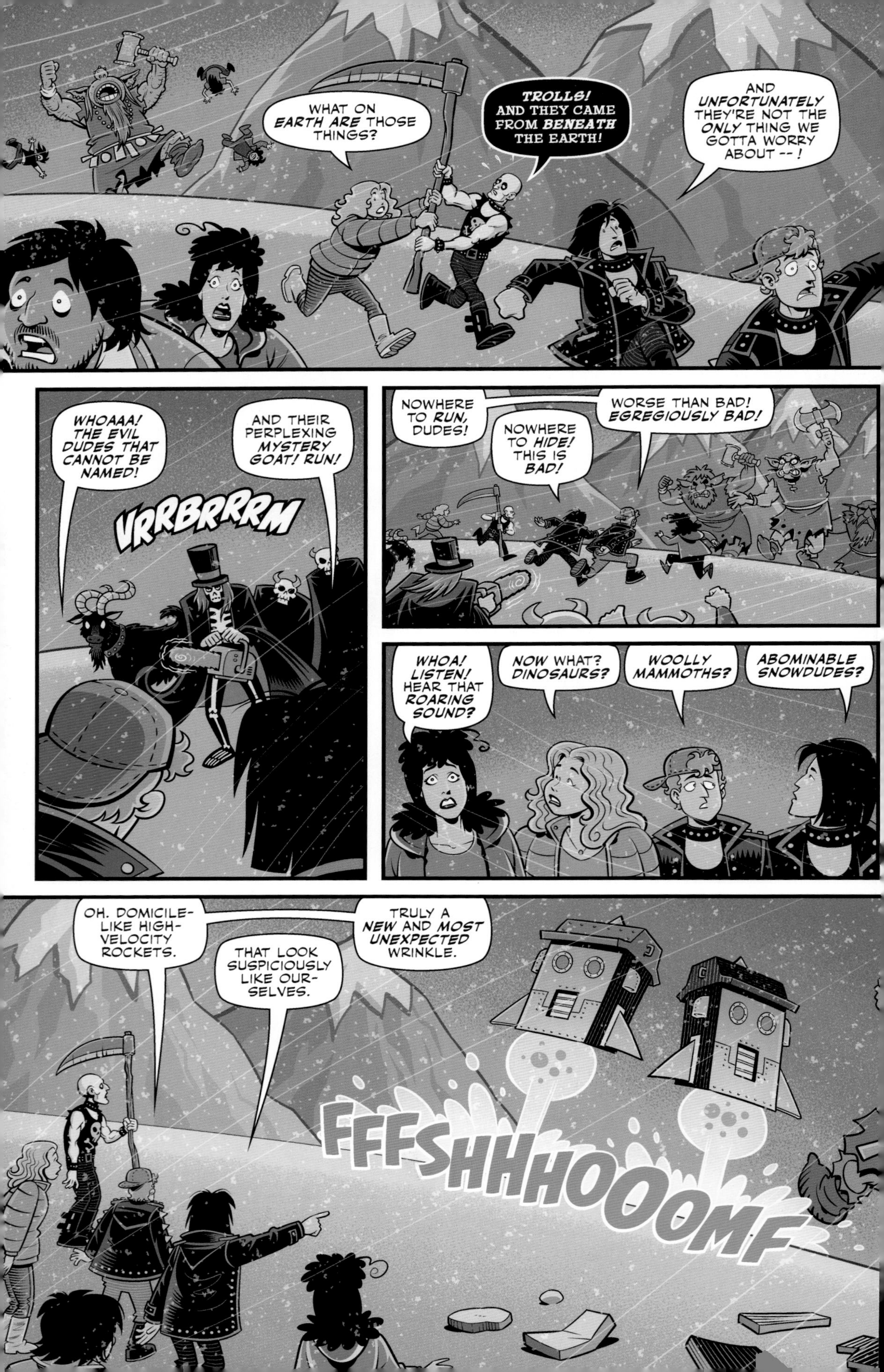
WHAT ON EARTH ARE THOSE THINGS?
TROLLS! AND THEY CAME FROM BENEATH THE EARTH!
AND UNFORTUNATELY THEY'RE NOT THE ONLY THING WE GOTTA WORRY ABOUT -- !
WHOAAA! THE EVIL DUDES THAT CANNOT BE NAMED!
AND THEIR PERPLEXING MYSTERY GOAT! RUN!
VRRBRRRM
NOWHERE TO RUN, DUDES!
NOWHERE TO HIDE! THIS IS BAD!
WORSE THAN BAD! EGREGIOUSLY BAD!
WHOA! LISTEN! HEAR THAT ROARING SOUND?
NOW WHAT? DINOSAURS?
WOOLLY MAMMOTHS?
ABOMINABLE SNOWDUDES?
OH. DOMICILE-LIKE HIGH-VELOCITY ROCKETS.
THAT LOOK SUSPICIOUSLY LIKE OUR-SELVES.
TRULY A NEW AND MOST UNEXPECTED WRINKLE.
FFFSHHHOOOOMF

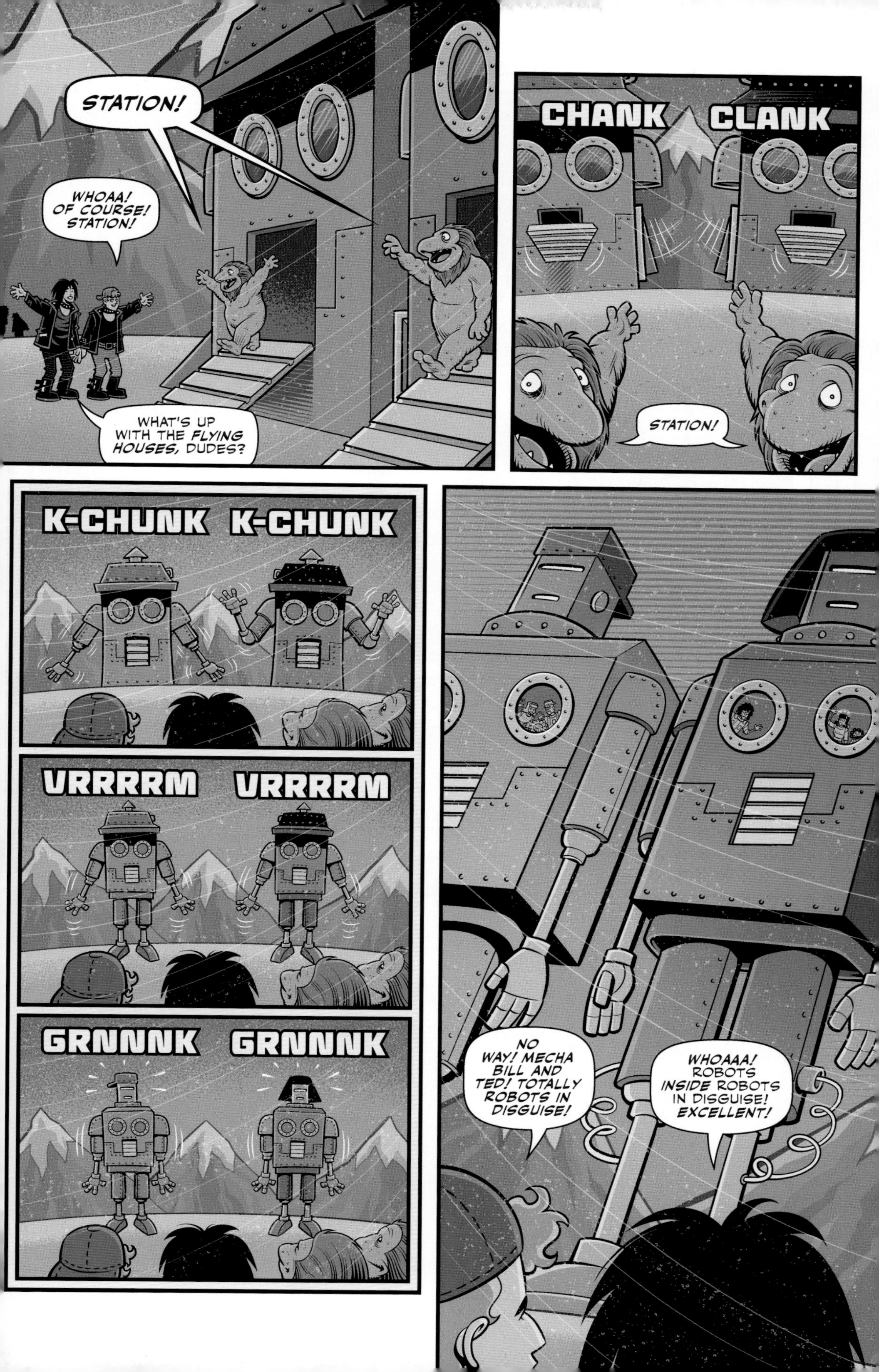
STATION!
WHOAA! OF COURSE! STATION!
WHAT'S UP WITH THE FLYING HOUSES, DUDES?
CHANK
CLANK
STATION!
K-CHUNK
K-CHUNK
VRRRRM
VRRRRM
GRNNNK
GRNNNK
NO WAY! MECHA BILL AND TED! TOTALLY ROBOTS IN DISGUISE!
WHOAAA! ROBOTS INSIDE ROBOTS IN DISGUISE! EXCELLENT!

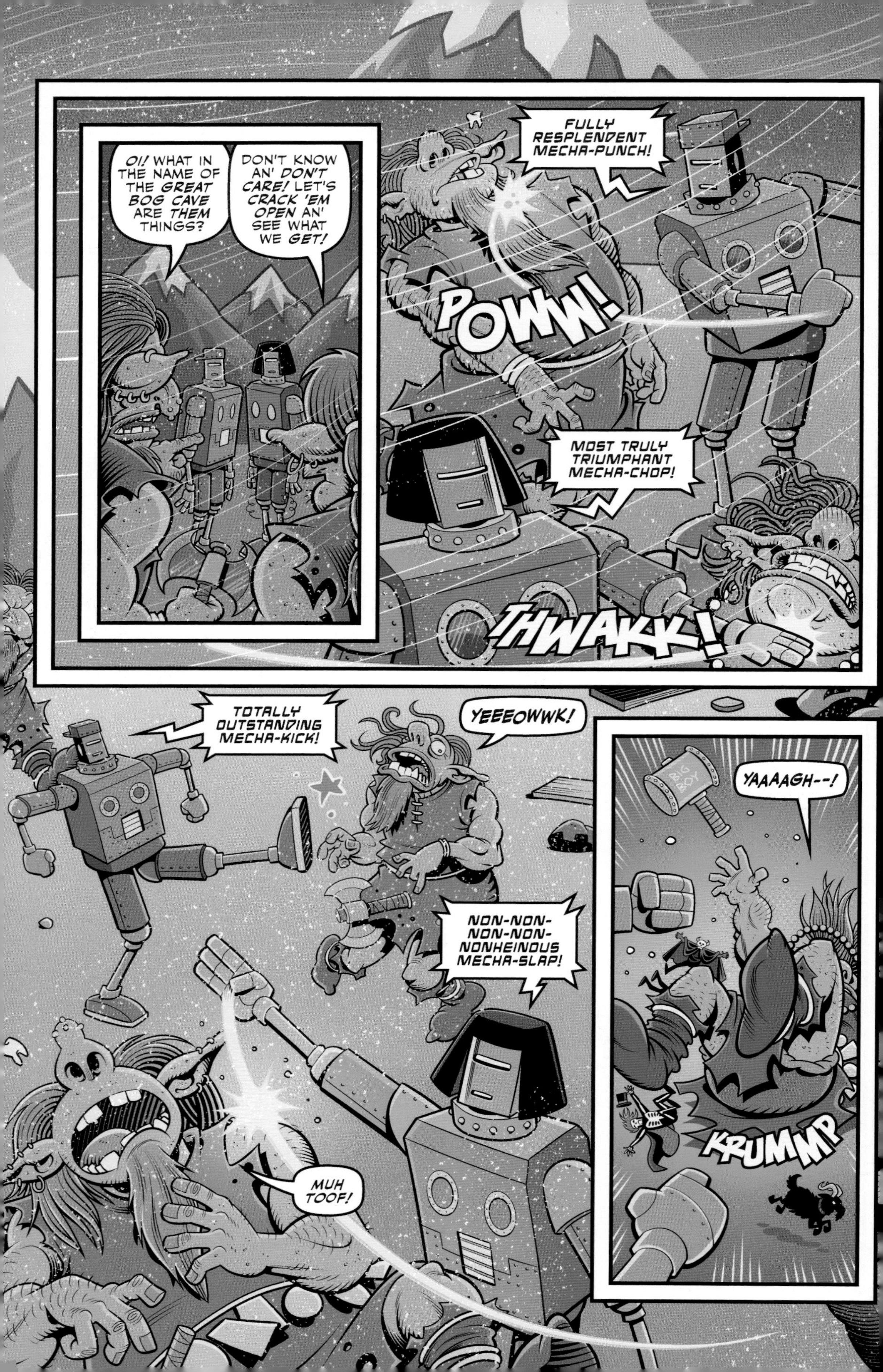
OI! WHAT IN THE NAME OF THE GREAT BOG CAVE ARE THEM THINGS?
DON'T KNOW AN' DON'T CARE! LET'S CRACK 'EM OPEN AN' SEE WHAT WE GET!
FULLY RESPLENDENT MECHA-PUNCH!
POWW!
MOST TRULY TRIUMPHANT MECHA-CHOP!
THWAKK!
TOTALLY OUTSTANDING MECHA-KICK!
YEEEOWWK!
NON-NON-NON-NON-NON-NONHEINOUS MECHA-SLAP!
MUH TOOF!
BIG BOY
YAAAAGH--!
KRUMMP

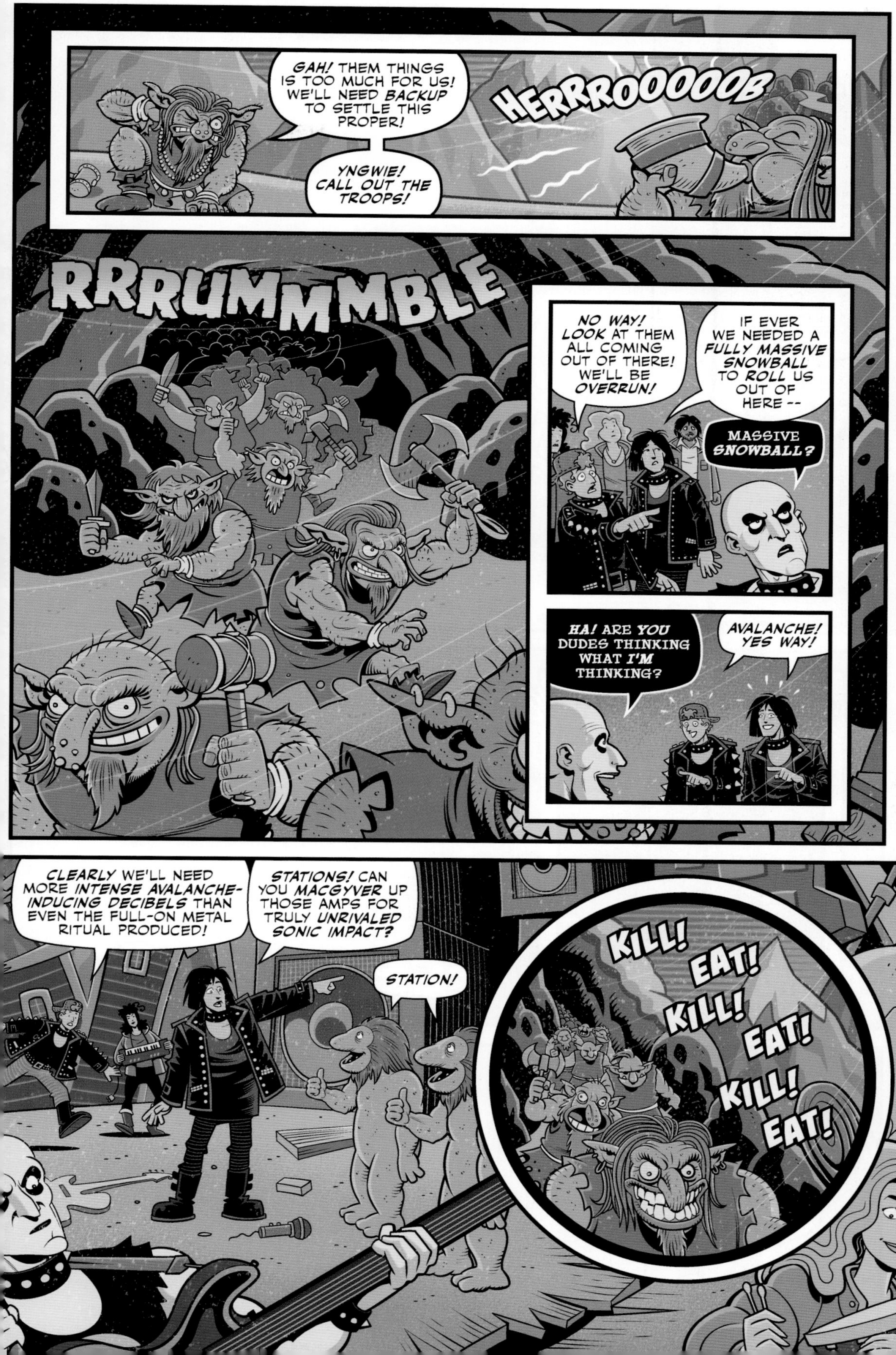
GAH! THEM THINGS IS TOO MUCH FOR US! WE'LL NEED BACKUP TO SETTLE THIS PROPER!
YNGWIE! CALL OUT THE TROOPS!
HERRROOOOOB
RRRUMMMBLE
NO WAY! LOOK AT THEM ALL COMING OUT OF THERE! WE'LL BE OVERRUN!
IF EVER WE NEEDED A FULLY MASSIVE SNOWBALL TO ROLL US OUT OF HERE --
MASSIVE SNOWBALL?
HA! ARE YOU DUDES THINKING WHAT I'M THINKING?
AVALANCHE! YES WAY!
CLEARLY WE'LL NEED MORE INTENSE AVALANCHE-INDUCING DECIBELS THAN EVEN THE FULL-ON METAL RITUAL PRODUCED!
STATIONS! CAN YOU MACGYVER UP THOSE AMPS FOR TRULY UNRIVALED SONIC IMPACT?
STATION!
KILL! EAT! KILL! EAT! KILL! EAT!

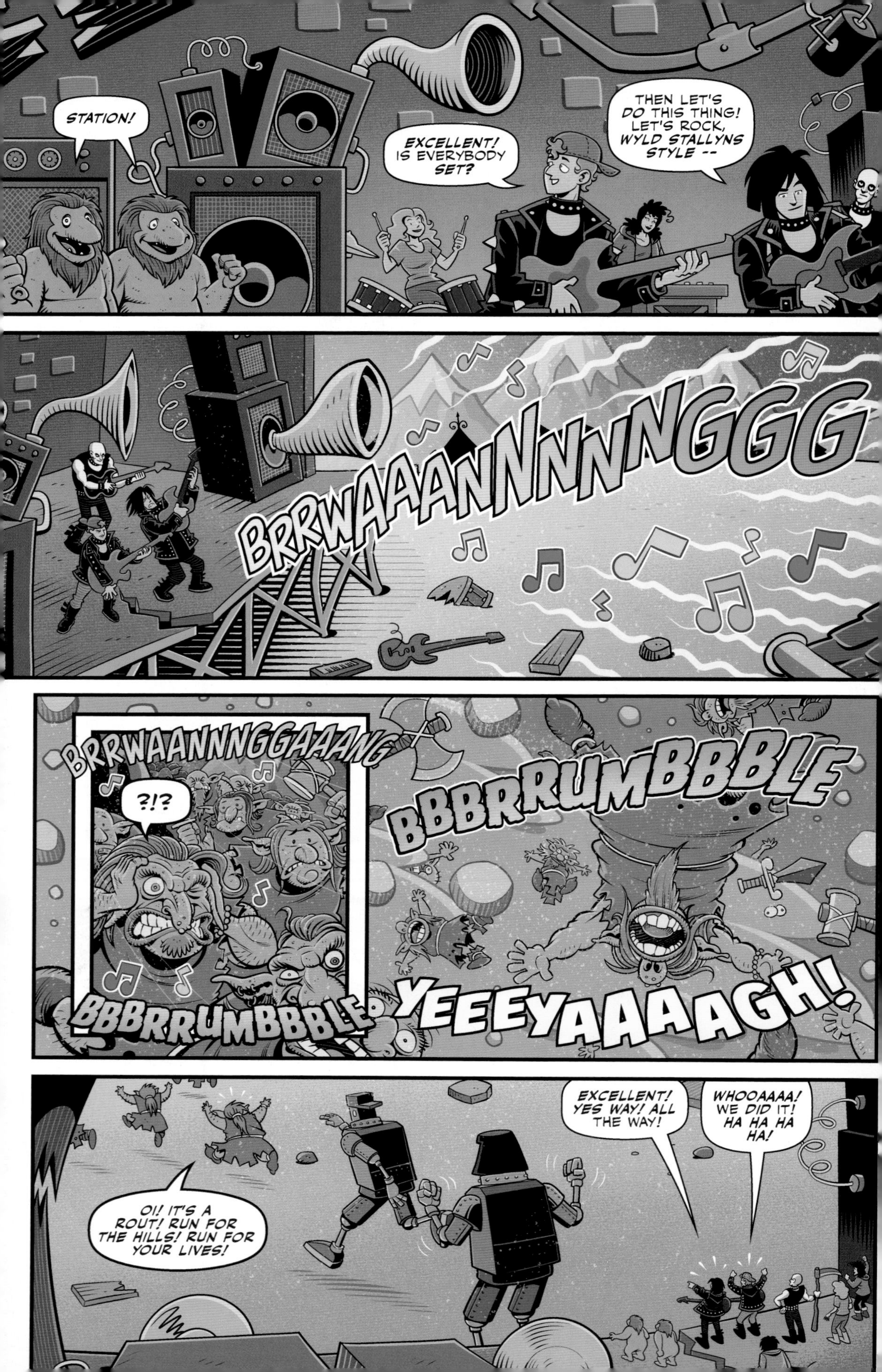
STATION!
EXCELLENT! IS EVERYBODY SET?
THEN LET'S DO THIS THING! LET'S ROCK, WYLD STALLYNS STYLE --
BRRWAAANNNNNGGG
BRRWAANNNGGAAANG
?!?
BBBRRUMBBBLE
BBBRRUMBBBLE
YEEEYAAAAAGH!
OI! IT'S A ROUT! RUN FOR THE HILLS! RUN FOR YOUR LIVES!
EXCELLENT! YES WAY! ALL THE WAY!
WHOOAAAA! WE DID IT! HA HA HA HA!

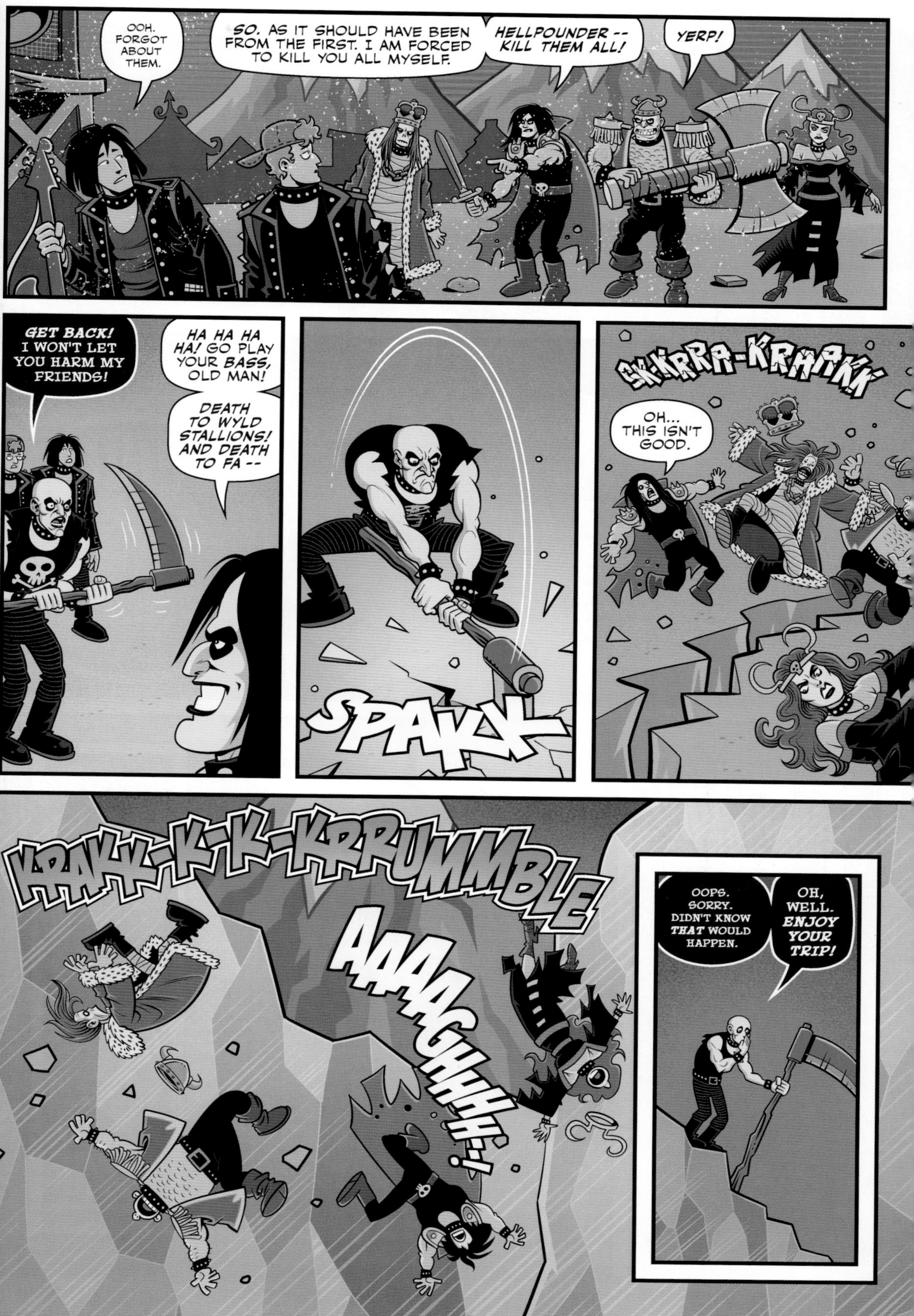
OOH. FORGOT ABOUT THEM.
SO. AS IT SHOULD HAVE BEEN FROM THE FIRST. I AM FORCED TO KILL YOU ALL MYSELF.
HELLPOUNDER -- KILL THEM ALL!
YERP!
GET BACK! I WON'T LET YOU HARM MY FRIENDS!
HA HA HA HA! GO PLAY YOUR BASS, OLD MAN!
DEATH TO WYLD STALLIONS! AND DEATH TO FA --
SPAKK
SK-KRRA-KRAKK
OH... THIS ISN'T GOOD.
KRAKK-K-K-KRRUMMBLE
AAAAGHHHH--!
OOPS. SORRY. DIDN'T KNOW THAT WOULD HAPPEN.
OH, WELL. ENJOY YOUR TRIP!

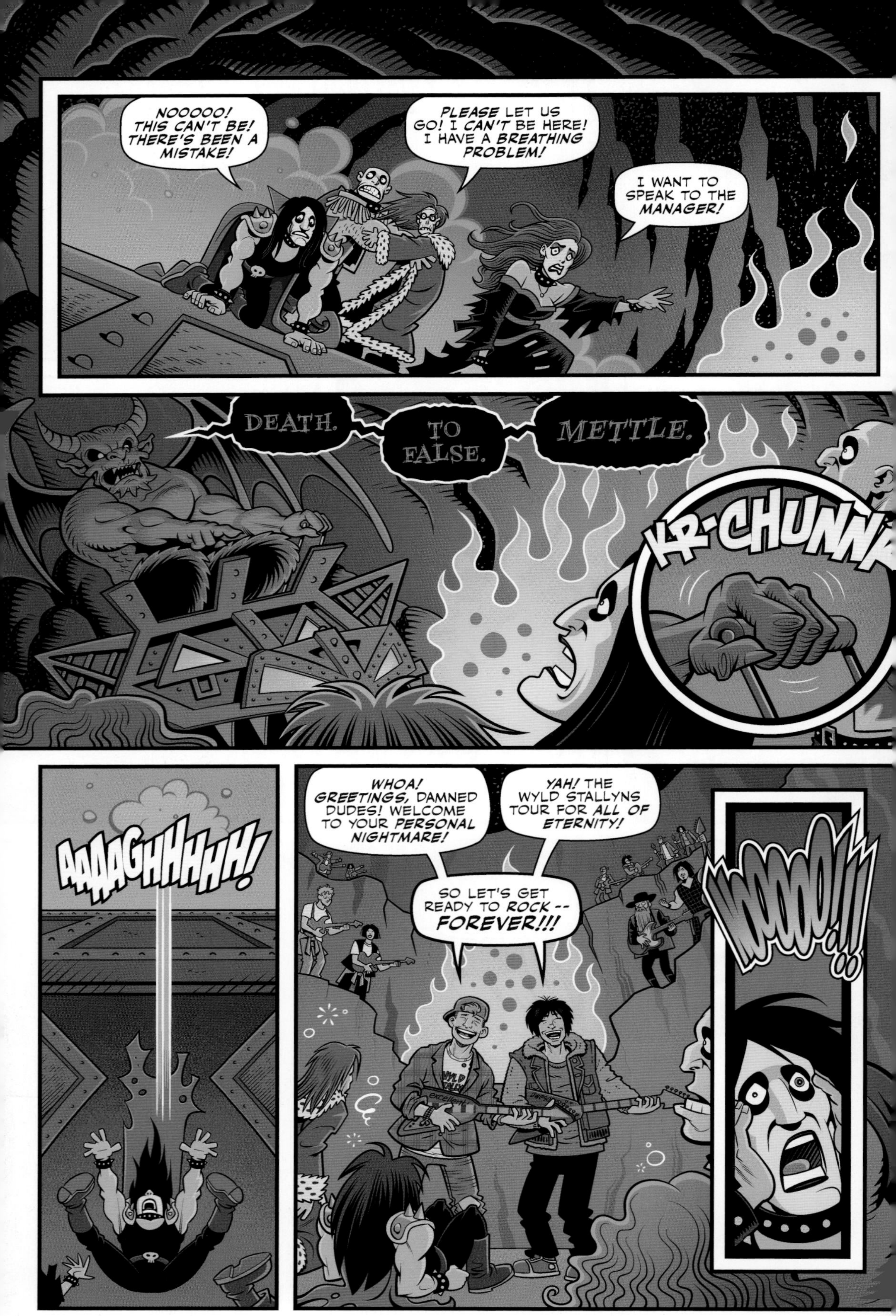
NOOOOO! THIS CAN'T BE! THERE'S BEEN A MISTAKE!
PLEASE LET US GO! I CAN'T BE HERE! I HAVE A BREATHING PROBLEM!
I WANT TO SPEAK TO THE MANAGER!
DEATH.
TO FALSE.
METTLE.
KR-CHUNNK
AAAAGHHHHH!
WHOA! GREETINGS, DAMNED DUDES! WELCOME TO YOUR PERSONAL NIGHTMARE!
YAH! THE WYLD STALLYNS TOUR FOR ALL OF ETERNITY!
SO LET'S GET READY TO ROCK -- FOREVER!!!
NOOOO!!!

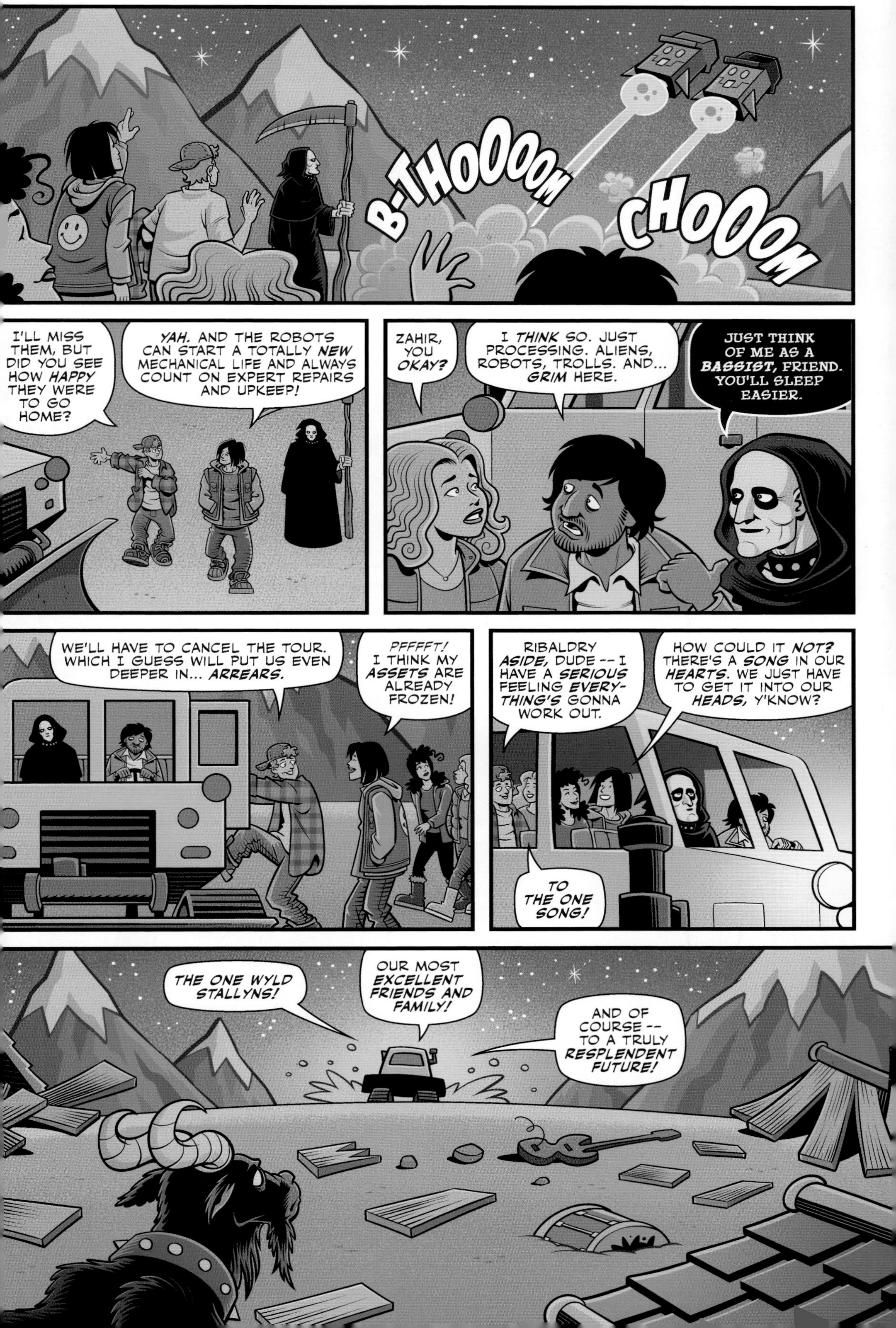
B-THOOOOM
CHOOOM
I'LL MISS THEM, BUT DID YOU SEE HOW HAPPY THEY WERE TO GO HOME?
YAH. AND THE ROBOTS CAN START A TOTALLY NEW MECHANICAL LIFE AND ALWAYS COUNT ON EXPERT REPAIRS AND UPKEEP!
ZAHIR, YOU OKAY?
I THINK SO. JUST PROCESSING. ALIENS, ROBOTS, TROLLS. AND... GRIM HERE.
JUST THINK OF ME AS A BASSIST, FRIEND. YOU'LL SLEEP EASIER.
WE'LL HAVE TO CANCEL THE TOUR. WHICH I GUESS WILL PUT US EVEN DEEPER IN... ARREARS.
PFFFFT! I THINK MY ASSETS ARE ALREADY FROZEN!
RIBALDRY ASIDE, DUDE -- I HAVE A SERIOUS FEELING EVERYTHING'S GONNA WORK OUT.
HOW COULD IT NOT? THERE'S A SONG IN OUR HEARTS. WE JUST HAVE TO GET IT INTO OUR HEADS, Y'KNOW?
TO THE ONE SONG!
THE ONE WYLD STALLYNS!
OUR MOST EXCELLENT FRIENDS AND FAMILY!
AND OF COURSE -- TO A TRULY RESPLENDENT FUTURE!

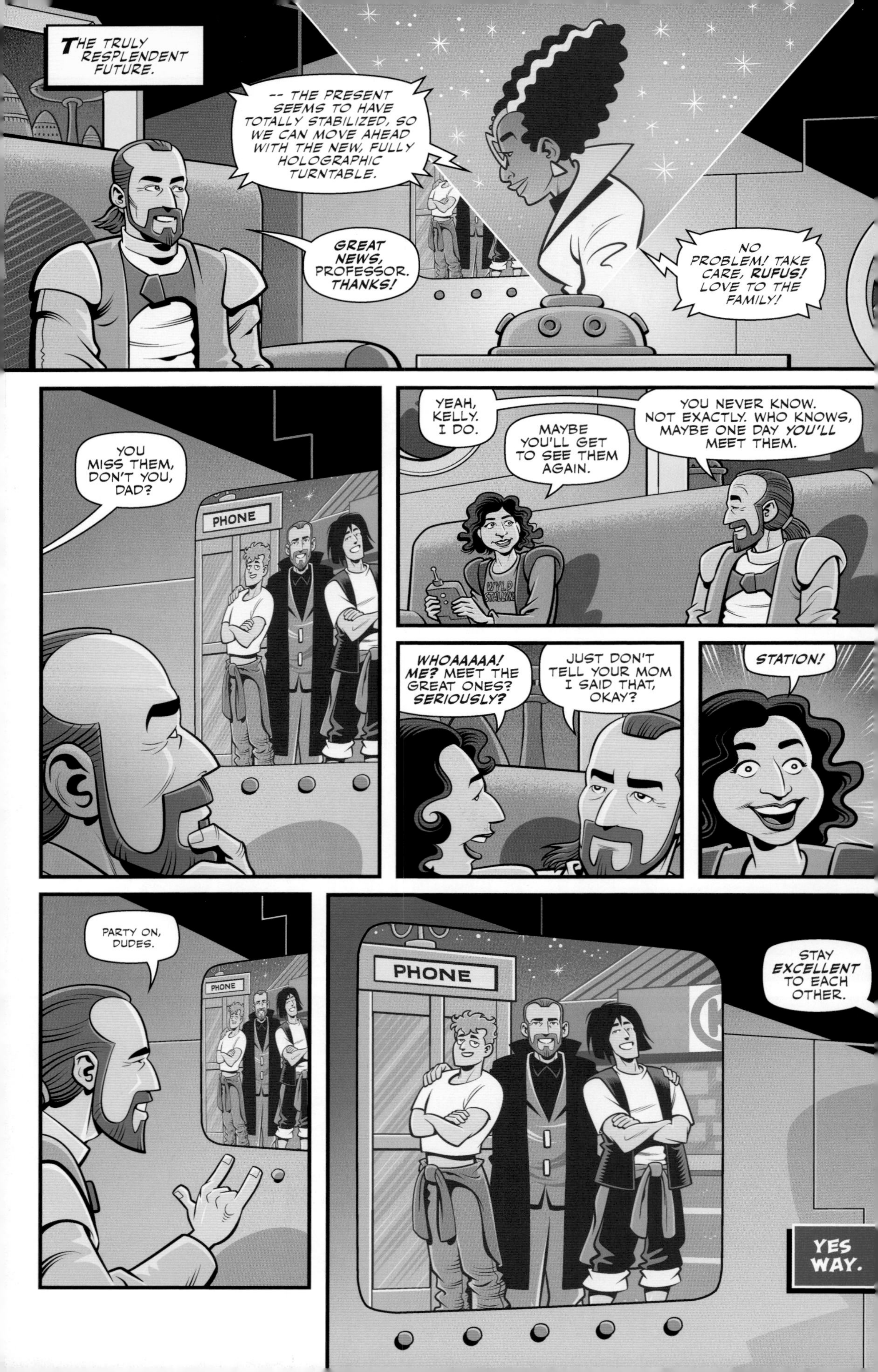
THE TRULY RESPLENDENT FUTURE.
-- THE PRESENT SEEMS TO HAVE TOTALLY STABILIZED, SO WE CAN MOVE AHEAD WITH THE NEW, FULLY HOLOGRAPHIC TURNTABLE.
GREAT NEWS, PROFESSOR. THANKS!
NO PROBLEM! TAKE CARE, RUFUS! LOVE TO THE FAMILY!
YOU MISS THEM, DON'T YOU, DAD?
PHONE
YEAH, KELLY. I DO.
MAYBE YOU'LL GET TO SEE THEM AGAIN.
YOU NEVER KNOW. NOT EXACTLY. WHO KNOWS, MAYBE ONE DAY YOU'LL MEET THEM.
WYLD STALLYNS
WHOAAAAA! ME? MEET THE GREAT ONES? SERIOUSLY?
JUST DON'T TELL YOUR MOM I SAID THAT, OKAY?
STATION!
PARTY ON, DUDES.
PHONE
PHONE
STAY EXCELLENT TO EACH OTHER.
YES WAY.

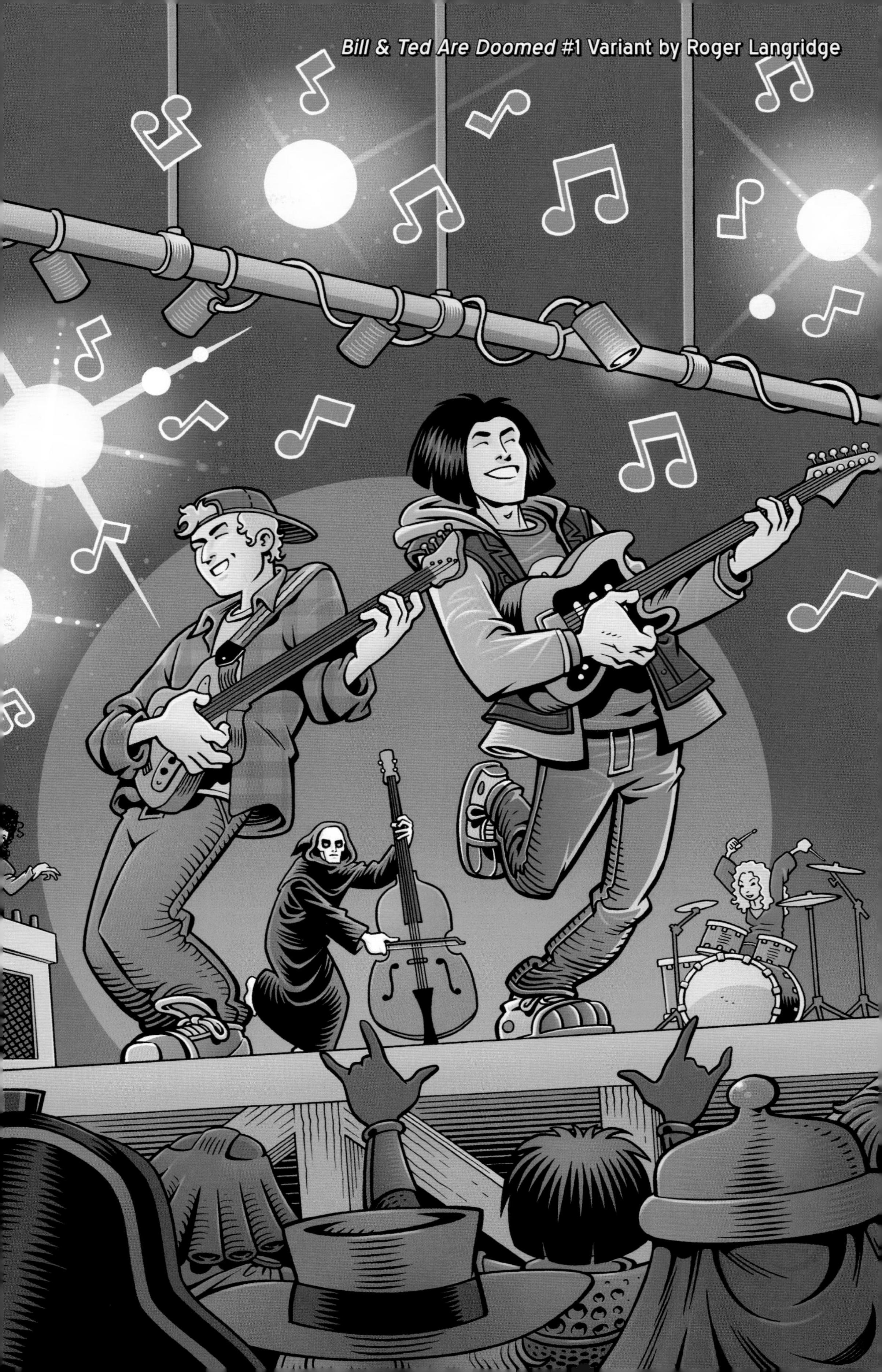

Bill & Ted Are Doomed #1 Variant by Roger Langridge

Bill & Ted Are Doomed #2 Variant by Tyler Crook

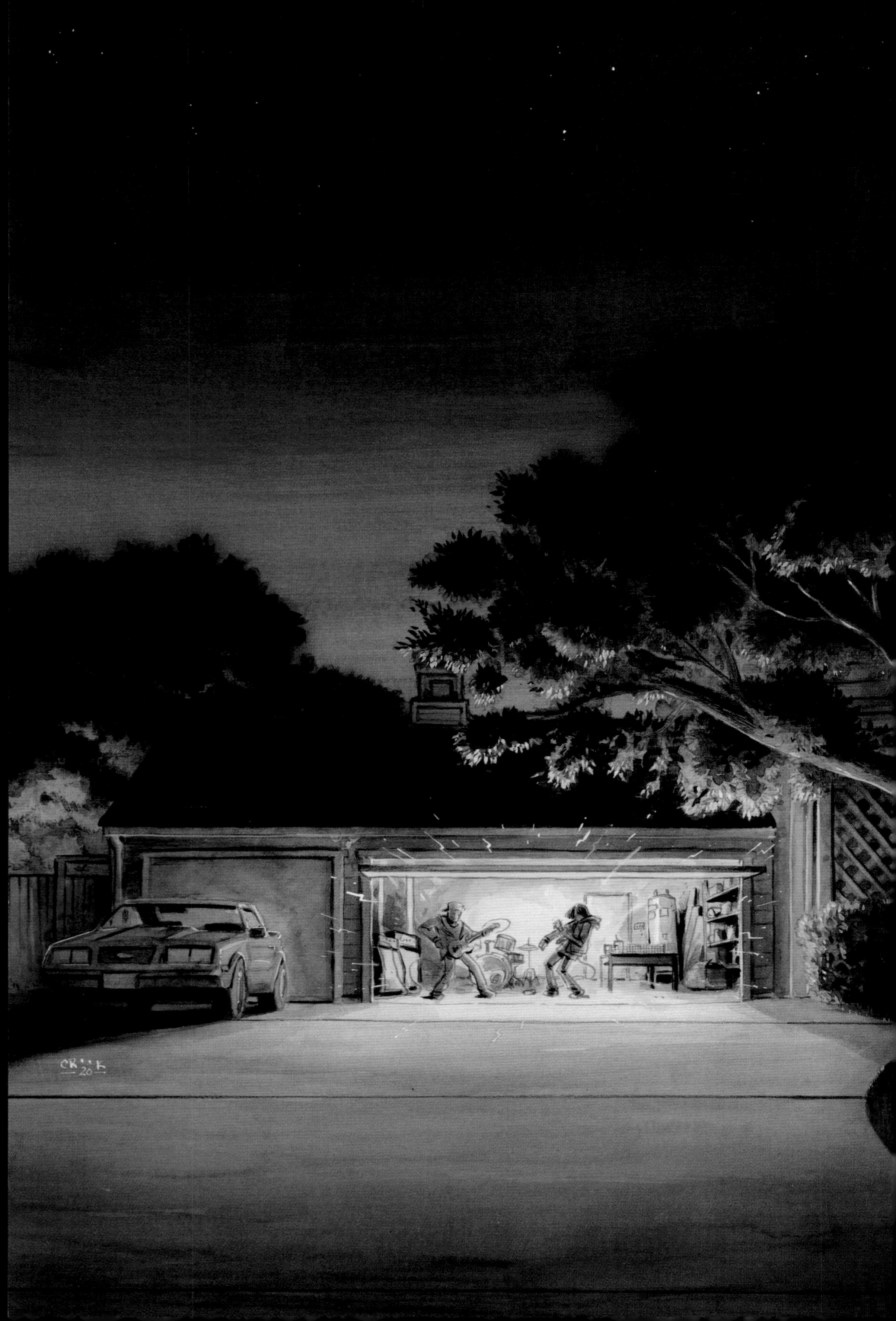

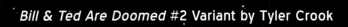

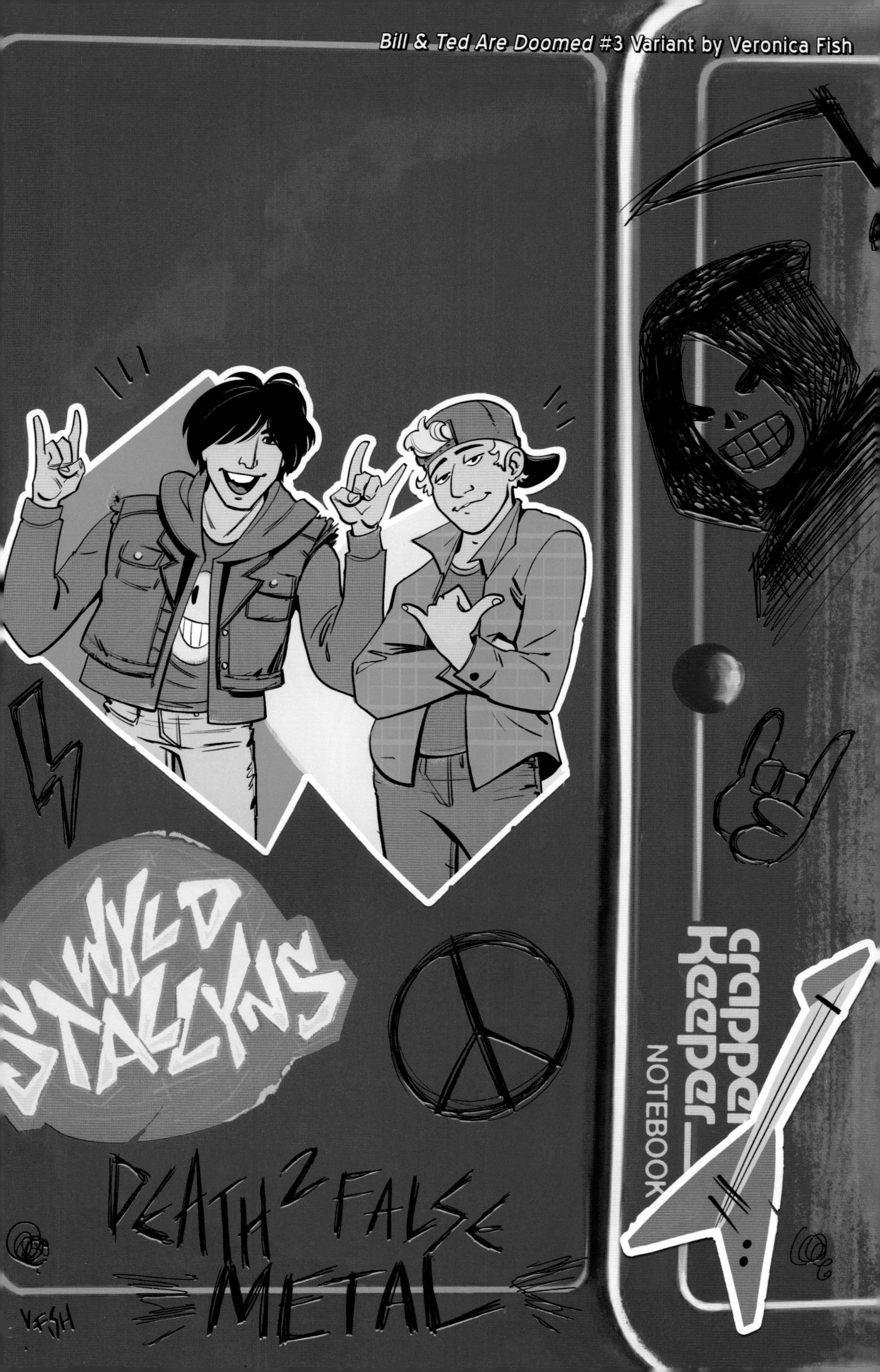
WYLD STALLYNS
DEATH 2 FALSE METAL
Crapper Keeper
NOTEBOOK
V.FISH
Bill & Ted Are Doomed #3 Variant by Veronica Fish

Bill & Ted Are Doomed #4 Variant by Benjamin Dewey

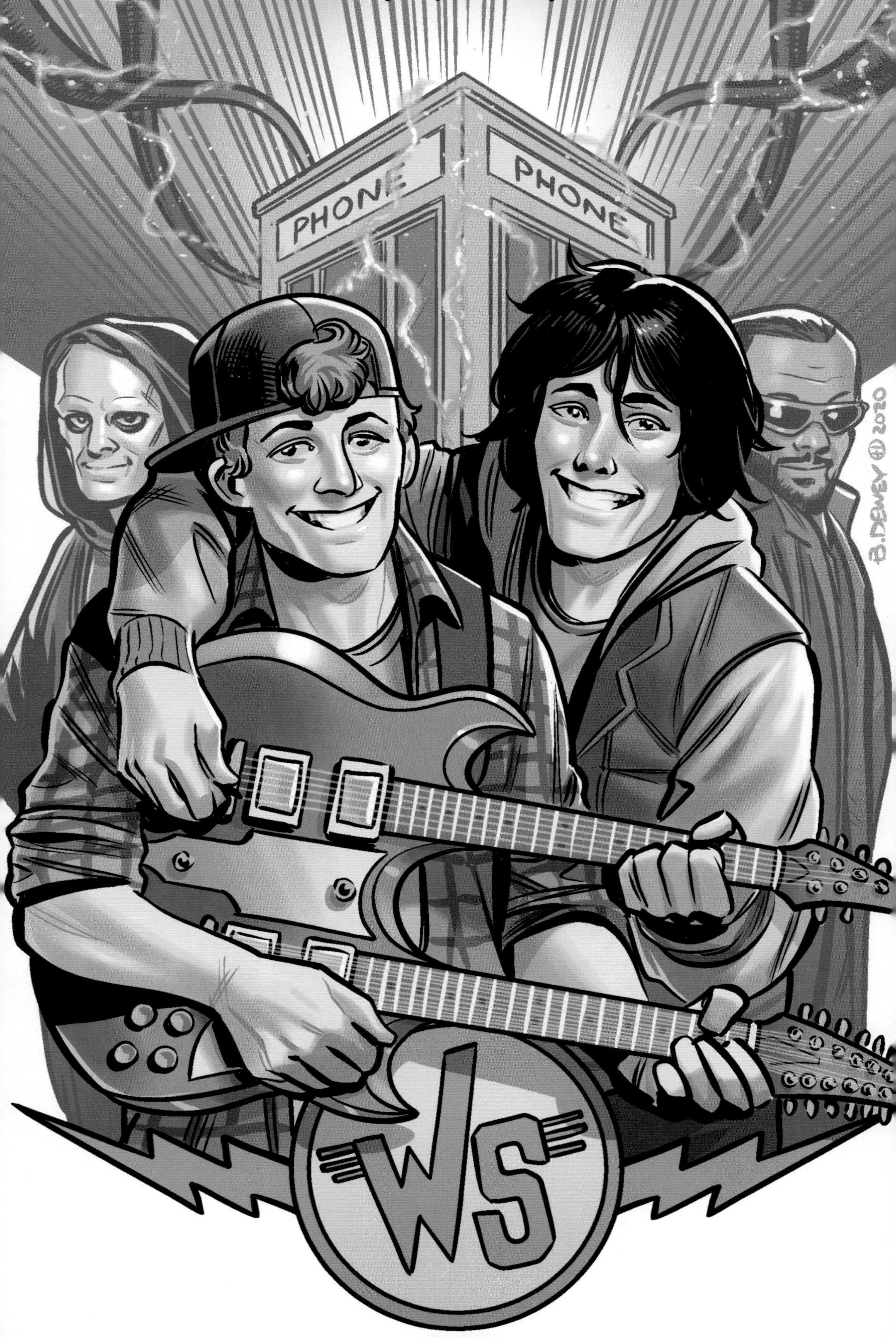
PHONE
PHONE
WS
B.DEWEY 2020

BILL & TED ARE DOOMED

SKETCHBOOK

NOTES BY ROGER LANGRIDGE AND EVAN DORKIN

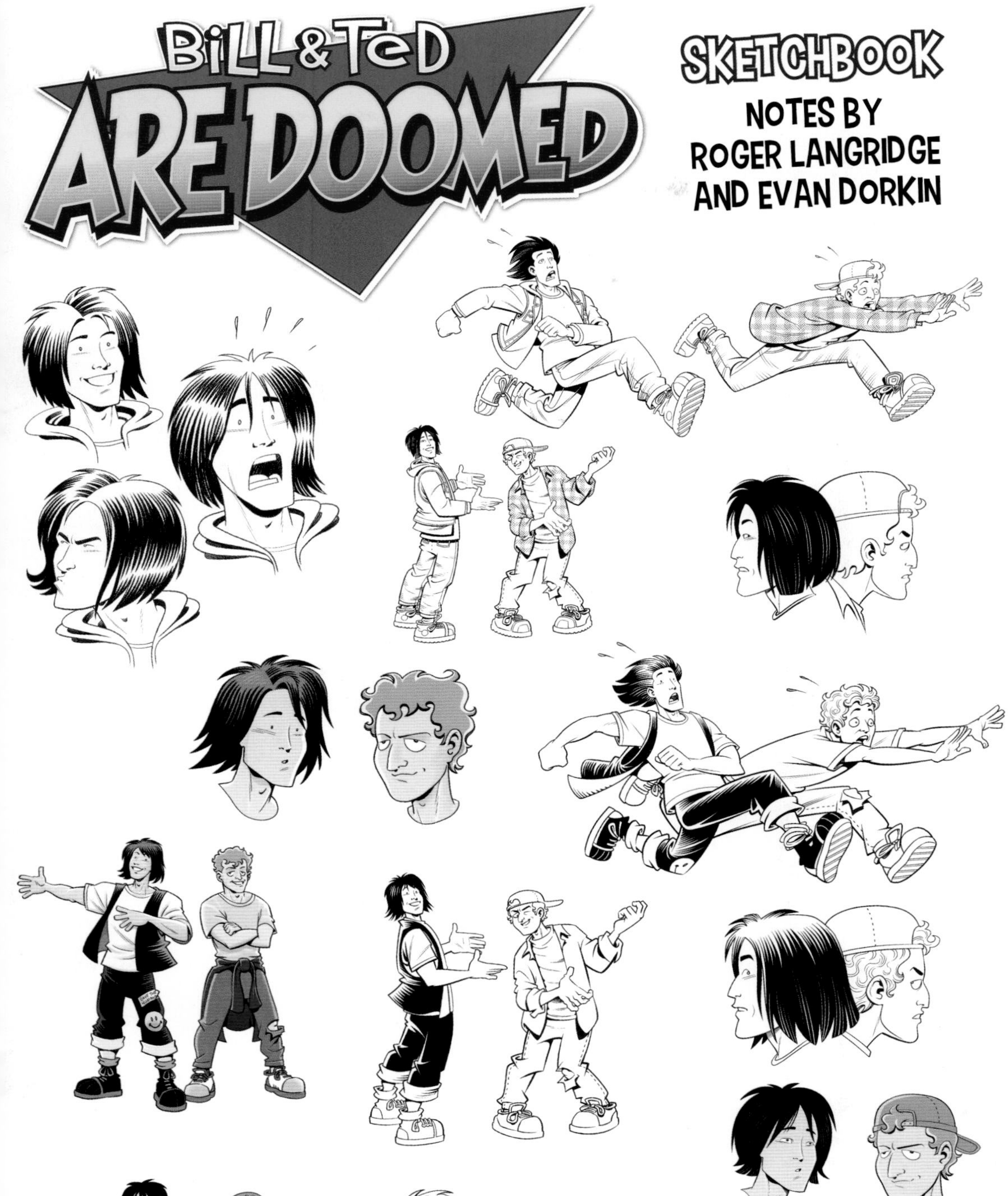

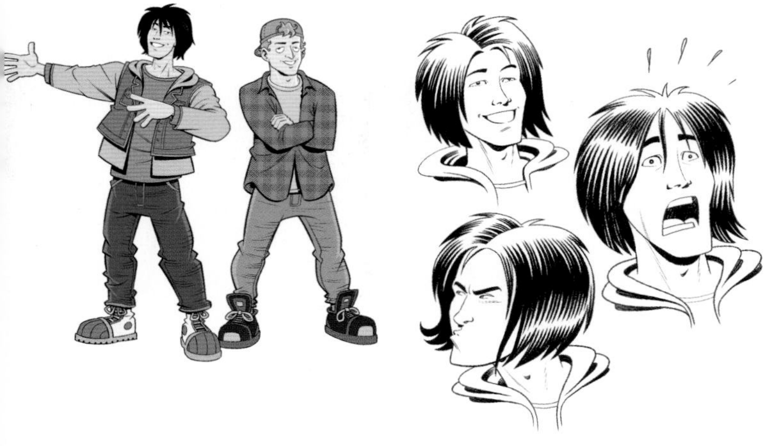

These are some initial drawings I did for the studio to sign off on before I started working on the book. I wasn't sure what outfits to draw them in—the first round of drawings used their Excellent Adventure costumes—but I was asked to have them looking more like their Bogus Journey incarnations, so that's what we eventually went with. The amount of cartooniness went back and forth a bit before it settled down, too.

—ROGER LANGRIDGE

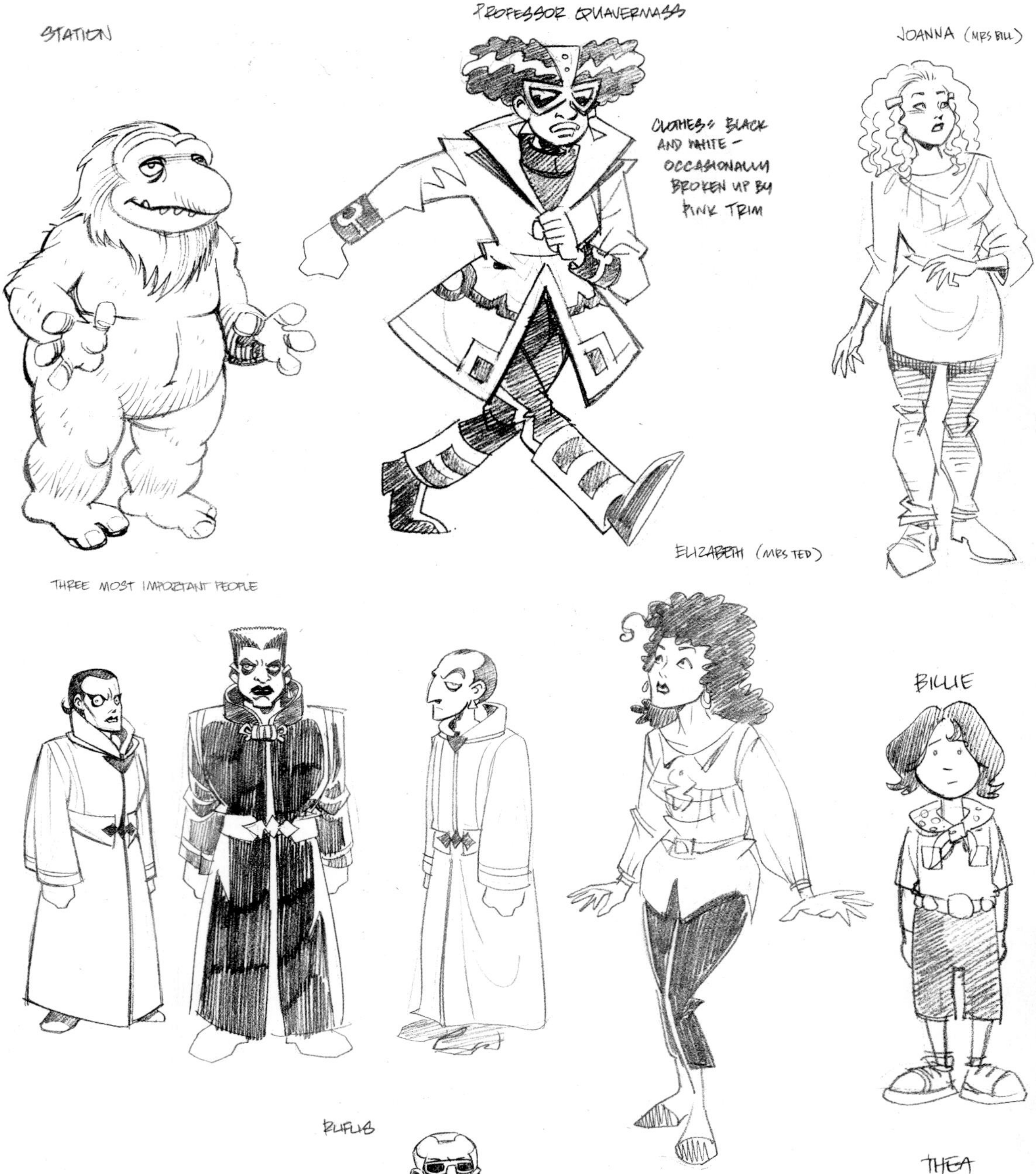
STATION
PROFESSOR QUAVERMASS
JOANNA (MRS BILL)
CLOTHES: BLACK AND WHITE - OCCASIONALLY BROKEN UP BY PINK TRIM
ELIZABETH (MRS TED)
THREE MOST IMPORTANT PEOPLE
BILLIE

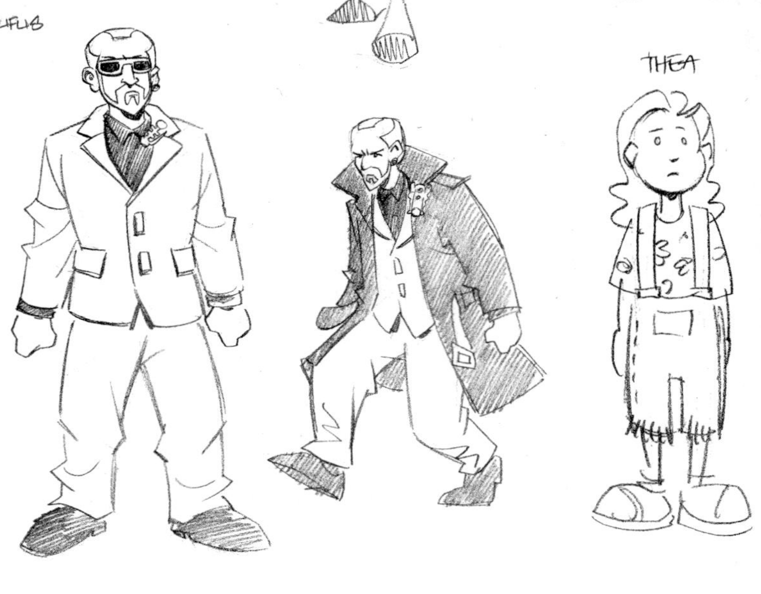
RUFUS
THEA

The drawings here were purely for my own reference. I was fairly new to the world of Bill and Ted, so I had these pinned above my drawing board as reminders of who everyone was and how they looked. Professor Quavermass was the only one I had to design from whole cloth, although I've only just noticed I seem to have ignored my own colour notes; everyone else was either based on their movie incarnations or (in the case of Billie and Thea) extrapolated from stills I found online.

–ROGER LANGRIDGE

The skull dropped into the background on the first cover was a visual "doomed" cue as well as a nod to the skeletal Death I drew in the old Marvel Bill and Ted comics.

-EVAN DORKIN

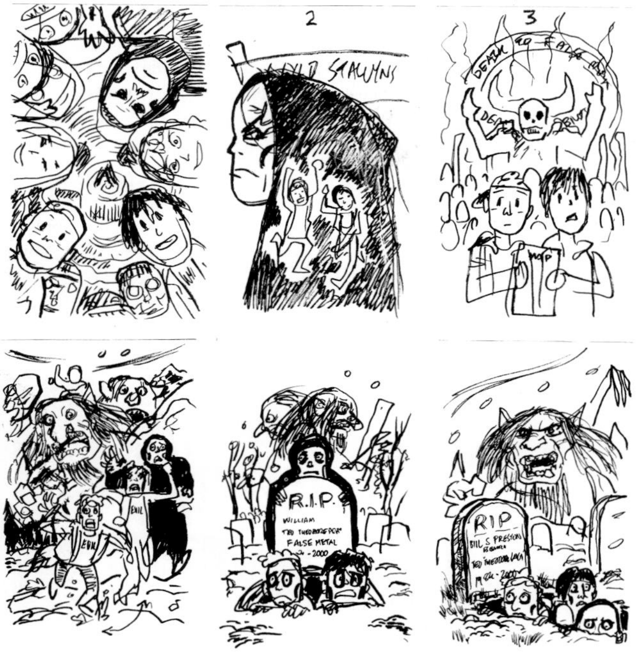

2
3
WYLD STALLYNS
R.I.P.
WILLIAM
FALSE METAL
RIP

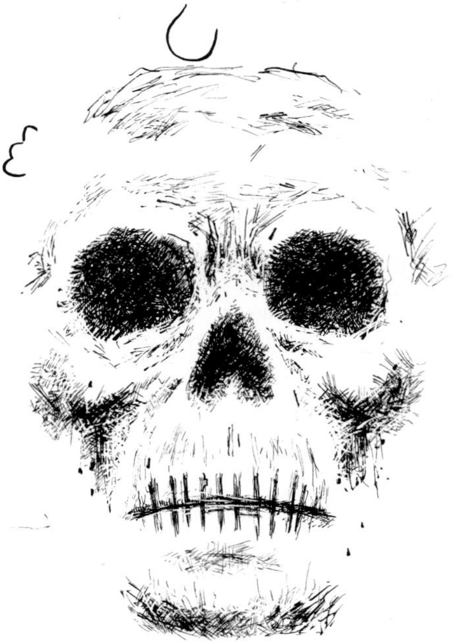

sketched my cover ideas on 3" x 5" index cards to try to keep things simple. If sketch bigger, I compulsively start adding too many details, which is what the enciling stage is for (ha ha).

-EVAN DORKIN

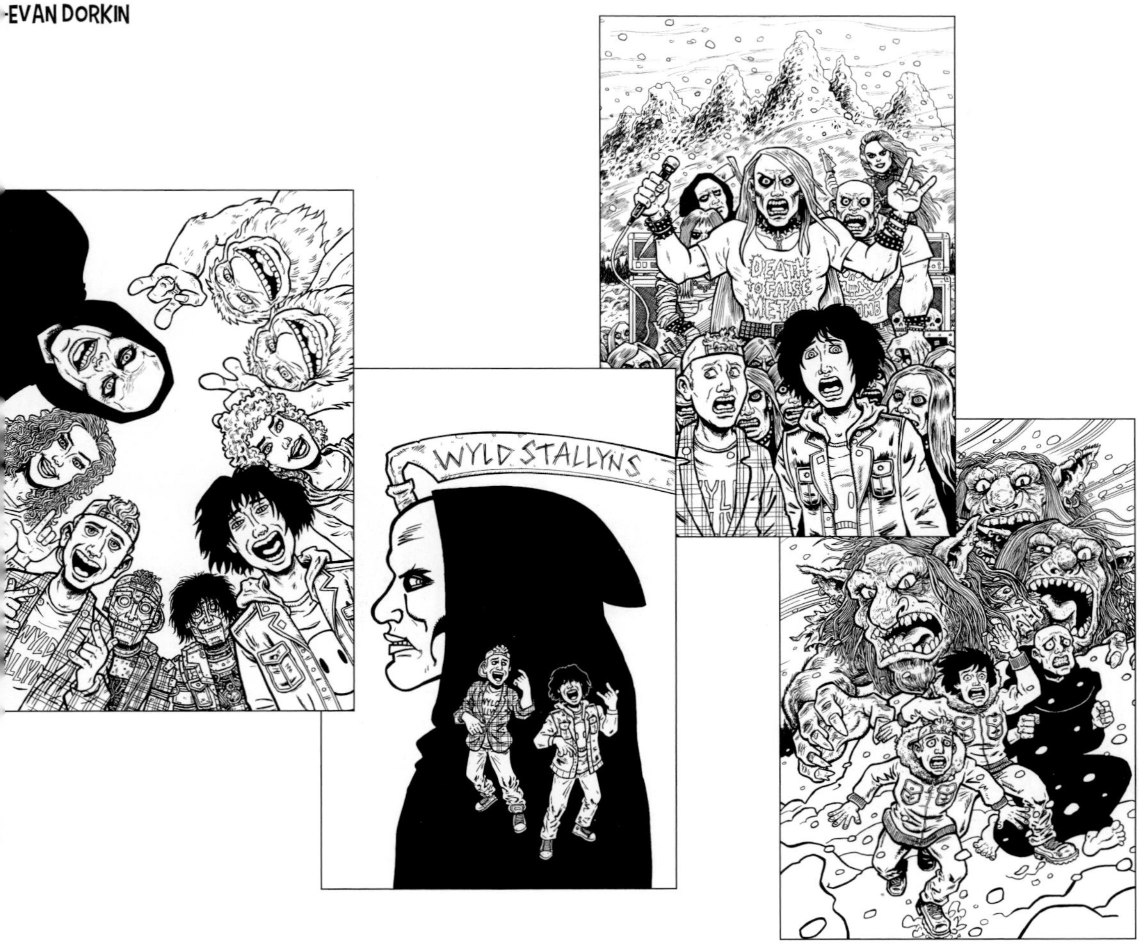

WYLD STALLYNS
DEATH TO FALSE METAL

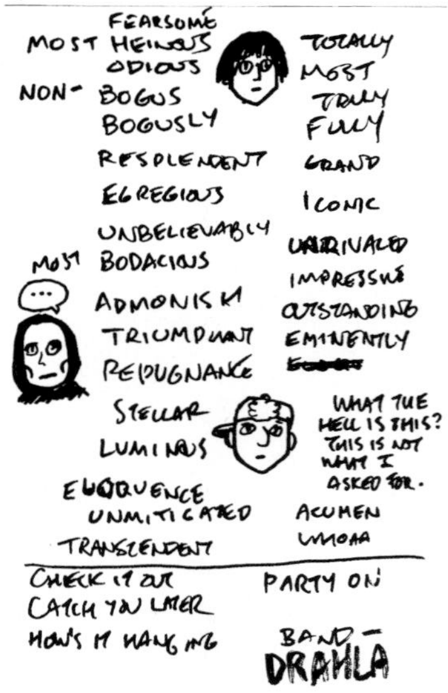
FEARSOME
MOST HEINOUS
ODIOUS
NON- BOGUS
BOGUSLY
RESPLENDENT
EGREGIOUS
UNBELIEVABLY
MOST BODACIOUS
ADMONISH
TRIUMPHANT
REPUGNANCE
STELLAR
LUMINOUS
ELOQUENCE
UNMITIGATED
TRANSCENDENT
TOTALLY
MOST
TRULY
FULLY
GRAND
ICONIC
UNRIVALED
IMPRESSIVE
OUTSTANDING
EMINENTLY
WHAT THE HELL IS THIS? THIS IS NOT WHAT I ASKED FOR.
ACUMEN
WHOAA
CHECK IT OUT
CATCH YOU LATER
HOW'S IT HANGING
PARTY ON
BAND -
DRAHLA

The other card is a basic "Bill and Ted speak" list I could refer to for dialog while writing/revising. If I needed to go off the list, I'd hit the thesaurus up for a word that I hoped sounded natural for them.

—EVAN DORKIN

These index card thumbnail sketches were done to pace things out and see if the beats worked on the page. I didn't send these to Roger, so it's interesting to compare how Roger and I each approached the page.

—EVAN DORKIN

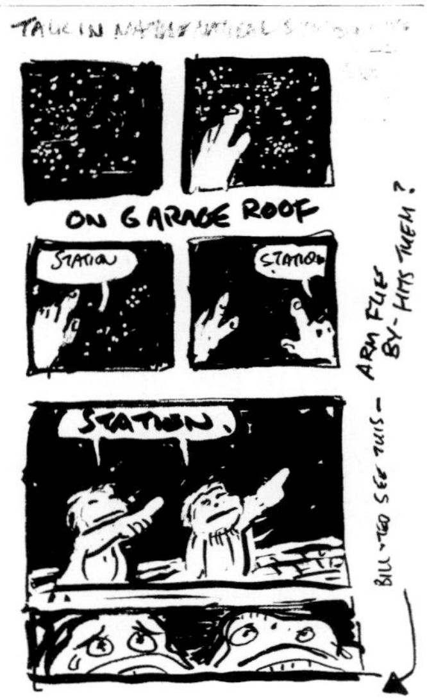
ON GARAGE ROOF
STATION
STATION
STATION
ARM FLIES BY- HITS THEM?
BILL + TED SEE THIS -

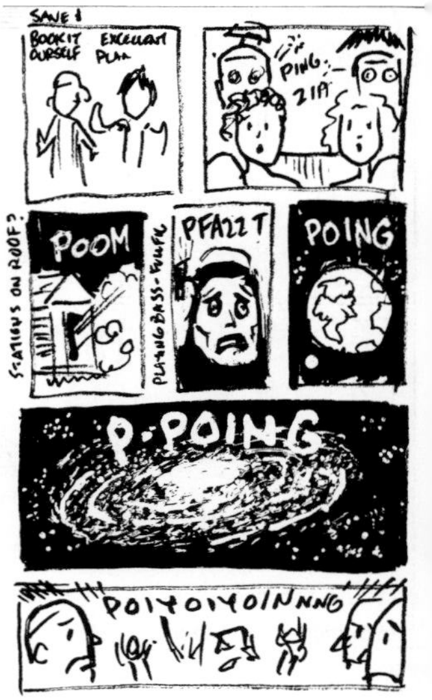
EXCELLENT PLAN
PING
STATIONS ON ROOF?
POOM
PFAZZT
POING
P-POING
POIYOIYOINNNG

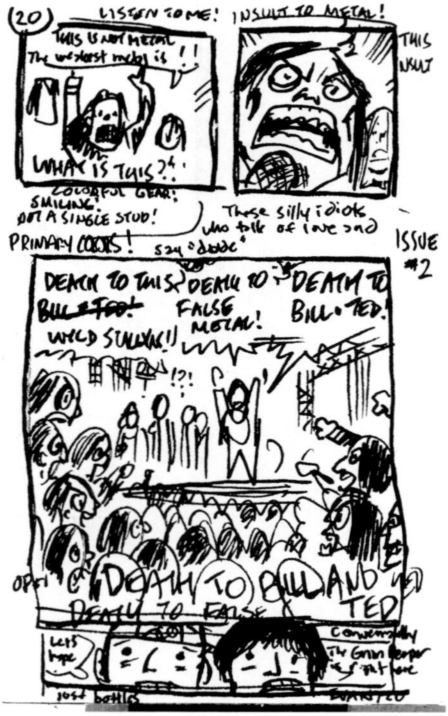
20
LISTEN TO ME!
INSULT TO METAL!
THIS INSULT
WHAT IS THIS?!
COLORFUL GEAR! SMILING! NOT A SINGLE STUD!
PRIMARY COLORS!
These silly idiots who talk of love and say "dude"
ISSUE #2
DEATH TO THIS!
DEATH TO FALSE METAL!
DEATH TO BILL + TED!
WYLD STALLYNS!
DEATH TO BILL AND TED

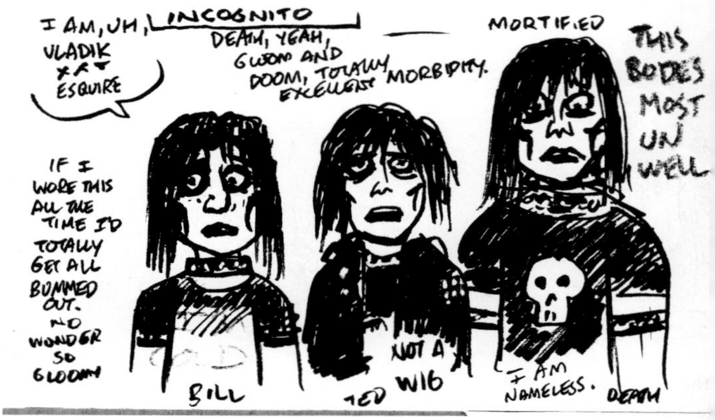
I AM, UH, INCOGNITO
VLADIK ESQUIRE
DEATH, YEAH, GLOOM AND DOOM, TOTALLY EXCELLENT MORBIDITY.
MORTIFIED
THIS BODES MOST UNWELL
IF I WORE THIS ALL THE TIME I'D TOTALLY GET ALL BUMMED OUT. NO WONDER SO GLOOMY
NOT A WIG
I AM NAMELESS.
BILL
TED
DEATH

A take on the last page of issue #2 with Vile Empire, and a doodle of Bill, Ted, and Death in Evil Metal incognito outfits and some stabs at dialogue. I wanted them to make up ridiculous "metal" names for themselves, but there wasn't room for the bit.

—EVAN DORKIN

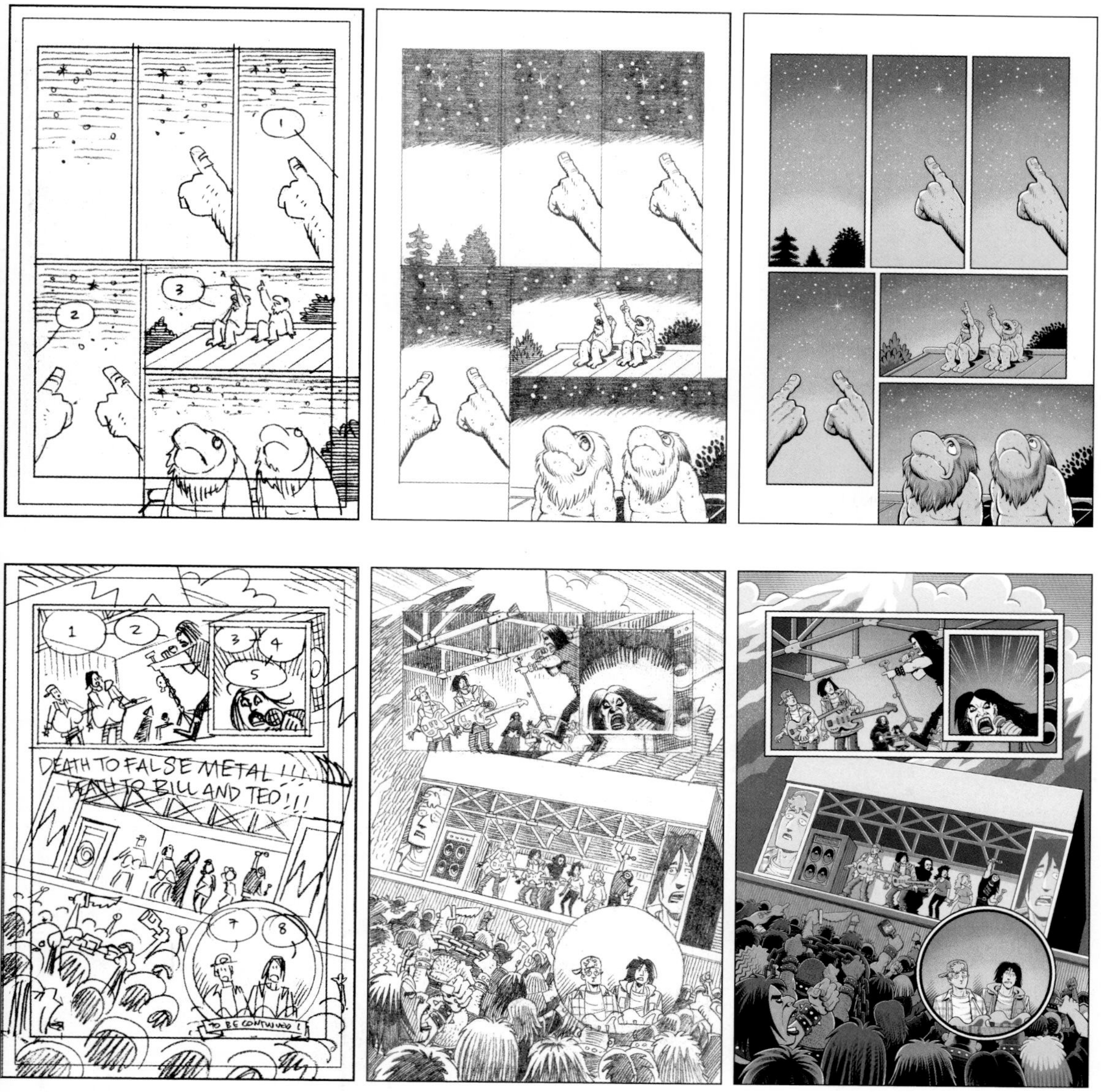
DEATH TO FALSE METAL !!!
DEATH TO BILL AND TED!!!

The evolution of a few pages, from initial thumbnail layouts (drawn about 2.5" x 3.75" on copier paper) to pencil art (also drawn on copier paper) to final "ink" art with gray tones (drawn digitally, over the scanned pencils). The idea of adding gray tones at the inking stage was to give me less to do at the coloring stage, which worked about 50% of the time. I'm sure I shaved off five minutes somewhere. It's fascinating to see Evan's own thumbnails, which I'm seeing here for the first time, both for their similarities and their differences from my own approach.

–ROGER LANGRIDGE

The montage panel here was fun—Evan's script essentially gave me a shopping list of stuff to work in to it, and I think I managed to get it all in without it seeming too cluttered or disjointed. It feels like a harmonious whole. And I like the fact that it shows the band actually having some fun and enjoying what they do, which we don't usually see a whole lot of.

–ROGER LANGRIDGE

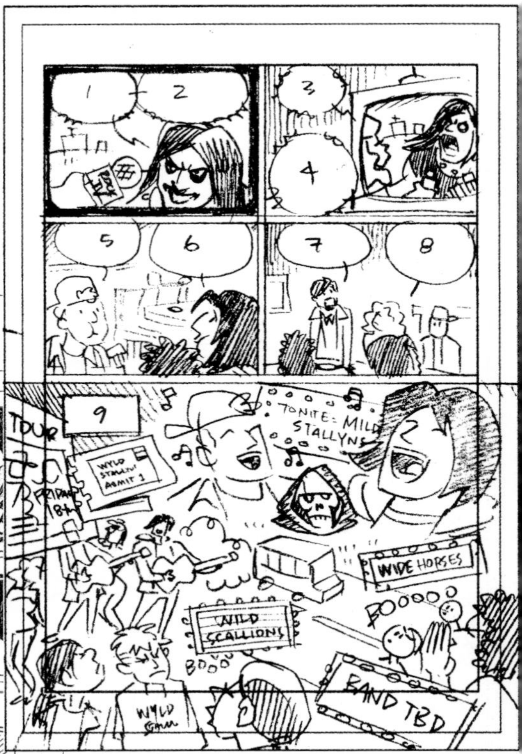

1
2
3
4
5
6
7
8
9
TOUR
TONITE: MILD STALLYNS
WYLD STALLYNS ADMIT 1
WIDE HORSES
WILD SCALLIONS
BAND TBD

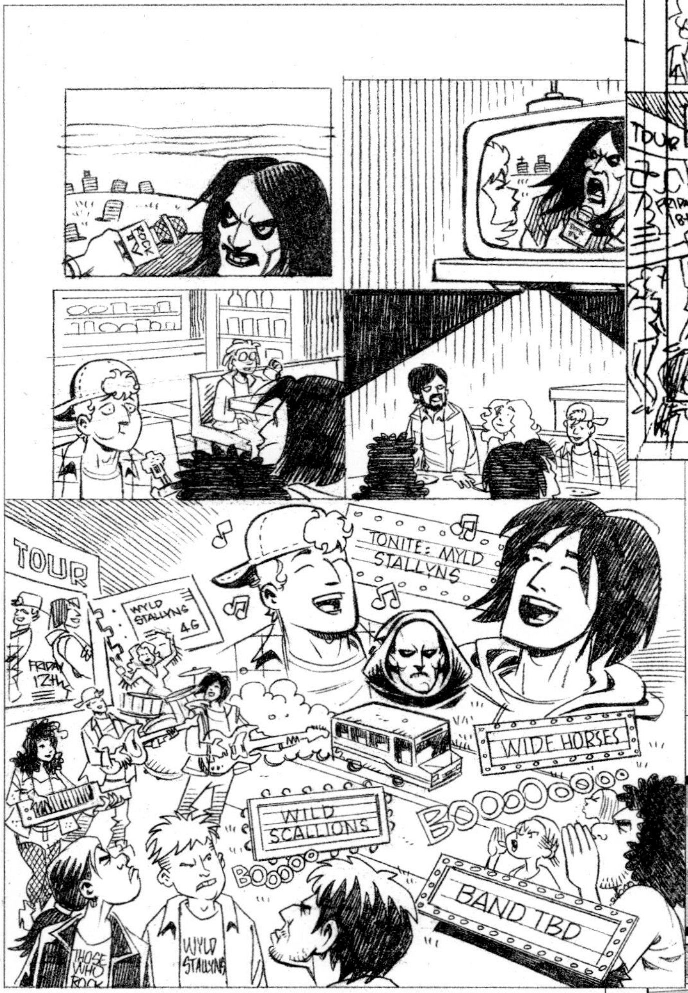

TOUR
TONITE: MYLD STALLYNS
WYLD STALLYNS 4G
FRIDAY 12th
WIDE HORSES
WILD SCALLIONS
BAND TBD
WYLD STALLYNS
THOSE WHO ROCK

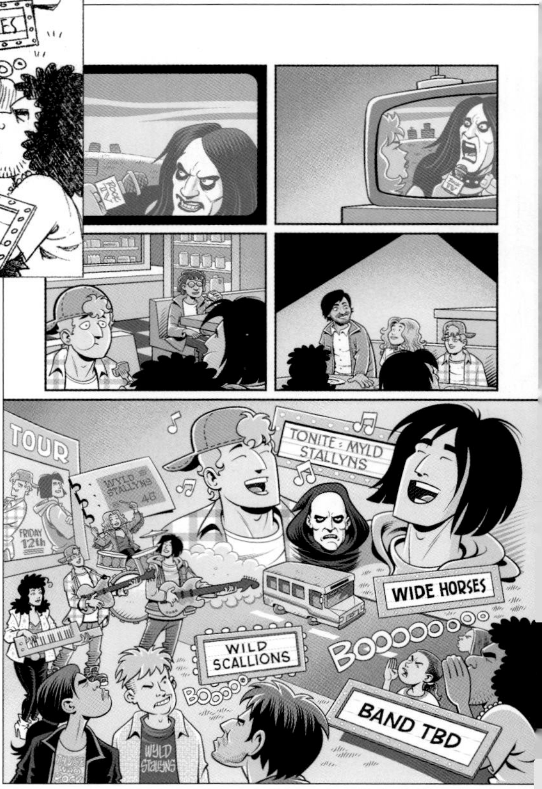

TOUR
TONITE: MYLD STALLYNS
WYLD STALLYNS 4G
FRIDAY 12th
WIDE HORSES
WILD SCALLIONS
BAND TBD
WYLD STALLYNS

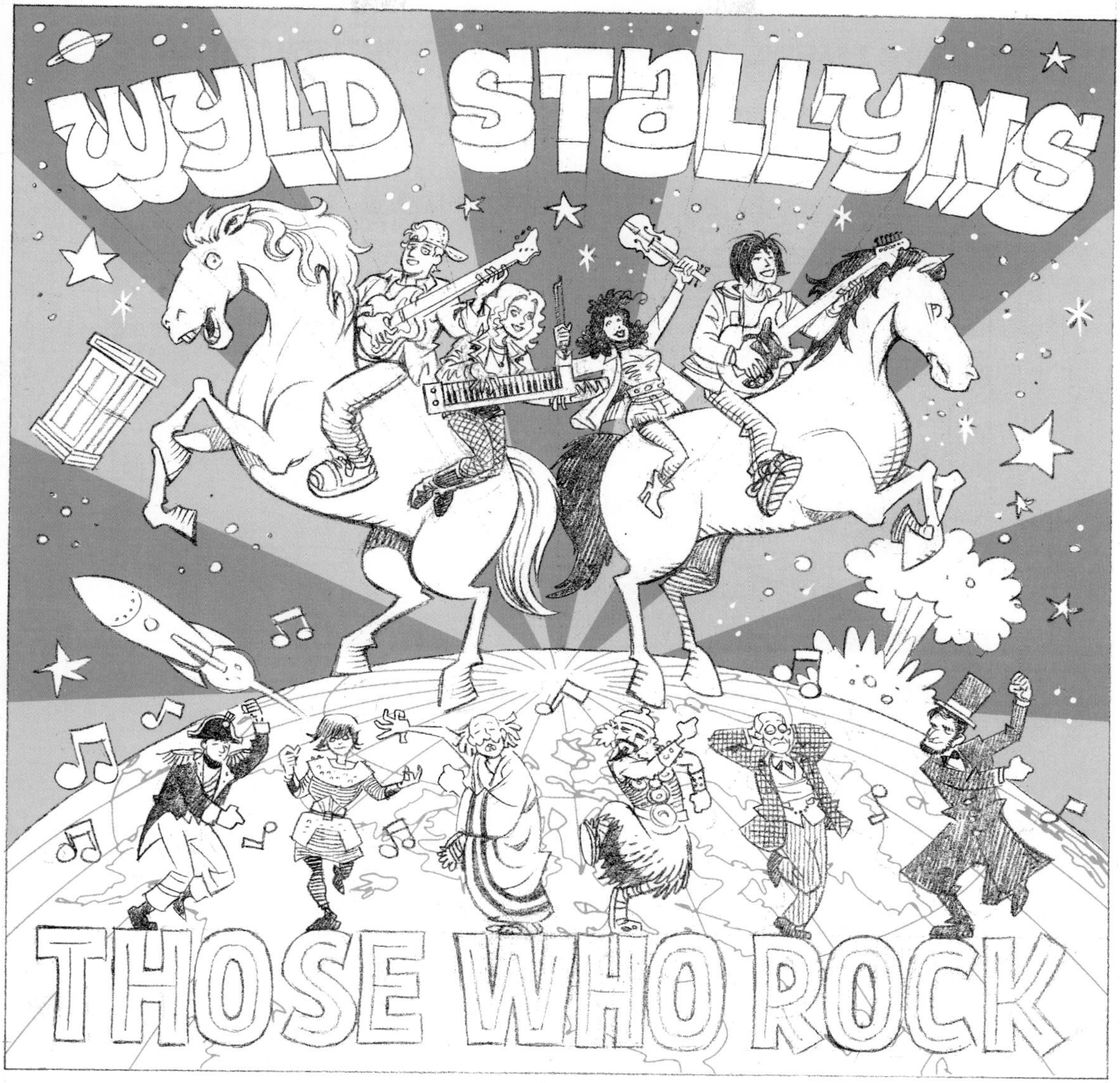
WYLD STALLYNS
THOSE WHO ROCK

There was a brief moment when it looked as though a made-up Wyld Stallyns album cover drawn by me might end up in the opening sequence of the movie. I spent a few days of back-and-forth with the studio trying to come up with something they liked, but eventually it was decided that my style wasn't quite what they wanted after all. There's an album cover by another artist in the final movie, which is tonally more in line with what they were after. I'm still quite fond of the dancing historical figures along the bottom—they make me laugh—but it's probably far too much detail for something that would only flash across the screen for a second.

–ROGER LANGRIDGE

EVAN DORKIN

EISNER AND HARVEY AWARD WINNER

"BRILLIANT."—*FORBIDDEN PLANET INTERNATIONAL*

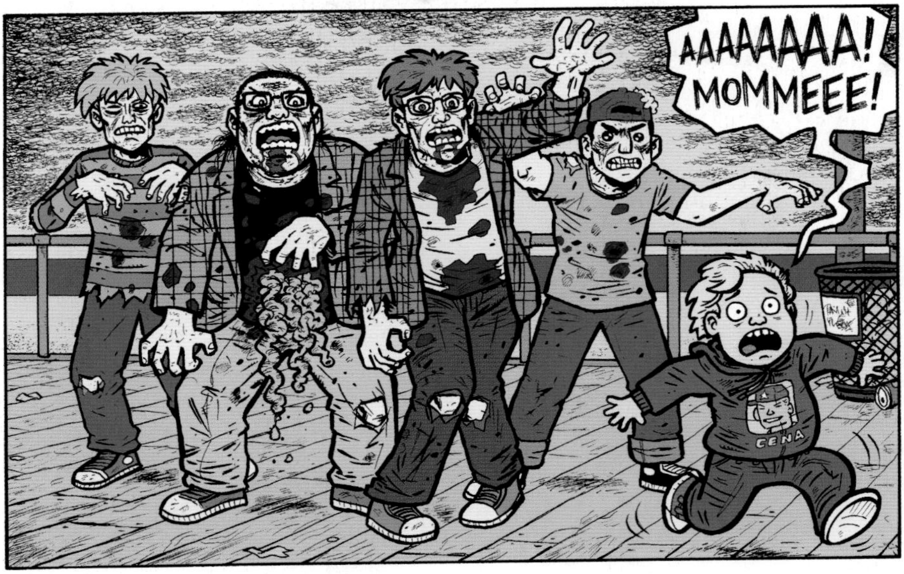
AAAAAAAA! MOMMEEE!
CENA

BEASTS OF BURDEN: NEIGHBORHOOD WATCH
Written by Evan Dorkin, Sarah Dyer, and Mike Mignola, art by Jill Thompson and Benjamin Dewey
978-1-50671-410-3 | $22.99

BEASTS OF BURDEN: WISE DOGS AND ELDRITCH MEN
Written by Evan Dorkin, art by Benjamin Dewey
978-1-50670-874-4 | $22.99

BEASTS OF BURDEN: ANIMAL RITES
Written by Evan Dorkin, art by Jill Thompson
978-1-50670-636-8 | $19.99

BILL AND TED ARE DOOMED
Written by Evan Dorkin, art by Roger Langridge
978-1-50672-252-8 | $19.99

CALLA CTHULHU
Written by Evan Dorkin and Sarah Dyer
Art by Erin Humiston, Mario A. Gonzalez, and Bill Mudron
978-1-50670-293-3 | $12.99

MILK AND CHEESE: DAIRY PRODUCTS GONE BAD
By Evan Dorkin
978-1-50670-571-2 | $19.99

THE ELTINGVILLE CLUB
By Evan Dorkin
978-1-61655-415-6 | $19.99

DORK!
By Evan Dorkin
978-1-50670-722-8 | $19.99

BLACKWOOD
Written by Evan Dorkin, art by Veronica Fish and Andy Fish
978-1-50670-742-6 | $17.99

BLACKWOOD: THE MOURNING AFTER
Written by Evan Dorkin, art by Veronica Fish and Andy Fish
978-1-50671-692-3 | $19.99

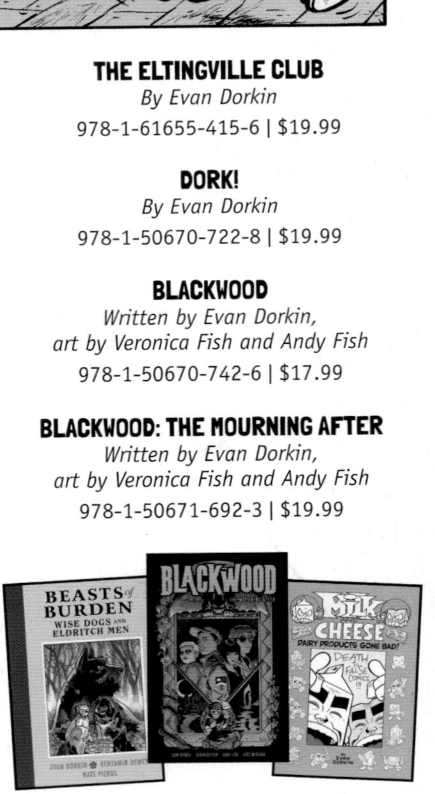
BEASTS of BURDEN
WISE DOGS AND ELDRITCH MEN
EVAN DORKIN BENJAMIN DEWEY
BLACKWOOD
MILK CHEESE
DAIRY PRODUCTS GONE BAD!
DEATH to FALSE COMICS!!
BY EVAN DORKIN